Tobacco Culture

TOBACCO CULTURE

The Mentality of the Great

Tidewater Planters on

the Eve of Revolution

*

With a new preface by the author

T. H. BREEN

PRINCETON UNIVERSITY PRESS

PRINCETON AND OXFORD

Copyright © 1985 by Princeton University Press
Published by Princeton University Press, 41 William Street,
Princeton, New Jersey 08540
In the United Kingdom: Princeton University Press,
3 Market Place, Woodstock, Oxfordshire OX20 1SY

First paperback edition, 1987

Ninth printing, and second paperback edition, with a new preface, 2001

Library of Congress Cataloging-in-Publication Data

Breen, T. H.
Tobacco culture : the mentality of the great Tidewater planters on the eve of
revolution / T. H. Breen ; with a new preface by the author.
p. cm.
Includes bibliographical references and index.
ISBN 0-691-08914-0 (alk. paper)
1. Virginia—History—Colonial period, ca. 1600–1775. 2. Plantation
owners—Virginia—History—18th century. 3. Plantation life—Virginia—
History—18th century. 4. Tobacco industry—Virginia—History—18th century.
5. Virginia—History—Revolution, 1775–1783—Causes—Case studies.
6. United States—History—Revolution, 1775–1783—Causes—
Case studies. I. Title.

F229.B8 2001
975.5'02—dc21   2001019854

British Library Cataloging-in-Publication Data is available

This book has been composed in Linotron Janson

Printed on acid-free paper. ∞

www.pup.princeton.edu

Printed in the United States of America

9   11   13   15   17   16   14   12   10

For Susan

CONTENTS

LIST OF ILLUSTRATIONS

PREFACE TO THE SECOND
PAPERBACK EDITION

The release of a new edition of *Tobacco Culture* provides a welcome opportunity to acknowledge a personal intellectual debt to Landon Carter. This delayed tribute may strike an odd note. After all, Carter was a somewhat truculent eighteenth-century Virginia planter. But, as I now have come to appreciate more fully than I did when the book first appeared, Carter taught me something fundamental about writing social and cultural history.

We should start with the man himself. No one in late colonial Virginia questioned Landon Carter's high standing among the region's great planters, least of all himself. A person of wealth and power, his world turned on the production of tobacco. What distinguished Carter from most of his peers was an extraordinary diary, a massive accounting of the daily challenges confronting him at Sabine Hall, a Carter plantation situated on the Rappahannock River. The detailed entries over almost a quarter century document a continuing struggle. Within a cycle of routine agricultural chores—seeding, transplanting, weeding, hoeing, topping, suckering, cutting, curing, and prizing—Carter depicted a personal contest against an uncooperative human and physical environment that frequently defied his own best efforts.

At the height of the growing season in July 1766, for example, Carter attempted to estimate the size of the coming harvest. With a flourish of mathematical precision barely disguising the crudeness of his calculations, Carter stated, "Tobacco I tend at least 280,000." He assumed that if "15 plants in the present way will make 1 pound of tobacco, then 280,000 will neat [yield] but 18,638 pounds of tobacco." Numbers of this sort demanded careful scrutiny. Did the figures represent a proper return on the investment of time and labor? Perhaps Carter had misjudged the crop, been too smart by half. He wondered if he should have thinned the fields. Perhaps he should have allowed five plants to the pound. Each year the diary recorded similar problems. Sometimes it was too much rain; sometimes slaves failed to carry out his precise instructions. Whatever his experience, the arrival of spring always signaled for Carter a renewed confrontation with the forces of nature.

When initially attempting to reconstruct the mentality of the great planters of Virginia, I found documents such as Carter's diary frustrating, often to the point of irritation. For all their prosaic detail about the production and marketing of tobacco, these materials never seemed to speak directly to my immediate research concerns. I wanted to know more about the political values of Carter's generation, a worthy project in my estimation. After all, this group of men behaved in a quite unexpected manner. The Virginia gentry encouraged a complex provincial society, one deeply divided by antipathies of class and race, to take up arms against the most powerful military empire the world had ever seen. The risks were extraordinary. Each act of corporate resistance raised new, frequently unwelcome possibilities within Virginia of wider participation in the political process. During the run-up to independence no one in the colony fully comprehended what it would mean to establish a genuinely republican government.

I had assumed that the personal papers of the great planters would contain extensive discussions of topics such as the limits of parliamentary sovereignty, natural rights and human equality, political virtue and corruption, liberty and a balanced constitution. But surviving records refused to cooperate with the project. Instead of chronicling the evolution of republican thought, the archives spoke more passionately about making tobacco than about sustaining a colonial rebellion. To be sure, some Virginia planters such as Richard Bland authored important pamphlets and newspaper essays, but links between the personal experience of the great planters and their political ideology at a moment of profound imperial crisis remained obscure.

Research for *Tobacco Culture* was well advanced before Carter and his friends persuaded me that I was not making very productive use of my time. My error—one not all that rare among contemporary historians of political ideas—was assuming that social context has very little effect upon the character of basic values such as freedom and liberty. But, as I discovered rapidly enough, context cannot be so easily dismissed. My misstep resulted from a stubborn insistence that the great planters speak to me across the centuries about my own analytic concerns in a form and language that I could readily comprehend. Not surprisingly, I transformed the leaders of Revolutionary Virginia into enlightened gentlemen, well-read, broadly philosophical, in other words, reflective people who possessed the leisure and intellect to explore formal political thought as if they were participants in a modern academic seminar. From this point of view, it made sense for me to ferret out discussions of liberty, equality, and independence.

In time, however, I learned how to listen more attentively to what Landon Carter and other members of the Virginia ruling class were actually trying to communicate about the structure of their lives. These were most certainly not men of leisure. They had obligations to meet, debts to pay, judgments to make about slaves and servants, not to mention the worry and time involved with the purchase of new lands, the quality of tobacco, and the ordering of expensive manufactured goods from Great Britain. The list of pressing daily responsibilities could be easily expanded. The point is obviously that it was a mistake to divorce the great planters from the busy and demanding world in which they actually lived. For some readers of this book, the discovery that mythic figures such as George Washington were actively engaged in managing large economic enterprises—in his case one involving the oversight of several hundred slaves and many thousands of acres of land—may come as a surprise, even a disappointment, but such a reaction seems unwarranted. This knowledge makes their support of a problematic colonial rebellion even more perplexing. Put simply, they had a lot to lose.

Tobacco Culture argues that the great planters of Virginia negotiated social identity in part through the crop that occupied so many of their waking hours. It is important that this claim not be misunderstood. The production of tobacco was certainly not their only source of identity. To insist on such a proposition would amount to a species of agricultural determinism. As cultural historians now understand, identity resists reduction to a single cause. Men like Carter and Washington derived a strong sense of self in this particular colonial setting through a constantly reinforced awareness that they were white rather than black, male rather than female, Protestant rather than Catholic, and British American rather than French.

In equal measure, however, the dominant crop itself provided a compelling vehicle for situating oneself within a complex world of other great planters, poorer white farmers, servants, slaves, and merchants. By the 1760s tobacco enjoyed the sanction of local history. For nearly a century and a half the wealthiest, most powerful men in Virginia had cultivated this export for distant markets. The Byrds and Carters, the Wormeleys and Beverleys were known to be makers of tobacco. Their reputation as growers of good leaves inspired pride; the work calendar defined a way of life, a set of shared rituals. They were the living representatives of a tradition tying the present generation to a familiar past, one that had come to define the distinct character of the "Tobacco Coast" or the "Tobacco Colony." In this sense, the great tobacco planters—much like the great sugar planters of the Caribbean and the major rice growers of the Carolinas—created over time an elaborate symbol system organized around the productive and marketing demands of a colonial staple.

Interpreted as the core of a late-eighteenth-century symbol system, tobacco provided a fresh perspective on the political culture of Virginia. In their intimate jottings about plantation work and sale to merchants the great planters may not have had much to say about abstract categories of republican thought. But these sources did contain many observations about the desirability of securing personal independence, about the fear of falling into dependence, and about the values that the leaders of this society projected onto distant strangers—merchants in Glasgow, Liverpool, and London— with whom they conducted business. Within the context of these relationships the great planters defined honesty and corruption, trust and betrayal. Indeed, during a period of severe financial instability throughout the Atlantic world, the marketing of tobacco became a lens through which they reassessed their status as provincials within the British Empire.

Not surprisingly, great planters who described their own plantations as rocks of independency had a very hard time comprehending why their crops, so lovingly attended, increasingly reduced them to the status of whining colonial debtors, often forcing them during the late 1760s to beg British merchants for help in avoiding insolvency. No persuasive evidence supports the claim that the great planters became revolutionaries largely to escape indebtedness. They would have found such a proposition insulting. Rather, the argument put forward in this volume is that planters such as Carter and Washington brought a fierce commitment to personal autonomy, a set of expectations about honest negotiations with British merchants, and a deep sense of pride to the fractious debate with Parliament over American sovereignty. In other words, experience with the culture of tobacco in itself did not generate a political ideology, but during the controversy with Great Britain it made some ideological positions seem a lot more credible than others.

Intended originally both as a contribution to the history of Virginia on the eve of revolution and as a model for a certain kind of interdisciplinary analysis, *Tobacco Culture* spoke to several different audiences. Drawing upon the literature of cultural anthropology, the book set forth an innovative framework for interpreting the relation between work experience and the social values that gave meaning to the lives of ordinary men and women. To that end, the study wove personal stories—Washington's often pathetic efforts to persuade a deadbeat neighbor to pay his debts, for example—into a broader understanding of a provincial ruling class at a moment of profound political crisis. This narrative strategy reflected my strong belief that individual testimony, however curious and interesting, must yield generalizations that inform larger comparative debates about topics such as race and class, capitalism and imperialism, subjects that continue to energize the best comparative history. Otherwise accounts of human struggle become the stuff only of antiquarian curiosity, tales told for no particular purpose. With a marvelous clarity that is derived from hindsight, of course, I might confess to a need to expand or to soften certain assertions, but on the whole, I remain confident that I have provided insight into the mentality of a planter elite that not only rebelled against Great Britain, but also played a major role in shaping the political culture of the new republic.

II

When *Tobacco Culture* first appeared reviewers had trouble placing it within a recognized subfield of historical debate. Some thought the book was an example of the "new political history." Others praised it as "environmental history." The volume won a prize for "agricultural history." Whether I actually set out to contribute to these areas of analysis is of no real importance. The more significant point is that the volume seemed to address several different sets of questions, in other words, to invite multiple responses.

Inventive reading and re-reading is an ongoing, creative process. Indeed, publication of a second edition provides me with a chance to consider how *Tobacco Culture* might be made to speak to the interpretive interests of a new generation of social and cultural historians. One exciting field known as the "new imperial history" serves this purpose very well. The word "new" in this context is obviously intended to distinguish it from an "older" imperial history. That literature—perhaps most closely identified with the great early-twentieth-century historian Charles M. Andrews—focused primarily on evolving institutional and legal structures that gave coherence to the British Empire before the American Revolution. Scholars such as Andrews mapped out an expanding regulatory system, explaining often in brilliant detail how royal governors and customs collectors went about the hard business of enforcing British statutes in distant provinces. These historians traced the development, especially after the Glorious Revolution of 1688, of an increasingly bureaucratic framework of laws and instructions, tariffs and fees, forms and reports. Missing from these splendidly researched works, however, was a sense of the human dimensions of empire, a grittier chronicle of controversy, resistance, and accommodation.

The newer imperial history, which is just now coming into its own as a respected subfield of early modern Anglo-American history, defines empire in less institutional terms than did Andrews and his contemporaries. A list of some of the more innovative voices in this area would certainly include scholars such as John E. Crowley, Nicholas P. Canny, Kathleen Wilson, Colin Kidd, Peter Marshall, and C. A. Bayly. Although it is hazardous to generalize about the shared characteristics of so many different works, it is safe to assert that most of the new imperial historians depict the eighteenth-century British Empire in cultural and social terms. They explore informal, nongovernmental connections that linked ordinary people in the North American colonies to those in Great Britain. Collectors of rare plants, itinerant evangelical ministers, and small-time frontier traders figure as centrally in this analysis of empire as do royal governors and admiralty court judges. In this story some persons were losers, shoved aside by those in power who disdained different races, classes, and ethnic groups. Other characters in this loosely integrated empire presented themselves as marvelous schemers, putting forward for anyone who would listen bold plans for land development and exploitation of natural resources.

Within this vast arena of human interaction ordinary men and women made judgments about other British subjects, some of whom had darker skin or did not speak English, creating a process of mutual imaginings that was as likely to sustain crude stereotypes as to promote meaningful understanding. From this perspective, the eighteenth-century British Empire perpetually generated resistance and accommodation, pride and irritation, freedom and enslavement. As in any complex cultural system, men and women sorted themselves out as best they could, forging identities that made sense within the context of small local communities without thereby abandoning claims, however tenuous, to a common Britishness. Even those who celebrated an imagined British identity sometimes had difficulty squaring local knowledge with the expectations and assumptions of others who found themselves living somewhere else in the same empire.

A book about the mental world of elite Tidewater planters such as Landon Carter may seem an unpromising inspiration for a broader, more inclusive imperial history. Whatever the limitations of the original study, however, I simply want to suggest how one might take into account other groups whose lives were closely bound up with the production and sale of tobacco. The focus is on mutual imaginings, on the often fumbling, sometimes totally mistaken attempts to comprehend what others were thinking about making and selling a good crop.

The Scottish merchants who came to Virginia to operate little stores where tobacco was exchanged for imported goods such as cloth and ceramics provide a case in point. As *Tobacco Culture* explains, the great planters consigned most of their crop directly to large London houses. But they occasionally dealt with local Scottish factors, as colonial store managers were called, and the large planters seem to have regarded them with suspicion, bordering on contempt. The storekeepers appeared to the Virginia leaders as too pushy, too ambitious, untrustworthy, and on the eve of revolution, a potential fifth column. Drawing on common ethnic stereotypes, the great planters situated the Scots unfavorably within a commercial framework linking local growers to distant European smokers.

By the same token, the Scots who worked in the scattered Virginia stores projected motives and values onto the great planters, many of them less than flattering. *Tobacco Culture* asserted that men like Carter did not have more than a superficial knowledge of how the European market actually worked, and in their ignorance and confusion about the highly technical aspects of international exchange, they relied on trust and good will, urging their London representatives to look out for the planters' commercial interests. But whatever the London merchants thought about this rhetoric, the local Scots viewed colonial trade from a strikingly different perspective. They insisted that the great planters were actually canny businessmen, eager to manipulate prices for tobacco and manufactured goods and capable in a number of subtle ways of taking advantage of the hapless factors. In 1771 one person in charge of a provincial string of stores instructed a new arrival from Scotland, "I need not recommend to you to live on good terms with your neighbours." He warned, however, "allow me to say that too great an intimacy with any of them may be attended with bad consequences. Secrecy in all our transactions of business, even to the most simple, is what I would strongly recommend." In another note of advice this leading factor expanded the point. "Intimacies and much visiting at the planters' houses I strongly advise you against. It gives them a pretense of taking great liberties at the store when you must fix upon a proper policy to be observed invariably."

The more the Scots practiced secrecy and rejected social invitations, of course, the more they seemed exactly what the great planters had claimed all along, people working against the real interests of Virginia. These two groups confronted each other frequently in face-to-face relations over tobacco, at county courthouses and rural taverns where they entered into cultural conversations that seem to have had little positive impact on the character of their mutual imaginings. Although the Scottish factors as well as the great planters wanted to make a profit within a commercial empire, their exchanges were unproductive, a source of political tension during the controversy with Parliament.

The perception of the great planters as skilled masters of agriculture—persons whose high professional self-regard might be compared to the major wine makers in modern France and California—ran counter to what contemporary writers were publishing in England. How much the Virginians knew of this literature is not known, but if they had bothered to examine encyclopedic volumes examining the flow of commerce within the eighteenth-century British Empire, they would have encountered a less than complimentary depiction of their contribution to the tobacco trade.

One popular publication, perhaps authored by Edmund Burke, declared that the colonial export of tobacco brought a lot of money to the English. "It produces a vast sum," claimed the *Account of the European Settlements in America*, "and yet [it] appears to lay but a very inconsiderable burden upon the people in England." How could one explain such a surprisingly one-sided exchange? The answer was that the great planters were not very astute businessmen. "All the weight [of the trade]," this writer announced, "in reality falls upon the planter, who is kept down by the lowness of the original price. . . . They have no prospect of ever bettering their condition; and they are less able to endure it as they live in general luxuriously, and to the full extent of their fortunes." If the Virginians come off here as improvident provincial rubes, the English merchants appear as near geniuses, heroes of the British Empire. "However the planters may complain of the tobacco trade, the revenue flourishes by it, for it draws near three hundred thousand [pounds] a year from this one article alone, and the exported tobacco, the far greater part of the profits of which come to the English merchant, brings almost as great a sum annually into the kingdom."

Another volume entitled *Observations on the Commerce of the American States* appeared soon after the Revolution. The author, John Lord Sheffield, did not worry much about the disruption of the Virginia market. After all, he concluded, almost anyone could grow tolerably good tobacco. He consoled English readers over the recent loss of the colonies, observing "if we cannot have an advantageous trade for tobacco with America, we may encourage the growth round our factories in Africa. The superior soil, and low price of labour there, if the natives can be obliged or induced to work, will give great advantage. It would, in some degree, civilize the natives, and increase the demand for our manufactures there." By implying that the great planters of Virginia had managed to achieve only a primitive level of civilization through the production of tobacco, Sheffield denied them special standing within the empire. They were somehow less than Englishmen, another category entirely. At the end of the day Sheffield assumed that even Africans could grow as fine a leaf as did white Virginians, a claim that would not have pleased the great planters. No doubt, reading this volume, Carter would have experienced the sting of injured pride, wondering privately in his diary why his talents as a crop master were so little appreciated by the English.

One might ask why, within this vast field of mutual imaginings that we term the British Empire, formal writers painted such a negative picture of the great planters of Virginia. One might speculate that their knowledge of the tobacco region may have been derived in part from popular novels, a literary genre then in its infancy. Early in the eighteenth century Daniel Defoe published two remarkable works allegedly describing life in colonial Virginia. Both titles still enjoy considerable popularity. *Moll Flanders* and *Colonel Jack* depict the distant plantation society as a place of exile. It was a raw society, given over to violence and exploitation, where unscrupulous men or women might overcome embarrassing English pasts and reinvent themselves sufficiently on tobacco plantations to merit a return to real civilization. In these novels the great planters remain shadowy figures, and one has the impression that Defoe did not regard them as in any way morally superior to his own flawed protagonists.

Another novel of this type—one that many modern historians have overlooked—appeared in 1754. We do not know how many English people read Edward Kimber's *History of the Life and Adventures of Mr. Anderson: Containing his Strange Varieties of Fortune in Europe and America, Compiled from his Own Papers*, but in so much as fiction shaped public perceptions of the empire during this period, Kimber's production certainly countered the great planters' sense of themselves as virtuous, fair-minded British gentlemen who just happened to live in America. Much about Kimber's career is obscure. He visited the colonies at mid-century and later published a short travel journal of no particular distinction. It is possible that Kimber drew upon his encounters in Virginia and Maryland while working on the *Adventures of Mr. Anderson*.

This curious gothic romance recounts the experiences of poor Tom Anderson, who as a boy of only seven years was kidnapped off the streets of London and sent as an indentured servant to a large Maryland tobacco plantation. Tom had a heart of gold. Despite ill-treatment, he worked hard, took the initiative, and earned the trust of almost everyone in the little

Tidewater community. Tom also made the mistake of falling in love with his master's daughter, a sweet, pure, convivial woman whose hand in marriage had already been promised to the son of a dominant Virginia family who just happened to be named Carter. The girl's father was an overbearing patriarch, and he was not about to let his daughter run off with Tom, however appealing he may have been.

The crisis in the narrative occurs when the father forces the daughter to visit the Carter mansion, a house of horrors as she soon discovers. Although her suitor proclaims himself a respected member of the ruling class, he is in fact a lout. In a clumsy attempt to win her affection, Carter promises material happiness. "As soon as we are tack'd together, d'ye see, father says we shall keep a coach, and I am sure it will be the first kept at *Worcester* county, 'pon my soul will it _____ then who but we _____ ha? What a figure you'll make at Church, and I at the *Court-house*." The woman's utter lack of enthusiasm for the good life in Virginia only encourages Carter. After the marriage, he rhapsodizes, "You shall have all the finery that can be bought from *England*, and wear nothing but silks and sattins [sic], and jewels and gold and silver _____ egad, we'll out-do all the country and buy out all the little folks about us." Still, she remains unmoved by the prospect of marriage to Carter. In one final attempt to change her mind, he explains that in Virginia "your coach shall be drawn by *Negroes* instead of horses. What d'ye say to it?" What she declares is that he appears to be a crude, disgusting person whose "education has been amongst your slaves."

In eighteenth-century England the woman's strong rejection might have ended the negotiations. But this was not the case in Kimber's Virginia. The cunning suitor devises a plan that involves his entire family. Sometime during the night he would break into her room and rape her in her own bed. Just as it seems that the heroine is doomed, the Carter slaves rise in rebellion, burn down the mansion, kill all the members of their master's family, and escape to western Virginia where they apparently planned to live free. These were not just any slaves. They were Gold Coast Africans, who carried with them to America a more robust sense of liberty and independence than the likes of Carter could ever understand. The rebels do not murder the visiting woman because they sympathize with her plight and because an old slave named Squanto assures them that she is a "goodee mistress" who loves the "poor Negroe, no beatee them _____ no whippee!" And, of course, she is eventually reunited with Tom, who has endured as many trials as she. Whatever its literary merits, Kimber's novel inverted the world of the great planters, awarding top marks to the Gold Coast African, whose own cultural values only highlighted the tyranny and violence of the Carter household. We have no evidence that Landon Carter of Sabine Hall was aware of Kimber's writing. One can only speculate how he might have reacted to this particular rendering of his world on the Rappahannock River.

The Adventures of Mr. Anderson reminds us that for all the great planters' pride in producing a good crop of tobacco, the agricultural work was actually performed by hundreds of unfree laborers such as Squanto. Except in studies of the slave trade, it is rare to encounter these men and women in discussions of the eighteenth-century British Empire. Most research has focused on the plantation itself, a bounded space where masters and slaves continuously negotiated small victories and endured little defeats, each group testing the other's power through strategies of accommodation and resistance. No one questions how deeply Africans in America desired freedom. But in point of fact, most Virginia slaves of this period did not rise in rebellion against the planter class. To have followed Kimber's Gold Coast Africans to the forests of the Ohio Valley would have meant certain death, and most black men and women spent their working hours tending tobacco.

In the more inclusive history of empire sketched out here, one might ask whether the slaves of Virginia cared about the quality of the crops being shipped to London and Glasgow. Did they see their own welfare as somehow intimately bound up with the tobacco prices that Carter and others received on the world market? Did the prospect of a rich harvest persuade them to work harder? To such queries, it is currently impossible to provide persuasive answers. We know that under certain conditions masters did break up slave families, selling off loved ones to distant plantations. Such events usually occurred after an original owner died, and his property—in this case many human beings—was distributed among scattered heirs. Bankruptcy could also precipitate such personal disasters. Whatever the slaves' knowledge of the marketplace—and they might have heard conversations on such topics around the master's dinner table or at the courthouses where people of both races went for recreation—they had a strong interest, in no way connected to the fear of punishment, in producing quality tobacco plants. Good prices may not have yielded freedom, but they certainly did suggest the possibility of better clothes.

Such concerns may have been on Sukey's mind, a slave woman at Sabine Hall, when she confronted Landon Carter at the edge of a tobacco field. After he questioned her judgment as a planter, she countered hotly that the acres she tended would "see a good crop of Tobacco, for she knew the ground." Never a man to retreat on matters associated with growing tobacco, Carter expressed skepticism, a reaction that only served to further anger Sukey. She told him in no uncertain terms, "she would be hanged if any planter seeing the ground would not say the tobacco stood tolerably well." Much as Carter himself might have done among his social peers, Sukey protested that "she knew the ground, knew how it was dunged, and would be hanged if it did not turn out good Tobacco."

By seeing the British Empire not as a formal regulatory system or as an expression of geopolitics but rather as a rich and contested field of imagination, we might come to a fuller understanding of how a crop such as tobacco promoted an amazing range of cultural conversations, some open-ended, others less so, but all feeding over time into an informal yet powerful sense of how different peoples might sort themselves out within a complex chain of relations that included Sukey as well as Landon Carter, Edward Kimber as well as John Lord Sheffield, and of course, all those merchants who negotiated more or less successfully the conflicting interests of so many producers and consumers.

Greensboro, Vermont
September 2000

PREFACE

Tobacco Culture explores the mental world of the great Tide-water planters of mid-eighteenth-century Virginia. It does not, however, analyze in detail their formal philosophical or political ideas. About these topics intellectual historians have written a great deal. This study concentrates instead on how a group of wealthy tobacco planters gave meaning to daily experience. It ties together the planting cycle, the psychology of the planters, and a political ideology. In other words, the book explores the construction of a specific social reality. By understanding these mental processes, we learn how these men perceived agricultural and economic changes over which they exercised little control, and more, why on the eve of the American Revolution many great Tidewater planters cham-pioned a radical political ideology. This loose bundle of ideas, sometimes called republicanism, sometimes radical Country thought, is described in Chapter I.

This type of historical study—the French call it *l'histoire des mentalités*—often focuses upon bizarre activities or beliefs, upon witchcraft, or, in the case of one recent essay, upon the massacre of cats by disgruntled Parisian artisans.[1] While such an approach to an alien culture may be perfectly acceptable, this book concentrates on more prosaic aspects of daily life in colonial Virginia: the production and marketing of tobacco. For some time agricultural history—in the early American pe-riod at least—has amounted to little more than an investiga-tion of who grew how many bales or bushels of some crop. *Tobacco Culture*, however, finds agriculture rich in cultural and symbolic meanings. The book looks at tobacco in eighteenth-century Virginia the way that a modern anthropologist might view coffee or sugar in contemporary Caribbean societies. It sees the planters' economic life not simply as an effort to max-

[1] See Robert Darnton, *The Great Cat Massacre and Other Episodes in French Cultural History* (New York, 1984) and Carlo Ginzburg, *The Cheese and the Worms: The Cosmos of a Sixteenth-Century Miller* (Baltimore, 1980).

imize financial returns, but rather as a series of highly personal, value-laden relationships. As we shall discover, it was in the fields and the marketplace that these Tidewater gentlemen sorted out society and defined their place within it. The tobacco mentality (discussed in Chapter II) imposed social and moral imperatives on the great planters, and by relating these imperatives to a pattern of debt and credit in Virginia, we begin to appreciate why these men valued a political ideology that stressed personal autonomy and abhorred corruption.

The mental path from tobacco to politics, from agrarian experience to political protest, was tortuous. During the 1760s many great Tidewater planters discovered that accumulating debts to British merchants threatened to undermine the Virginians' personal autonomy, the core value of the tobacco mentality. The planters reacted to this crisis as best they could, alternately apologizing and complaining, devising strategies to produce more tobacco, and vowing to live more frugally. But however they responded, they did so as individuals. They discussed their problems in personal correspondence with the merchants. The character of this private discourse in which the planters explained the local meaning of debt and credit is explored in Chapters III and IV.

At some time during the late 1760s, the great Tidewater planters transformed these private conversations into public discourse. They began to realize—largely because of growing external pressures—that they must cooperate. As we shall learn in Chapter V, it was during this period that they reached a new stage of consciousness. To escape a growing sense of dependence upon the merchants they drew up nonimportation agreements, counselled each other to practice frugality and simplicity, and suggested schemes for general moral reform. This discourse was not yet political. It was not aimed at king or Parliament and therefore should be seen as existing quite apart from the other, more familiar discourse over constitutional rights and liberties.

Only in the years following 1772 did the commercial and constitutional discourses merge into a single powerful expression of discontent. The great planters politicized tobacco and debt. They now regarded the merchants not simply as the instruments of economic control, but as the agents of a degenerate society. To achieve personal independence—indeed, to restore personal honor and virtue—they had to break with the economic and political system that threatened to enslave them.

Not all Tidewater planters travelled the full route. Some backed away from the escalation of ideas that was sweeping their neighbors toward revolution. They refused to conflate economic and political, trusting that somehow they could work themselves free of debt without separating from the mother country. But other planters, such as Thomas Jefferson, welcomed the shattering of the old order. They envisioned a new society in which wheat farmers would replace tobacco planters, yeomen displace aristocrats, and free republicans liberate themselves from the clutches of the tobacco mentality. Jefferson's aversion to Alexander Hamilton's financial schemes and the development of a distinctive agrarian republicanism after the revolution of the 1790s can in large measure be traced to this earlier crisis of the tobacco culture.

The limits of this study should be made clear at the very beginning. *Tobacco Culture* does not argue that planter debt or, for that matter, a particular agrarian mentality *caused* the American Revolution. Such monocausal explanations are seldom persuasive, and they usually ignore other factors that mobilized mass protest. We shall probably never know the reasons why thousands of Virginians risked and lost their lives in the fight for independence. Nevertheless, we should appreciate the evidence that has survived. If the planters' perceptions of debt and their fears over the loss of personal autonomy were not sufficient causes for revolution, they were certainly necessary. The crisis of the tobacco culture helped crystallize inchoate elements in a political ideology. It compelled planters to rethink assumptions and in some cases, to contemplate radical possibilities of reform. As one historian who has studied prerevolutionary Virginia concluded, "Still the question of whether planter debts influenced the coming of the Revolution, being far broader than a single incident, demands further consideration. Certainly the endless discus-

sions of increasing debts, depressed tobacco prices, and short-
ages of currency that occupy so large a part of the surviving
correspondence of Virginians suggests the possibility of a link
between economic conditions in the colony and the Revolutionary movement."[2]

Second, there is the question of timing. This study concentrates on the experiences of the great Tidewater planters during the years before independence. It concentrates upon perceptions, on how the gentry made sense out of the events that
seemed to be transforming their culture. Many of these
gentlemen feared that they might go bankrupt, that they
would be forced to sell their estates. Moreover, not a few
Virginians believed that they would have to give up tobacco
and cultivate another crop. Looking back from the 1790s we
see that they were wrong, or at least that their fears were
exaggerated. Most great planters managed to remain solvent;
some even prospered in the new republic. The change from
tobacco to wheat did occur, especially in a section of the
Tidewater known as the Northern Neck, but the process was
slow and uneven. None of this, however, has much bearing
on the prerevolutionary experience. The planters were not
prescient. In 1772 they dreamed of liberating themselves from
an enslaving crop and economic dependence. It is our responsibility to focus attention upon the social and cultural context
in which these ideas flourished.

Tobacco Culture attempts to recast how we think about the
complex interplay between ideology and experience. If nothing else, the study reminds us that economic relations and
agricultural production are appropriate objects for cultural
analysis. They reveal the mental categories that the men and
women who inhabited historical societies projected onto the
rush of daily events.

Research Triangle Park, North Carolina
September 1984

[2] Thad W. Tate, "The Coming of the Revolution in Virginia: Britain's
Challenge to Virginia's Ruling Class, 1763-1776," *William and Mary Quarterly*
[hereinafter cited as *W&MQ*], 3rd ser., 19(1962), 333.

ACKNOWLEDGMENTS

Among other topics, *Tobacco Culture* explores how the great Tidewater planters perceived debt on the eve of the Revolution. Like those Virginians, I have acquired many personal obligations over the last five years that I suspect can never be fully repaid. While writing this book, I received the unstinting encouragement of friends and colleagues. I also enjoyed the hospitality of two marvelous research centers. This study is offered as partial compensation to those people who gave so unselfishly of their time and to those institutions that provided much-needed financial support.

This book could not have been completed without the generosity of the Institute for Advanced Study in Princeton, New Jersey. I was a member of the Institute during the academic year 1978-79 and want to thank Professors Morton White, Albert Hirschman, Clifford Geertz, and other members of the Institute faculty for their encouragement. I finished the manuscript while a fellow at the National Humanities Center in North Carolina. Charles Blitzer, Kent Mullikin, John S. Reed, Harold Woodman, John Seelye, David Shi, Paul Rahe, and the members of the Center staff provided a splendid intellectual environment in which to write.

A number of librarians provided invaluable assistance along the way. I want to thank in particular the archivists at the Virginia Historical Society in Richmond, at the Virginia State Library (Jon Kukla), and at the Research Division of Colonial Williamsburg (Linda Rowe and P. Maccubbin). They located microfilm editions of planter letterbooks, searched for illustrations, and suggested other sources that I might otherwise have overlooked.

And, of course, progress on this book would have been seriously delayed had it not been for the support of Northwestern University. To Robert Wiebe, Emory Evans, Thad

Tate, Stephen Foster, John Murrin, Josef Barton, James Pea-
cock, Edmund S. Morgan, Richard Beeman, Jake Lassner,
and the many other individuals who read and criticized drafts
of this work and who forced me to push the analysis, I express
my gratitude. Mark H. Friedland, a person who appreciates
the practical problems of doing history, provided timely research funds. It has been a pleasure working with Herbert S.
Bailey, Jr., Gail Ullman, and Marilyn Campbell of the
Princeton University Press. Susan, Sarah, and Bant bore the
whole experience with love and patience.

Chapter II originally appeared in substantially different
form as "The Culture of Agriculture: The Symbolic World
of the Tidewater Planter, 1760-1790" in *Saints and Revolutionaries: Essays on Early American History* edited by David D. Hall,
John M. Murrin, and Thad W. Tate (New York, 1984), 247-
84. Except in passages where the meaning was unclear, I have
not modernized the spelling of the eighteenth-century
sources.

Tobacco Culture

"Virginia?

"Yes, don't you see? Virginia is where it will begin. And it is where there are men who will do it. Just as it was Virginia where it all began in the beginning, or at least where the men were to conceive it, the great Revolution, fought, won it, and saw it on its way. They began the Second Revolution and we lost it. Perhaps the Third Revolution will end differently.

"It won't be California after all. It will be settled in Virginia, where it started.

"Virginia!"

WALKER PERCY, *Lancelot*

CHAPTER I

AN AGRARIAN CONTEXT
FOR RADICAL IDEAS

One early spring day several years ago, I visited Westover, a magnificent Georgian mansion built by William Byrd II during the eighteenth century. The house is located on the James River about twenty-five miles west of Williamsburg. To reach it, one leaves the main state highway and then follows a gravel road that cuts across several large working farms. When I arrived, men were just beginning to cultivate the fields. Some handsome cattle had been let out to pasture. It was too early in the season for the Byrd plantation to attract tourists and schoolchildren, and the grounds of Westover itself appeared deserted. After parking my car, I walked along the river bank, idly surveying places where in colonial times vessels might have docked. In such a setting, it was easy to let my imagination slip back into an agrarian world of the great eighteenth-century planters of Tidewater Virginia.

I suspect that like many other colonial historians, I had taken such ordinary agricultural sights and smells and sounds largely for granted. I had forgotten, or perhaps never even bothered to consider, that the gentry of prerevolutionary Virginia spent most of their waking hours thinking about crops and livestock. I had previously regarded these particular planters, many of whom achieved fame as founding fathers, as somehow divorced from their physical environment—indeed, from work of any sort. I had come to see these men as rural *philosophes* thoroughly absorbed in the writings of Enlightenment thinkers, especially the essays of John Locke, and it appeared to me, at least, that these abstracted Virginians regarded the imperial crisis of the 1760s and 1770s largely as an intellectual problem. I could not comprehend how the ex-

periences of everyday life fit into this traditional image of the
Tidewater planters.

The problem seemed all the more curious because, as we
now know, these Virginians embraced a political ideology
that most contemporary Englishmen regarded as radical. For
a group of wealthy, slaveowning tobacco planters to have
made such a commitment required explanation. After all,
they seem to have had so much to lose, so little to gain, by
upsetting the traditional political order. And yet that is precisely what they did. After mid-century they stressed the importance of personal autonomy and, in language that after
1765 became increasingly strident, warned of growing corruption in Great Britain, secret plots against liberty, and betrayal
of public trust.

This radical Country ideology, as it was termed, apparently struck a responsive chord in the social knowledge of a
group of articulate tobacco planters. But what was the fit between ideas and experience? What elements in their daily lives
predisposed Tidewater gentlemen to think of politics in these
terms? No claim is made that either the experience of cultivating tobacco or the popularity of Country ideas in themselves "caused" the Revolution in Virginia. The movement
toward independence was obviously too complex to be reduced to a single explanation. Nevertheless, by exploring the
relation between a particular agrarian experience and a set of
radical political ideas, we better understand how during the
1770s radical Country thought acquired sufficient moral force
to bring at least some planters to Revolution.

                              I

During most of the nineteenth century, historians encountered little difficulty in defining those ideas that had sparked
the Revolution. Scholars such as George Bancroft regarded
that great event as the inevitable result of the rise of liberty.
Americans fought the British to preserve human rights and
representative government. In the flowery, self-confident
prose so popular in the 1850s, Bancroft explained, "In Great

I. William Byrd's Westover viewed from the James River

Britain, the house of commons had become so venal that it might be asked whether a body so chosen and so influenced was fit to legislate even within the realm. . . . The knell of the ages of servitude and inequality was rung; those of equality and brotherhood were to come in."[1]

During the early decades of the twentieth century, a group of so-called Progressive historians broke with this dominant patriotic tradition. Arthur M. Schlesinger and Carl L. Becker—to cite just two prominent examples—argued that the colonists' dispute with the mother country involved little more than a clash of economic interests. Ideas such as human liberty and natural rights were mere window dressing, rationalizations for the Americans' "real" motives. Progressive scholars concluded that while the leaders of rebellion spoke

[1] Cited in Edmund S. Morgan, ed., *The American Revolution: Two Centuries of Interpretation* (Englewood Cliffs, N.J., 1965), 73.

eloquently of freedom and liberty, they were actually concerned with the preservation of property, which translated into a stubborn avoidance of parliamentary taxation and resistance to commercial regulations that threatened to erode profit.[2]

Soon after World War II, the economic interpretation of the coming of the American Revolution fell into disfavor. To label this shift of focus as revisionism would be misleading, for it involved a total rejection of the basic premise of Progressive scholarship. During the 1950s historians such as Edmund S. Morgan insisted that political principles should be treated as independent variables, fully capable in themselves of sparking violent protest. Americans did not consult their pocketbooks before taking up arms. Even humble artisans and farmers viewed British policy before 1776 as an assault on cherished constitutional rights; by rioting against the Stamp Act or by throwing tea into Boston harbor, the colonists transformed these intellectual abstractions into political action. The entire process seemed remarkably rational, as if the patriot leaders were involved in an orderly philosophical debate rather than a turbulent revolutionary movement.[3]

This idealistic approach still dominates the historiography

[2] Gordon S. Wood provides an excellent review of this literature in "Rhetoric and Reality in the American Revolution," *W&MQ*, 3rd ser., 23(1966), 3-32.

[3] Edmund S. Morgan, "The American Revolution Considered as an Intellectual Movement," in *Paths of American Thought*, ed. Arthur M. Schlesinger, Jr., and Morton White (Boston, 1963), 11-13; Morgan, *Birth of the Republic, 1763-89* (Chicago, 1956); Jack P. Greene, "The Flight from Determinism: A Review of Recent Literature of the Coming of the American Revolution," *South Atlantic Quarterly*, 61(1962), 235-59. The fullest account of this historiography is John M. Murrin, "The Great Inversion, or Court versus Country: A Comparison of the Revolution Settlements in England (1688-1721) and America (1776-1816)," in *Three British Revolutions: 1641, 1688, 1776*, ed. J.G.A. Pocock (Princeton, 1980), 371-76. Murrin correctly observes that the so-called Wisconsin school of colonial historians that flourished under the guidance of Merrill Jensen at the University of Wisconsin asked many of the same questions that had occupied the Progressives. Jensen's students generally fault ideological interpretations of the coming of the Revolution for ignoring economic and social issues (373-74).

of the American Revolution. There has, however, been a major shift in emphasis. Scholars devote less attention to the analysis of high-sounding principles. This change occurred rather suddenly in the mid-1960s; while historians such as J.G.A. Pocock, Caroline Robbins, Isaac Kramnick, Joyce Appleby, and Gordon Wood contributed to the reinterpretation, this new understanding of the character of revolutionary ideology is chiefly associated with the work of Bernard Bailyn. He originally set out to reexamine the contents of familiar revolutionary pamphlets, but, to his surprise, he did not encounter the reasoned discourse about representative government and property rights that he had expected to find. Instead, he discovered an amalgam of political assumptions and beliefs that appeared emotional, irrational, even frenzied. Earlier historians had dismissed this excited rhetoric as sheer hyperbole, a kind of polemic static that should not be allowed to distract one's attention from the patriots' central ideas. Bailyn rejected that assessment. To him, these peculiar excesses offered an important key to reconstructing the ways in which revolutionary Americans actually perceived political reality.[4]

Establishing the intellectual genealogy of these political assumptions has proved unrewarding. Efforts have been made, of course, to isolate specific concepts and then to attribute

[4] Bernard Bailyn, *The Ideological Origins of the American Revolution* (Cambridge, Mass., 1967); Gordon Wood, *The Creation of the American Republic 1776-1787* (Chapel Hill, N.C., 1969); Caroline Robbins, *The Eighteenth-Century Commonwealthman; Studies in the Transmission, Development, and Circumstances of English Liberal Thought from the Restoration of Charles II until the War with the Thirteen Colonies* (Cambridge, Mass., 1959); J.G.A. Pocock, *The Machiavellian Moment: Florentine Political Thought and the Atlantic Republican Tradition* (Princeton, 1975); Edmund S. Morgan, *American Slavery—American Freedom: The Ordeal of Colonial Virginia* (New York, 1975), chapter 18; Zera S. Fink, *The Classical Republicans: An Essay in the Recovery of a Pattern of Thought in Seventeenth-Century England* (Evanston, Ill., 1945); Charles Blitzer, *An Immortal Commonwealth: The Political Thought of James Harrington* (New Haven, 1960); Joyce Appleby, *Capitalism and a New Social Order: The Republican Vision of the 1790s* (New York, 1984); Appleby, "The Social Origins of American Revolutionary Ideology," *Journal of American History*, 64(1978), 935-58; and Isaac Kramnick, *Bolingbroke and His Circle; The Politics of Nostalgia in the Age of Walpole* (Cambridge, Mass., 1968).

them to a certain theorist, a John Locke or a James Harrington, for example. But the division of ideas into precise "units" of thought is an artificial as well as anachronistic exercise. During the eighteenth century, the set of ideas that we have called radical Country ideology owed its origins to the confluence of various streams of political ideas, streams that were at any moment pushed forward by the genius of a particular man but that were not solely the product of his creative insight. It is useful, therefore, to speak in terms of a general idiom of eighteenth-century British opposition politics.[5] This bundle of ideas—the one that Bailyn discovered in the revolutionary pamphlets—cohered around perceptions of personal autonomy, political corruption, and civic virtue. The idiom bears several names: republicanism, Commonwealthman ideas, radical Whig ideology, radical opposition, and dissenting ideology. Radical Country thought is probably no better or worse than these alternative labels. The point to remember is that we are dealing with a loose collection of assumptions that drew moral force from an idiosyncratic reading not only of classical and Renaissance history but also of contemporary political events.[6]

One strand of this opposition idiom deserves special attention: republicanism. Though this body of thought probably originated in Renaissance Italy, some believe it can be traced back to ancient Greece and Rome. Whatever its roots may have been, it spread to England, and during the civil wars of the mid-seventeenth century, republican ideas flourished. A few of the more radical republicans advocated abolition of the monarchy. James Harrington is perhaps the most famous of the early English republicans. The others were relatively obscure pamphleteers, and, following the restoration of the

[5] The concept of a political idiom was sugggested by Robert Darnton in his review essay, "Working-Class Casanova," *New York Review of Books*, 28 June 1984, 32-37.

[6] Bailyn, *Ideological Origins*, passim; Pauline Maier, "The Beginnings of American Republicanism 1765-1776," in *The Development of a Revolutionary Mentality* (Washington, D.C., 1972), 99-117; Robert E. Shalhope, "Toward a Republican Synthesis: The Emergence of an Understanding of Republicanism in American Historiography," *W&MQ*, 3rd ser., 29(1972), 49-80.

Stuart monarchy in 1660, most Englishmen abandoned republicanism almost as rapidly as puritanism. Republicanism survived the English Civil Wars as a dissenting tradition, a political ideology celebrated by the likes of Marchamont Nedham and Algernon Sidney—hardly household names even in their own times. During the first half of the eighteenth century, the story is much the same; republican essayists on the border of intellectual and social respectability turned out tracts which, for all their fire and thunder, were apparently read by very few. Personal zeal rather than financial reward seems to have sustained writers of this political persuasion. By this time most English republicans had made their peace with the monarchy, at least the mixed variety created by the Glorious Revolution of 1688. What worried them the most was the possibility that one element of the balanced constitution—king, lords, or commons—would acquire dominant power and in the process destroy popular liberties.[7]

Other eighteenth-century spokesmen for the radical Country ideology achieved brief notoriety in England for their virulent attacks on Sir Robert Walpole's government. Thomas Gordon and John Trenchard, two Commonwealthmen, hammered away at an unappreciative British audience in a series of essays collectively entitled *Cato's Letters*. While Henry St. John, Viscount Bolingbroke, had little in common socially with the likes of Trenchard and Gordon, this alienated Tory aristocrat shared many of their assumptions about liberty and power, corruption and vice. Bolingbroke's writings were widely republished, often without attribution since it was feared that his scandalous private life might repel people who would ordinarily sympathize with his political philosophy. None of these Country authors welcomed the commercial revolution that was sweeping the British economy. They looked back nostalgically to an ill-defined past when country gentlemen and yeomen farmers had successfully preserved their moral and political independence.[8]

---

[7] Pocock, *Machiavellian Moment*; and Fink, *Classical Republicans*.

[8] William D. Liddle, " 'A Patriot King, or None': Lord Bolingbroke and the American Renunciation of George III," *Journal of American History*, 65(1979), 451-70; and Kramnick, *Bolingbroke and His Circle*.

These various figures—republicans, Commonwealthmen, disaffected Tory noblemen—contributed to a body of ideas that became the commonplaces of eighteenth-century opposition thought. Fear of centralized power lay at the heart of the Country ideology. Writers like Trenchard and Gordon described such power in the shrillest terms. It was aggressive, rapacious, grasping, tenacious, and encroaching. It posed an omnipresent threat to all virtuous citizens for, as radical Country writers repeatedly warned, the exercise of political authority inevitably corrupted rulers, transforming seemingly good people into tyrants. Unless checked by vigilant freemen, despots would destroy popular liberties. One could not be too careful. As *Cato's Letters* explained, "Whatever is good for the People, is bad for their Governors; and what is good for the Governors, is pernicious to the People." The pages of history contained a dreary tale of prosperous republics succumbing to luxury, tolerating venality, and consequently suffering enslavement.[9]

Englishmen who subscribed to the Country idiom could easily spot the danger signs. Attempts by the government to muzzle the press, creation of a standing army, obstruction of free trade, all such policies indicated that conspiracy against liberty had taken root. Even when the commonwealth seemed in perfectly good health, Country essayists warned against secret plots. Great Britain's famed balanced constitution provided some protection against tyrants, but not much. Indeed, corruption of the legislature by the executive branch was the overwhelming fear of the opposition writers. For them, patronage was a form of bribery, a means to undermine a representative's political independence. The Bank of England and the establishment of a funded national debt seemed simply to be instruments of ministerial corruption.

Responsibility for maintaining liberty ultimately rested with England's freemen. This was a crucial point. When Country writers addressed this topic, their rhetoric took on a

---

[9] David L. Jacobson, ed., *The English Libertarian Heritage, From the Writings of John Trenchard and Thomas Gordon* (Indianapolis, 1965); Bailyn, *Ideological Origins*, 22-54; Wood, *Creation of the American Republic*, 3-45.

highly moral, almost religious tone. It was not sufficient for the citizen to monitor the policies of the central government. He was expected to lead an ethical life as well, to exemplify simplicity, rectitude, and incorruptibility. These were the essential attributes of eighteenth-century virtue; they defined the character of the true patriot. The spread of luxury and idleness—indeed, private vices of all sorts—indicated that the people were no longer worthy of liberty. An anonymous Virginian stated the Country view as succinctly as did any of his contemporaries. Luxury and idleness, "Brutus" explained, "bring on a general deprivation of manners, which sets us loose from all the restraints of both public and private virtue, and diverts our thoughts from examining the behaviour and politics of artful and designing men, who meditate our ruin. . . . From immorality and excesses we fall into necessity, and this leads us to a servile dependence upon power, and fits us for the chains prepared for us."[10]

The radical Country ideology received a far more enthusiastic reception in the colonies than it did in the mother country. In England the opposition writers remained marginal, on the fringe of political life, and even the country gentry who sat in Parliament generally took a more flexible stance on public issues than did the essayists who allegedly spoke in their behalf.[11] The story was quite different in America. The Country writers enjoyed broad popularity, and by mid-century the works of Trenchard and Gordon regularly appeared in the provincial press. In the southern colonies Bolingbroke was a favorite, and planters cited his ideas in letters, often without the slightest notion of where those ideas had originated.[12] In fact, what had been a dissenting ideology became in the colonies the dominant political idiom.

[10] *Virginia Gazette* (Rind), 1 June 1769.

[11] Pocock, "1776: The Revolution Against Parliament," in his *Three British Revolutions*, 267-73; and Lance Banning, *The Jeffersonian Persuasion: Evolution of a Party Ideology* (Ithaca, N.Y., 1978), 71.

[12] Robert M. Weir, "The Role of the Newspaper Press in the Southern Colonies on the Eve of the Revolution: An Interpretation," in *The Press and the American Revolution*, ed. Bernard Bailyn and John B. Hench, (Worcester, Mass., 1980), 99-150; and H. Trevor Colbourn, *The Lamp of Experience: Whig*

One example will suffice to show how thoroughly Virginians absorbed the Country perspective. In 1768 the *Virginia Gazette* ran a short essay by "Fabricius," entitled "Salus Populi Est Suprema Lex." The piece was a pastiche of radical Country truisms. If tyranny ever took root in Great Britain, Fabricius warned, the colonists would discover "that servile fear and dependence which the abuse of power naturally creates, shall bind them down in chains; and they shall, at length, become willing slaves ready to sacrifice every generous assertor of their rights and liberties to the power, rage, and malice of their Governors." The author solemnly reminded his readers that "Liberty, when once lost, is scarce ever recovered." And, as was clear enough to those who shared this ideological perspective, "if the executive power be in possession of a right to govern by caprice, there is an end of liberty."[13] It is doubtful that anyone in Virginia—except perhaps the royal governor—found this statement objectionable.

The popularity of radical Country ideas presents historians of the American Revolution with a difficult challenge. The idealist interpretation, however brilliantly argued by scholars like Bailyn, fails to explain why mid-eighteenth-century Americans—and especially the great planters of Tidewater Virginia—would have found this particular idiom so persuasive, so moving.[14] The colonists presumably could have selected other sets of ideas, other ways to make sense out of political and social reality. After all, the appeal of the Country rhetoric eluded most contemporary Englishmen. The Americans' choice, therefore, suggests a close connection between Country ideas and everyday experience. Ideologies do not float freely above human affairs. Nor, for that matter, are

---

History and the Intellectual Origins of the American Revolution (Chapel Hill, N.C., 1965), 142-56.

[13] *Virginia Gazette* (Rind), 9 June 1768.

[14] Several historians have criticized the idealist interpretation on these grounds. See, for example, Jack P. Greene, "The Preconditions for American Republicanism: A Comment," in *The Development of a Revolutionary Mentality* (Washington, D.C., 1972), 119-24; and Pauline Maier, "Why Revolution? Why Democracy?" *Journal of Interdisciplinary History*, 6(1976), 711-32.

they mere rationalizations for material conditions. The relation between ideology and experience is complex, contingent, mutually reinforcing, and it is only within a specific cultural and social context that the kind of intellectual abstractions described by Bailyn acquire the power, the vitality, the moral force necessary to sustain revolution. To be sure, experience does not always generate an ideology, but it does predispose men and women to prefer one set of ideas over another.

The more one thinks about this interpretative problem, the more perplexing it becomes. Eighteenth-century American society would certainly not appear to have been a fertile ground for the reception of an imported, rather shrill, slightly paranoid set of ideas about the corrupting influence of political power. No wonder historians have been at pains to explain exactly why Americans living in stable, prosperous circumstances governed by representatives largely of their own choosing paid the slightest attention to the scribblings of Trenchard and Gordon.

Bailyn provided a possible solution. Radical country ideas, he maintained, made good sense within the colonists' unusual political environment. Mainstream Whig theories developed in Great Britain after 1688 to explain the smooth operation of the balanced constitution—kings, lords, and commons—did not fit the political realities of eighteenth-century America. Royal governors, for example, claimed independent executive authority, but, as they soon discovered, prerogative power counted for very little without the support of the provincial assemblies. Since no genuine aristocracy evolved in America, it seemed absurd to equate a governor's council or a colonial upper house with the British House of Lords. The franchise was much broader in the colonies than it was in the mother country. There were no rotten boroughs in America. This list of structural dissimilarities could be extended. Bailyn's argument is that as early as 1720, such glaring differences made orthodox English political theory appear both arbitrary and irrelevant in the American context. As colonists grew more sensitive to the contrast between British rhetoric and

American reality, they found in the Country ideology a ready explanation for political tensions within the empire.[15]

Another historian, Gordon Wood, sketched out a different way of looking at the problem of fitting ideology to experience. In an influential essay entitled "Rhetoric and Reality in the American Revolution," he argued that the insights of Progressive scholars should not have been so hastily dismissed. To be sure, those historians had been tendentious, their deterministic explanations for political behavior smacking of crude materialism. Nevertheless, Wood insisted that the Progressives raised vital questions about the social context in which a radical political idiom had found expression. "Since ideas and beliefs are ways of perceiving and explaining the world," he observed, "the nature of the ideas expressed is determined as much by the character of the world being confronted as by the internal development of inherited and borrowed conceptions."

The challenge for Wood—and it is the challenge of this book as well—was where one would be best advised to look for those "basic social experiences" that apparently caused colonists to prefer one "pattern of thought" over its competitors. He implied that Bailyn had not provided an adequate answer; that is, Wood did not view the structure of colonial political institutions as necessarily accounting for the Americans' enthusiasm for radical Country ideas. Rather, Wood urged historians to adopt more psychologically sophisticated research strategies, to search out severe "social strains," to reveal the sources of the fears and anxieties that often seemed to obsess eighteenth-century colonists.[16]

The work of Bailyn and Wood reveals—albeit implicitly— several elements that may have impeded our understanding of the mental processes that led eighteenth-century Americans to adopt a radical ideology. First, there is the question of the level of historical generalization. In other words, it may be a mistake to attempt to establish a social context for *all* colo-

[15] Bernard Bailyn, *The Origins of American Politics* (New York, 1967).
[16] "Rhetoric and Reality," 24-32.

nists, a uniform American experience. Perhaps the focus should instead be upon a specific region or culture? Second, and clearly related to the first consideration, is the problem of timing. Since colonists living in various parts of America took up Country ideas at different times ranging from the 1720s to the 1760s, it would seem expedient to concentrate upon the experiences of a group of people precisely during the period when the expression of Country ideology became most intense.

And third, while recognizing the role of political experience in shaping political ideology, we should also consider whether other, nonpolitical experiences such as cultivating tobacco contributed to the spread of Country ideas. People do not usually seal off one aspect of their lives from the rest, treating politics, or religion, or work, or family life as if it bore no relation to other forms of social experience. One can easily imagine, therefore, that strains within a religious community, alterations in the economy, or changes in the demographic structure might create a social situation in which certain political ideas would suddenly gain credibility over others.[17] This is not to suggest that when Americans complained about unconstitutional taxation or lack of representation, they were *really* speaking about God or their pocketbooks. Rather, we must be aware that the general idiom that helped the colonists to interpret political events may have helped them to make sense out of economic and social affairs as well.

II

The great planters of Tidewater Virginia seem to have conspired to frustrate modern social historians. These gentlemen thought a good deal about sex and marriage, of that there is

[17] See, for example, Michael Walzer, *The Revolution of the Saints: A Study in the Origins of Radical Politics* (Cambridge, Mass., 1966); Rhys Isaac, *The Transformation of Virginia, 1740-1790* (Chapel Hill, N.C., 1982). For valuable insights into this and many other topics raised in this book see, J. E. Crowley, *This Sheba, Self: The Conceptualization of Economic Life in Eighteenth-Century America* (Baltimore, 1974).

no doubt.[18] They appear to have loved their children, had opinions on theology and art, on a host of other intriguing subjects; but they remained stubbornly silent about most matters that arouse the curiosity of contemporary scholars. To be sure, a few planters—Landon Carter, for example—recorded their opinions on intimate topics, and it is not surprising that Carter's extraordinary diaries have become the major source for the social history of mid-eighteenth-century Virginia. While Carter's ascerbity is often entertaining, sometimes pathetic, one finds it difficult to ascertain whether he was just a crank, an anomaly in Tidewater society. By comparison, Carter's fellow Virginians—many of whom produced sizable letterbooks and rich personal correspondence—appeared willfully unreflective about what went on around them. To reconstitute the planter mentality, indeed, to recapture the social context in which Country ideas took root, seems on first consideration an impossibility.

To blame the Virginians, however, would be a mistake. One has to learn how to listen to these gentlemen, to appreciate what was on their minds. Only then does it become apparent that the great planters were quite articulate about matters that genuinely concerned them. Their correspondence contains especially revealing observations about two topics: tobacco and debt. This, of course, should come as no surprise. The Tidewater planters lived in a society dominated by agriculture, by the cultivation and marketing of a staple crop, and common sense alone suggests that they would have concentrated their attention upon those subjects most directly connected to their daily experience.

It is from this perspective that we begin to comprehend more fully the cultural and social context of Country ideas in prerevolutionary Tidewater Virginia. Tobacco and debt open windows onto an agrarian mentality, a pattern of values and personal perceptions that gave meaning to the experiences of

---

[18] See Jan Lewis, *The Pursuit of Happiness: Family and Values in Jefferson's Virginia* (Cambridge, 1983); and Daniel Blake Smith, *Inside the Great House: Planter Family Life in Eighteenth-Century Chesapeake Society* (Ithaca, N.Y., 1980).

everyday life. These topics—the cultivation and marketing of a staple crop—are important to us precisely because they were so very important to the great planters. By closely analyzing discussions of tobacco and debt, by following the language of commerce and agriculture, we can more fully appreciate how a group of proud, fiercely independent planters might have interpreted the far-reaching changes in agriculture and credit that occurred in the third quarter of the eighteenth century. That some of these men politicized these experiences, eventually becoming revolutionaries, illuminates a mental process that transformed an agrarian mentality into a justification for national independence.

III

However much Virginians wrote about tobacco, historians have seldom shown much interest either in its production or in its relation to the culture of the great Tidewater families: the Carters, Corbins, Fitzhughs, Lees, Byrds, Beverleys, and Washingtons. The reasons for this oversight are clear. Since many planters became patriot leaders, researchers have naturally emphasized the Virginians' grievances against the British imperial system and their thoughts about the structure of the new government. But the members of this particular group were unusual in another way. Unlike other landed elites that Western historians have studied, particularly the sugar lords of the Caribbean, this one actually directed the production of their staple crop. Virginia planters did not retire to metropolitan centers, divorcing themselves from the annual agricultural routine.

Twentieth-century scholars seem to find it difficult to comprehend the productive aspects of agrarian culture. In their analyses of preindustrial societies, they seize upon the familiar—the nuclear family or urban conflict, for example—while ignoring the daily activities of the great majority of the population. As a result of this bias, we possess abundant studies of colonial cities, urban artisans, and mob violence, but little

A
TREATISE
ON THE
CULTURE
OF THE
TOBACCO PLANT;
WITH THE
Manner in which it is usually cured.

ADAPTED TO
NORTHERN CLIMATES,
AND
DESIGNED FOR THE USE OF THE
LANDHOLDERS OF GREAT-BRITAIN.

TO WHICH ARE PREFIXED,

Two Plates of the Plant and its Flowers,

By JONATHAN CARVER, Esq.
Author of Travels through the Interior Parts of
North-America.

LONDON:
Printed for the Author,
And sold by J. Johnson, in St. Paul's Church-yard.
1779.

about the work culture of the early American planters and farmers.[19]

Modernization theory has exacerbated the interpretative difficulties. Colonial American historians—sometimes quite unconsciously—anticipate the birth of a new industrial society and therefore depict farmers and planters as persons whose lives must inevitably be transformed by market forces beyond their control. From this perspective, early American cultivators become a homogeneous group. No distinction is made between different kinds of agriculture; no attention is paid to different relations between crop and cultivator. Thus, all too often, the farmers of prerevolutionary America appear either as simple rural folk about to be overwhelmed by an expanding market economy or, less frequently, as agricultural innovators busily hustling their neighbors and themselves down the road toward modernity.[20]

To avoid anachronistic interpretations, one must understand the agrarian population on its own terms, as men and women bound by rules developed within a specific cultural

[19] Obvious exceptions to this generalization are Lewis Cecil Gray, *History of Agriculture in the Southern United States to 1860* (New York, 1941), and Ulrich B. Phillips, *Life and Labor in the Old South* (Boston, 1941), chapter 8. See also, James A. Henretta, "Families and Farms: *Mentalité* in Pre-Industrial America," *W&MQ*, 3rd ser., 35(1978), 3-32; and for a provocative discussion of the relation between planter culture and agricultural production at a slightly later time in American history, Eugene D. Genovese, *The Political Economy of Slavery; Studies in the Economy and Society of the Slave South* (New York, 1967), esp. chapters 1 and 6.

To appreciate the dimensions of this interpretative problem, one has only to compare what little we know about colonial farm life with the rich insights into early nineteenth-century factory culture that we have gained from scholars such as E. P. Thompson, Merritt Roe Smith, and Anthony Wallace. E. P. Thompson, "Time, Work-Discipline, and Industrial Capitalism," *Past and Present*, no. 38(1967), 56-97; Merritt Roe Smith, *Harpers Ferry Armory and the New Technology: The Challenge of Change* (Ithaca, N. Y., 1977); and Anthony F. C. Wallace, *Rockdale: The Growth of an American Village in the Early Industrial Revolution* (New York, 1978).

[20] I have discussed these issues at greater length in "Back to Sweat and Toil: Suggestions for the Study of Agricultural Work in Early America," *Pennsylvania History*, 49(1982), 241-58.

and physical environment. As anthropologists have shown, forms of cultivation can affect the character of a people's culture. Analysis of agricultural activities in narrow economic terms—as simply a matter of counting bushels and bales, of calculating profits and losses—obscures the more subtle relations between crop and cultivator. Plants often assume special significance for the grower, and over several generations the products of the fields may become associated with a particular set of regional values, a pattern of land tenure, a system of labor, even a festive calendar. This connection is especially obvious in communities relying upon a particular staple, such as sugar, cotton, rice, or coffee.[21] Whether the cultivation of certain plants generates cultural values and mental categories or merely reinforces those already present in the society is not clear. Probably both processes are at work, and the dominant crop both shapes and gives meaning to the local culture.

A comparative dimension is helpful here. In the study of Caribbean agriculture, the relation between crop and cultivator occupies a central place. Indeed, these island societies established staple economies at approximately the same time and under roughly similar conditions as did the Tidewater planters, and the Caribbean experience illuminates the development of Virginia's culture of agriculture. In the case of Cuba, for example, scholars speak of a "sugar mentality," a specific pattern of behavior and turn of mind connected with the production of sugar. In plantation societies dependent upon sugar cane, the crop affects the cultivators' attitudes about proper land use and work habits, about time and space, about the character of most human activities. As one anthro-

---

[21] See Clifford Geertz, *Agricultural Involution: The Process of Ecological Change in Indonesia* (Berkeley, 1963); Carville V. Earle, "A Staple Interpretation of Slavery and Free Labor," *Geographical Review*, 68(1978), 51-65; Richard Lyle Power, *Planting Corn Belt Culture: The Impress of the Upland Southerner and Yankee in the Old Northwest*, Indiana Historical Society Publications, 17(Indianapolis, 1953); and Pete Daniel, "The Crossroads of Change: Cotton, Tobacco, and Rice Cultures in the Twentieth-Century South," *Journal of Southern History*, 50(1984), 429-56.

pologist has put it, "Sugar . . . rules the Antilles."[22] In neighboring islands, where coffee was the chief staple, one finds a
similar cultural configuration. As one investigator of a subre-
gion of Puerto Rico discovered, "coffee culture is not merely
a business [it is also] . . . an environmental pattern and a social structure."[23]

Though colonial Virginians grew tobacco, the relation of
their culture to the dominant crop was much like that found
in the Sugar Islands. Indeed, in view of the centrality of a
single staple in the lives of the Tidewater planters, one can
write of a "tobacco mentality," a distinct culture that leaders
of eighteenth-century Virginia like Carter, Lee, and Washington took for granted. The relation between plant and planter
was far more complex than it might at first appear.

On one level, tobacco *shaped* general patterns of behavior.
The plant's peculiar physical characteristics influenced the
planters' decisions about where to locate plantations and how
to allocate time throughout the year. In other words, tobacco
added a dimension to the colonists' perceptions of time and
space; and without doubt, the details of the Virginia work
routine contributed powerfully to the development of a tobacco mentality.

On a second level, however, tobacco gave *meaning* to routine planter activities. It was emblematic not only of a larger
social order, its past, its future, its prospects in comparison
with those of other societies, but also of the individual producers. As we shall see, there was a crucial psychological link
between planter and tobacco. The staple provided the Lees
and Carters of mid-eighteenth-century Virginia with a means
to establish a public identity, a way to locate themselves
within a web of human relations. The crop served as an index
of worth and standing in a community of competitive, highly
independent growers; quite literally, the quality of a man's

---

[22] Sidney Mintz's foreword to Ramiro Guerra y Sánchez, *Sugar and Society in the Caribbean: An Economic History of Cuban Agriculture* (New Haven, 1964), xliv.

[23] Cited in Julian H. Steward et al., *The People of Puerto Rico: A Study in Social Anthropology* (Urbana, Ill., 1969), 171, also 93-94, 161-68.

tobacco often served as the measure of the man. Both aspects of the tobacco mentality—tobacco as shaper of everyday experience and tobacco as source of individual and corporate meaning—help to explain the intensity of the planters' commitment to the staple and to the personal relations that it spawned.

IV

The great planters of Tidewater Virginia were also obsessed with the topic of personal debt, a condition that after 1750 seemed to be an inevitable consequence of raising tobacco for a world market. In fact, after 1773 planter indebtedness precipitated a major cultural crisis. Surviving Virginia account books contain extensive commentary about the nature of trade, credit, and debt; these scattered observations can be employed to reconstruct a framework of commercial perceptions—what is here termed a "culture of debt"—that gave meaning to the great planters' economic affairs, and as we shall discover, to their political life as well.

Over the course of the eighteenth century, the great tobacco planters—those that produced the largest crops and sent them to the major merchant houses of London, Bristol, and Glasgow on consignment—developed an elaborate mental framework that gave meaning and coherence to commercial transactions, to ongoing exchanges with merchants living thousands of miles away and often involving complex credit arrangements. During the 1760s and 1770s instabilities in the international economy, over which the planters had no control, strained ties between merchant and producer. In these difficult circumstances the language of commerce, which had taken on idiosyncratic overtones in the Virginia context, acquired new meanings to fit changing external conditions. The transformation of how planters perceived their relations with British merchants seemed to undermine the core of the tobacco mentality and thus, especially after 1772, to demand a revolutionary response.

Unlike tobacco, debt has been the object of considerable

scholarly attention. Indeed, it has been a source of some embarrassment for Virginia historians, much like a ne'er-do-well relative whom a proper family chooses to ignore. The reasons for the uneasiness are clear enough. The great planters of Tidewater Virginia enjoy a special place in American history. They included some of the nation's ablest leaders, and without the likes of Washington and Jefferson, it is hard to see how Americans could have made good their claim to political independence.

Progressive historians of the early twentieth century rebelled against this filiopietism. Charles A. Beard and others have revealed that the great planters were in debt up to their ears, and it seemed obvious to the Progressives that whatever the Virginia patriots may have said about freedom and liberty, they actually regarded the Revolution as an opportunity to escape British creditors.[24] Lawrence H. Gipson pointedly reminded his readers of George Mason's remark to Patrick Henry at the conclusion of the Revolution: "If we now have to pay the debts due to British merchants, what have we been fighting for all this while?" If a patriot of Mason's credentials fought to avoid paying his bills, what are we to make of the other, less prominent planters? The answer, Gipson suggested, can be found in the fact that "most of the private debts owed to British creditors *were never paid.* . . ." None of Gipson's contemporaries apparently noticed that he had quoted Mason's statement grossly out of context.[25]

---

[24] Charles A. Beard, *Economic Origins of Jeffersonian Democracy* (New York, 1915); Isaac S. Harrell, *Loyalism in Virginia: Chapters in the Economic History of the Revolution* (Durham, N.C., 1926).

[25] Lawrence H. Gipson, "Virginia Planter Debts before the American Revolution," *Virginia Magazine of History and Biography* [hereinafter cited as *VMHB*], 69(1961), 276-77 (emphasis added). Mason's question was clearly rhetorical. He then answered it: "Surely not to avoid our just Debts, or cheat our Creditors; but to rescue our Country from the Oppression and Tyranny of the British Government, and to secure the Rights and Liberty of ourselves, and our Posterity; which we have happily accomplished." Mason's full letter can be found in Robert A. Rutland, ed., *The Papers of George Mason, 1725-1792* (Chapel Hill, N.C., 1970), II, 771-72. The author thanks Emory Evans for pointing out Gipson's misrepresentation of this evidence.

The image of the great planter as deadbeat did not sit well with historians of the Eisenhower generation. In an essay published in 1962, Emory Evans admitted that Virginians owed British creditors almost two million pounds on the eve of the Revolution, but after reviewing all of the relevant evidence both before and after 1776, Evans concluded that this burden of indebtedness had no appreciable effect upon the planters' perception of the Anglo-American crisis. Private finances certainly did not figure in the Virginians' formal protests sent to king and Parliament. "Despite the heavy indebtedness and the considerable frustration it produced," Evans concluded, "there does not seem to have been *any important connection* between the debts and the Revolutionary movement in Virginia before 1774."[26] The thoroughness of Evans's research effectively silenced the Progressives. He seemed to have conclusively demonstrated that in Virginia at least, the size of a man's debt provided no sure key to his politics.

The rout of the Progressives restored much of the planters' tarnished glory. Historians writing of Virginia thereafter could hardly contain their admiration for this remarkable group of men. Charles Sydnor and others described the gentry as students of classical history and common law, as commonsensical types who saw the imperial crisis almost exclusively as a matter of constitutional principle.[27] One did not need to know how much the planters owed their British merchants—indeed, one did not need to know much about social and economic experience—to understand why they so passionately defended the political rights of America. These ideas simply made good sense. Taxation without representa-

[26] Emory G. Evans, "Planter Indebtedness and the Coming of the Revolution in Virginia," *W&MQ*, 3rd ser., 19(1962), 511-33 (emphasis added). Since the appearance of his essay, Evans has modified his earlier estimate of the role of planter debt. In a letter to the author, he explained that "I now believe debt to be an important factor in the coming of the Revolution, but I do not believe it is the only explanation . . ." (5 June 1984). With that judgment, I fully agree.

[27] Charles S. Sydnor, *Gentlemen Freeholders: Political Practices in Washington's Virginia* (Chapel Hill, N.C., 1952).

tion was tyranny. In his study of Virginia's ruling elite, Thad W. Tate explained, "What remains as the fundamental issue in the coming of the Revolution, then, is nothing more than the contest over constitutional rights."[28] Historians who shared Tate's perspective transformed planter-debtors into constitutional lawyers, and in the process abstracted them from the world in which they lived.

By the mid-1960s the great planters' place of esteem in American historiography seemed secure. Scholars regularly described the leaders of Tidewater Virginia as children of the Enlightenment, imaginatively employing reason to solve the problems of Virginia and the new nation.[29]

The difficulty with this interpretation, one in which the question of planter debt played no role, was that it did not conform to what wealthy eighteenth-century Virginians said about their lives. When Gordon Wood and Jack P. Greene examined the personal papers of the Tidewater gentry, they encountered expressions of anxiety, often ill-focused to be sure, but sometimes involving doubts about the very survival of a traditional social order. The threat seemed as much internal as external, as if the planters themselves were partially responsible for the crisis. On the eve of the Revolution, according to Wood, there seemed "to have been something of a social crisis within the ruling group itself, which intensely aggravated the Virginians' antagonism to the imperial system."[30]

However tentative Wood's speculations may have been (his remarks on Virginia occupy only a few pages of a long essay),

[28] Thad W. Tate, "The Coming of the Revolution in Virginia: Britain's Challenge to Virginia's Ruling Class, 1763-1776," *W&MQ*, 3rd ser., 19(1962), 323-43.

[29] See, for example, Garry Wills, *Inventing America: Jefferson's Declaration of Independence* (Garden City, N.Y., 1978).

[30] Wood, "Rhetoric and Reality," 27; Jack P. Greene, *Landon Carter: An Inquiry into the Personal Values and Social Imperatives of Eighteenth-Century Gentry* (Charlottesville, 1965); Greene, "Society, Ideology, and Politics: An Analysis of the Political Culture of Mid-Eighteenth-Century Virginia," in *Society, Freedom, and Conscience: The American Revolution in Virginia, Massachusetts, and New York*, ed. Richard M. Jellison (New York, 1976), 14-76.

he called into question accepted interpretations of the mentality of the Tidewater planters. If, as he argued, the great planters felt threatened by tensions within their society, then it seemed less inexplicable why they might have embraced radical Country ideas. And by insisting that these particular colonial gentlemen were not *philosophes* divorced from the pressures of everyday agrarian life, Wood forced Virginia historians to reconsider the entire relation between political ideology and social experience. "It seems clear," he explained, ". . . from the very nature of the ideas expressed that the sources of the Revolution in Virginia were much more subtle and complicated than a simple antagonism to the British government. Constitutional principles alone do not explain the Virginians' almost unanimous determination to revolt."[31]

Wood did not pursue the difficult problems that he raised, at least not in the Virginia context. He barely considered the issue of planter debt, leaving it to others to discover exactly what might have conditioned the planters of mid-eighteenth-century Virginia to perceive politics in terms of lost virtue, personal betrayal, and possible enslavement.

The most original solution to this problem appeared in 1982. Drawing upon what he described as Wood's "seminal discussion of the social sources of the emotional appeal of ideology," historian Rhys Isaac argued that the great planters of colonial Virginia experienced a colossal failure of nerve.[32] Moreover, their anxiety was not the product of an overwrought collective imagination. It was rooted in actual experience, in everyday life.

After mid-century, according to Isaac, the traditional world

---

[31] Wood, "Rhetoric and Reality," 30.

[32] Isaac, *Transformation of Virginia*, 400. See Isaac, "Evangelical Revolt: The Nature of the Baptists' Challenge to the Traditional Order in Virginia, 1765 to 1775," *W&MQ*, 3rd ser., 31(1974), 345-68; and Isaac, "Preachers and Patriots: Popular Culture and the Revolution in Virginia," in *The American Revolution: Explorations in the History of American Radicalism*, ed. Alfred F. Young (Dekalb, Ill., 1976), 127-56. Also see, Jack P. Greene, " 'Virtus et Libertàs': Political Culture, Social Change, and the Origins of the American Revolution in Virginia, 1763-1766," in *The Southern Experience in the American Revolution*, ed. Jeffrey J. Crow and Larry E. Tise (Chapel Hill, N.C., 1978), 55-108.

of the great planters came increasingly under attack. Virginia gentlemen no longer received deference—or so they believed—from their poor neighbors. The small planters seemed to have developed a separate culture, a different set of assumptions about social and economic intercourse. This erosion of authority, Isaac maintained, could be traced to the spread of evangelical Protestantism, especially the Baptist faith, among the colony's less affluent whites. The Great Awakening produced scores of dissenting communities, congregations that, Isaac insisted, represented more than an expression of intense religious conviction. The evangelicals propagated a radically new system of values. They idealized humility and advocated equality, even to the point of questioning the morality of slavery. Isaac declared that the Baptists "aroused intense hostility amongst many gentry leaders . . . so that violence, riot, arrest, and imprisonment were not infrequent occurrences."[33] Such crude tactics backfired: gentry violence only turned "born-again" Virginians into local martyrs. Isaac concluded that what eventually preserved gentry hegemony was the timely appearance of Patrick Henry, a traditional planter who expressed himself like an itinerant preacher and thus managed to bridge the two cultures. Henry brought a fiery, emotional commitment to Country ideas, and during the difficult years preceding revolution, he transformed political protest into a moral crusade.

Isaac's argument was brilliantly presented and methodologically innovative, but ultimately unpersuasive. He exaggerated the impact of the Baptists on Virginia society before the Revolution. Their numbers were actually rather small (one estimate is that no more than 5 percent of white Virginians belonged to Separate Baptist churches in 1775), and the private papers of the great Tidewater planters reveal almost universal indifference to their activities. To be sure, an outspoken itinerant preacher occasionally annoyed the local gentry; it is, however, absurd to claim that the gentry of Tidewater Virginia terrorized their poorer Baptist neighbors. Robert Carter, one of the region's wealthiest planters, eventually con-

---

[33] Isaac, "Preachers and Patriots," 128.

verted to the new faith. And though some Baptists may have resented the privileges of the established church, they were neither barred from voting nor prohibited from worshipping as they pleased.[34] Despite the undeniable creativity of Isaac's book, therefore, it does not adequately explain why a radical Country ideology would have struck a responsive chord among the Tidewater gentry or how this particular political idiom could have acquired sufficient moral force to spark a revolution.[35] This criticism does not mean, of course, that Isaac simply invented the planters' crisis of confidence. The great planters did express considerable uneasiness about the future of their society and their place within it. No doubt, the Baptist challenge exacerbated the fears and anxieties of some Virginia gentlemen, but something so complex as the Revolution cannot be reduced to a single cause, be it aggressive dissenters or an insensitive English Parliament.

This discussion returns us to a reconsideration of planter debt, a topic after all about which the Virginians had a good deal to say. The Progressive historians correctly focused their attention on this aspect of the plantation economy. They went astray, however, by assuming that debt was simply a question of who owed whom how much. Their approach to the problem was that of the accountant rather than the anthropologist; they concentrated on total sums rather than mental categories. But, as we shall see, statistics provide little help in understanding eighteenth-century perceptions of debt. The magnitude of a man's financial obligations does not in itself determine how he thinks about debt, or more precisely, how he defines relations with persons to whom he happens to owe money. Such human exchanges involve values as well as pounds and pence. In other words, credit is a form of com-

[34] See Louis Morton, *Robert Carter of Nomini Hall: A Virginia Tobacco Planter of the Eighteenth Century* (Williamsburg, 1941); and Bernard Bailyn, "Political Experience and Enlightenment Ideas in Eighteenth-Century America," *American Historical Review*, 67(1962), 345-46.

[35] Herbert Sloan and Peter Onuf, "Politics, Culture, and the Revolution in Virginia: A Review of Recent Work," *VMHB*, 91(1983), 259-84. Also, Philip D. Morgan, "The Medium and the Message: The Transformation of Virginia," *Historical Studies*, 20(1983), 590-99.

munication, and throughout the world, societies discuss debt
in highly moral terms.[36] Some modern economists chide
Americans for talking of the national debt in language more
appropriate to family finances than to the funding of a large
government. The debt is seen as evil, fearful, morally suspect;
the government appears to engage in practices that would land
the private citizen in bankruptcy court. What the people are
doing, of course, is projecting assumptions drawn from personal experience—paying the light bill and mortgage—and
applying them to a budgetary problem so huge that it almost
defies comprehension. These examples suggest that when two
groups—in this case, Tidewater planters and British merchants—operating under different assumptions about the
meaning of credit and projecting different understandings
onto a common commercial vocabulary, come into conflict,
they would not only express cultural assumptions, usually la-
tent, with unusual clarity and force, but would also interpret
the other group's actions in the worst possible light.[37]

V

These interrelated systems of meaning, in agriculture as well
as in commerce, came unravelled on the eve of the Revolu-

[36] Edward L. Schieffelin, "Reciprocity and the Construction of Reality,"
Man, 15(1980), 502-17.

[37] My interpretation reflects an eclectic reading in anthropology and soci-
ology. Some of the titles I found most helpful are Conrad M. Arensberg, *The
Irish Countryman; An Anthropological Study* (Garden City, N.Y., 1968); Fredrik
Barth, "Introduction," *Ethnic Groups and Boundaries: The Social Organization of
Cultural Difference* (Boston, 1963), 9-38; Barth, "Economic Spheres in Dar-
fur," in *Themes in Economic Anthropology*, ed. Raymond Firth (London, 1967);
Barth, *Models of Social Organization*, Royal Anthropological Institute, Occasional Papers, 23 (London, 1966); Erving Goffman, *The Presentation of Self in
Everyday Life* (Edinburgh, 1958); Andrew Strathern, *Rope of Moka; Big-Men
and Ceremonial Exchange in Mount Hagen, New Guinea* (Cambridge, 1971); Anthony Giddens, *Central Problems in Social Theory: Action, Structure and Contra-
diction in Social Analysis* (Berkeley, 1979); Norman Long, *An Introduction to the
Sociology of Rural Development* (London, 1977); and Bernard Bailyn, "Com-
munication and Trade: The Atlantic in the 17th Century," *Journal of Economic
History*, 13(1953), 378-87.

tion. Chronically low prices forced Tidewater planters to contemplate seriously the abandonment of tobacco in favor of wheat. Some gentlemen actually dropped the staple. Though the change was gradual, it eroded the tobacco mentality, threatening a set of symbols and values traditionally associated with the cultivation of the leaf. The shift altered the basic language of agriculture. *Planters* became *farmers*. The gentry became innovators despite themselves. They were swept up by a tide of change that affected even the appearance of the fields, a psychological process that may have made the great planters more receptive to new ideas—even to a reformation of political society—than they would have been before.

Such was the agricultural context of a second, even more disruptive cultural change. International financial crises during the 1760s and 1770s compelled British merchants to call in longstanding debts, to challenge, however implicitly, the Virginians' independence, and the gentry felt betrayed. A commercial "friendship"—the term is theirs—had gone sour. Their autonomy had been questioned. They had been dishonored. Even worse, the merchants' insistent dunning forced each great planter to protect his own credit as best he could, to ward off bankruptcy, even if that course meant badgering his neighbors. These strains evoked a powerful desire to revitalize the traditional culture, to restore lost virtue and independence.

During the early 1760s, planters treated their debts largely as private matters. They carried on lengthy correspondence with distant merchants in which they complained that commercial relations that had once been reciprocal friendships had become a means to reduce Virginians to economic dependence, even slavery. In other words, they expressed their anger and embarrassment in language remarkably Country in character. Gradually, however, the planters became aware that other Virginians were suffering the same indignities. Debt was transformed from a private to a public concern. Planters condemned luxury and joined together to stem the flow of those British imports that had bought them into debt.

They vowed to lead simple, virtuous, uncorrupted lives; at least, they would try. In the early 1770s these issues became politicized. The great planters described the merchants as agents of an oppressive administration that seemed determined to crush constitutional liberties and economic prosperity in America. Though debt and tobacco did not bring the Virginians to Revolution, they hastened many planters down the road to independence and gave Country ideas a moral force that they might not otherwise have possessed.

VI

The great Tidewater planters dominated Virginia society. Historians have estimated their numbers at anywhere from 3 to 10 percent of the white heads of households. These are obviously rough figures, and modern scholars seem to have more difficulty identifying great planters than did the eighteenth-century colonists. Some contemporaries have described these gentlemen as haughty, overbearing, eager to impress their social inferiors with the trappings of wealth and power. The sight of a great planter riding his horse down a dusty Virginia road was sufficient to throw James Ireland, a young man of modest financial resources, into a panic. "When I viewed him riding up," Ireland reported many years after the Revolution, "I never beheld such a display of pride in any man, . . . arising from his deportment, attitude and gesture; he rode a lofty elegant horse . . . his countenance appeared to me as bold and daring as satan himself."[38]

Ireland, who later became an evangelical minister, may have exaggerated the hauteur of the great planters. Certainly, other Virginians did not remember the colony's leaders as being either particularly bold or daring. During the early years of the nineteenth century, for example, William Wirt

[38] Cited in Isaac, *Transformation of Virginia*, 161. The percentages are taken from D. Alan Williams, "The Small Farmer in Eighteenth-Century Virginia Politics," *Agricultural History*, 43(1969), 92; and Aubrey C. Land, "The Tobacco Staple and the Planter's Problems: Technology, Labor, and Crops," ibid., 78.

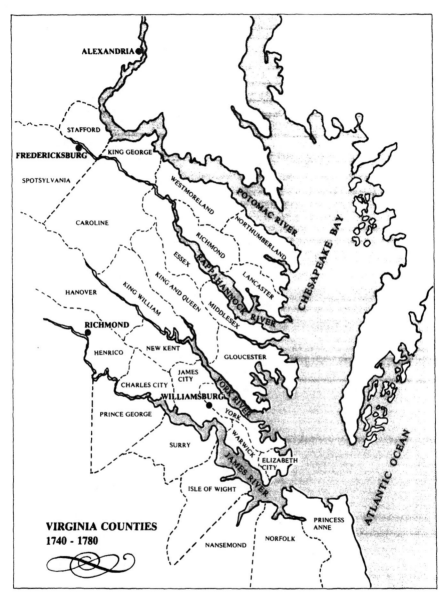

ALEXANDRIA

STAFFORD

FREDERICKSBURG   KING GEORGE

SPOTSYLVANIA

WESTMORELAND

POTOMAC RIVER

CAROLINE

RICHMOND

NORTHUMBERLAND

ESSEX

RAPPAHANNOCK RIVER

LANCASTER

HANOVER

KING WILLIAM

KING AND QUEEN

MIDDLESEX

RICHMOND

HENRICO   NEW KENT

GLOUCESTER

JAMES CITY

CHARLES CITY

WILLIAMSBURG

YORK RIVER

PRINCE GEORGE

YORK

WARWICK

SURRY

JAMES RIVER

ELIZABETH CITY

ISLE OF WIGHT

CHESAPEAKE BAY

ATLANTIC OCEAN

PRINCESS ANNE

VIRGINIA COUNTIES
1740 - 1780

NANSEMOND   NORFOLK

III. Tidewater Virginia at mid-century

asked St. George Tucker to criticize a draft of his *Life of Patrick Henry*. Tucker had arrived in Virginia in 1772 and thus had personally known many individuals who had figured in Henry's career. Wirt's manuscript amazed Tucker. It depicted the gentry in language that Ireland might have used. "The rich rode in Coaches, or Chariots, or on fine horses," Tucker explained, "but they never failed to pull off their hats to a poor man whom they met, & generally, appear'd to me to shake hands with every man in a Court-yard, or a Church-yard, and as far as I could judge the planter who own'd half a dozen negroes, felt himself perfectly upon a level with his rich neighbor that own'd a hundred." To Ireland and Wirt, a man who owned six slaves may have seemed something of an aristocrat. Whatever the case may have been, Tucker insisted that the great planters of prerevolutionary Virginia had been "a race of *harmless aristocrats*" who possessed neither the "Talent" nor "the Inclination, to do any political Injury."[39]

However civilly the great planters may have behaved, it is doubtful that any self-respecting European nobleman would have mistaken even the wealthiest Virginians for aristocrats. For one thing their genealogies did not bear close examination. The Virginia gentry traced its roots back to the mid-seventeenth century when the sons of middling English merchants travelled to the Chesapeake in search of economic opportunity. Many of these early migrants were roughnecks, men in a hurry to get rich and none too particular about the means they employed to achieve their goal. Tobacco provided good, though not spectacular, returns to those newcomers who could obtain the labor of white indentured servants. But progress was slow. The planters battled royal governors and each other for political advantage, and on several occasions these rivalries sparked open rebellion. Moreover, as we now know, these seventeenth-century Virginians entered a deadly disease environment. It was a struggle to survive, and most planters and servants died young. Indeed, the earliest repre-

[39] "Notes of St. George Tucker on Manuscript Copy of William Wirt's *Life of Patrick Henry* (September 25, 1815)," *W&MQ*, 1st ser., 22(1914), 252-53.

sentatives of the famous eighteenth-century families—the Byrds and Carters, for example—lived in modest wooden structures, homes that would not have impressed the contemporary English squirarchy. It was not until the 1720s and 1730s that elegant Georgian structures such as Westover, Sabine Hall, and Mount Airy began to appear along Virginia's major rivers.[40]

The construction of these mansions revealed changes that were reshaping the colony's social structure. Though it seems a truism to state that the rich were getting richer, the poor poorer, that is exactly what was occurring in early eighteenth-century Virginia. The sources of these growing social distinctions were obvious. The wealthier planters, those with a little cash to invest or with access to credit, purchased slaves. In fact, it was during this period that the colony's labor force became predominantly black. The small planters simply could not afford to purchase slaves, and since those colonists who owned blacks produced more tobacco, they inevitably found themselves in a position to buy additional Africans. The process continued until some planters like the Carters literally possessed hundreds of unfree workers.[41]

As this rising elite gained greater economic security, it seized control of the colony's political institutions. Not only did the great planters dispense justice for their less affluent neighbors, they also used their positions on the governor's

[40] See Bernard Bailyn, "Politics and Social Structure in Virginia," in *Seventeenth-Century America*, ed. J. M. Smith (Chapel Hill, N.C., 1959), 90-115; and Allan Kulikoff, "The Rise of the Chesapeake Gentry" (Paper presented at the annual meeting of the Organization of American Historians, New York, April 1978). Gloria Main provides an excellent account of material conditions in late seventeenth-century Chesapeake society in her *Tobacco Colony: Life in Early Maryland, 1650-1720* (Princeton, 1982). Also see, James Horn, "Everyday Life in Seventeenth-Century England and the Chesapeake: An Exercise in Comparative Local History" (Paper presented at the St. Mary's Conference, St. Mary's City, Maryland, May 1984).

[41] Willard F. Bliss, "The Rise of Tenancy in Virginia," *VMHB*, 58(1950), 427-41; Land, "The Tobacco Staple and the Planter's Problems," 69-86; and Darrett B. and Anita H. Rutman, *A Place in Time: Middlesex County, Virginia 1650-1750* (New York, 1984), chapter 6.

council or in the House of Burgesses to patent huge tracts of western lands. The local representatives of the crown winked at these practices; indeed, they carved out extensive pieces of real estate for themselves. The great planters held on to some choice pieces of property, insurance that their sons and daughters would have acreage on which to grow ever more tobacco, but most of it was resold to other Virginians and new immigrants at considerable profit. In other words, they were speculators on a grand scale. This cozy system lasted until the early 1750s when the French and Indian War, coupled with tighter imperial controls over the granting of western lands, cut the gentry off from one of its major sources of income.[42]

The great Tidewater planters, those who lived on the lower reaches of the colony's four largest rivers, sold their tobacco on consignment. Each year they shipped their harvest to an English merchant who not only sold the staple at the best price he could obtain, but also purchased various manufactured goods that the Virginians had ordered. During the first third of the eighteenth century, the gentry often bought tobacco produced by their poorer neighbors, and thus linked the small planters to the European market. Even after this system broke down, the wealthiest planters continued to sell on consignment. In fact, this marketing device became a badge of class, a means of distinguishing the great planters from those of lesser status.[43]

As they grew increasingly wealthy, the leading gentlemen of Virginia indulged themselves as consumers. They attempted to live like English gentry, and some men fulfilled their dreams. They imported luxury items, kept up with

---

[42] In conversation with the author (December 1979), John M. Hemphill of Colonial Williamsburg, Inc., Research Center pointed out the immense importance of land speculation in the rise of the great planter families. I thank him for sharing his ideas on this and related topics.

[43] Jacob Price, "Economic Growth of the Chesapeake and European Market, 1697-1775," *Journal of Economic History*, 24(1964), 506-507; Rutman and Rutman, *Place in Time*, 231; and Emory Evans, "Private Indebtedness and the Revolution in Virginia, 1776 to 1796," *W&MQ*, 3rd ser., 28(1971), 349.

standards of dress and reading set in London. In 1736 one surprised English visitor exclaimed on arrival in Yorktown, "You perceive a great Air of Opulence amongst the Inhabitants, who have some of them built Houses equal in Magnificence to many of our superb ones at St. James's; as those of Mr. Lightfoot, Nelson, &c. Almost every considerable Man Keeps an Equipage, tho' they have no Concern about the different Colours of their Coach Horses, driving frequently black, white, and chestnut, in the same Harness."[44] This last observation was the sort of backhanded compliment that was bound to offend ambitious Virginians. They hated to be reminded that despite all their expenditures they remained parvenu, and perhaps because of their fear of being exposed as provincials, they spent a little too heavily, gambled too much, and expected less wealthy Virginians to show them respect.

Questions immediately arise concerning the analysis of an agricultural mentality based on the experience of such a small elite group. Did other Virginians share the great planters' perceptions of tobacco? Of exchanges with British merchants? For the slaves the answer is obvious. For these people the relation between laborer and crop—the definition of work culture—was different from that of the gentry. It is inconceivable that the slaves could have imbibed the same fixation with quality, debt, and autonomy.[45]

The small planters present a more difficult interpretative problem. Though they were ubiquitous in the eighteenth-century records—often because of their propensity to run afoul of the law—they left only hints of their personal beliefs and assumptions. During the middle decades of the century, many of these poorer planters swarmed up Virginia's rivers to the newly opened lands of the Piedmont, and there, on small holdings without the benefit of slave labor, they har-

[44] " 'Observations on Several Voyages and Travels in America in the Year 1736,' from *The London Magazine*, July 1746," *W&MQ*, 1st ser., 15(1907), 222. The best account of the public aspects of gentry society in early eighteenth-century Virginia is Isaac, *Transformation of Virginia*, 11-138.

[45] See Gerald W. Mullin, *Flight and Rebellion: Slave Resistance in Eighteenth-Century Virginia* (New York, 1972).

vested thousands of pounds of tobacco. We simply do not have evidence whether these men felt pride of production, identified with the crop, or achieved meaningful social identity through an agricultural work culture. Whatever these people may have thought, the upper classes took it as a matter of faith that the small planters looked to their betters for social cues. In 1772 Philip Fithian, an observant young man who served as Robert Carter's tutor at Nomini Hall, claimed that "the People of fortune . . . are the *pattern of all behavior here.*"[46]

One hesitates, however, to accept the word of such well-placed visitors. The small planters were notoriously independent, and when it served their purposes, they distanced themselves from their wealthy neighbors. This was most evident in the marketing of tobacco. After the 1730s the little producers began selling their tobacco to resident Scottish factors, agents of the large Glasgow firms who provided cash and credit to Virginians who might otherwise have been dependent on the generosity of the great planters. The Scots landed huge contracts from the French tobacco monopoly, and in order to fulfill their employers' obligations, the factors bought in bulk. They could not be bothered with the higher-grade leaf grown on the Rappahannock and York Rivers. The French demanded quantity, not quality, and by supplying this market with tobacco, the small planters not only obtained European manufactures but also freed themselves from gentry control.[47]

Nevertheless, even when one takes the factor system into

[46] Fithian to Rev. Enoch Green, 1 December 1773, in *Journal and Letters of Philip Vickers Fithian*, ed. Hunter D. Farish (Williamsburg, 1945), 35 (emphasis added). At least one other contemporary report supports Fithian's observation. Just before departing for the meeting of the Continental Congress in Philadelphia, Benjamin Harrison, a wealthy Virginia planter, received a delegation of "respectable but uninformed inhabitants." These men announced, "You assert that there is a fixed intention to invade our rights and privileges; we own that we do not see this clearly, but since you assure us that it is so, we believe it. We are about to take a very dangerous step [declaring independence], but we have confidence in you and will do anything you think proper" (cited in Wier, "The Role of the Newspaper Press," 144).

[47] See Price, "Economic Growth of the Chesapeake," 506-10.

account, it would seem that the experiences of the small planters were not so very different from those of the wealthy gentlemen. The tobacco culture imposed the same moral and social imperatives on them as it did on the Byrds and Carters. They may not have been able to acquire slaves, but there is no evidence that they did not want to do so. They were bound by the planting cycle and grew tobacco—with hoe and shovel—in the same way that it was done on the largest plantations. And perhaps most significant, the small planters fell into debt to the Scottish factors. These deficits, often only a few pounds, represented a considerable percentage of the little man's annual income, and there is no reason to believe that he welcomed economic dependence more enthusiastically than did the Virginia gentry.

What one must understand is that the rhythms of debt were not the same for all planters. The great Tidewater planters were extremely hard pressed to meet their obligations in the early 1760s, a time when the small producers were holding their own. During this period, the little men did not sympathize with the plight of their richer neighbors. But in the early 1770s everyone found themselves in straitened conditions. The Scottish factors as well as the consignment merchants were seen as instruments of economic and political oppression. In fact, the great credit crisis of 1772 probably did more to unify white Virginians than did any regulatory act of Parliament.

CHAPTER II

TOBACCO MENTALITY

Late in the 1760s, Richard Henry Lee composed an essay entitled "The State of the Constitution of Virginea." Considering Lee's modern reputation as an outspoken defender of American liberties, one might assume that the manuscript dealt primarily with British corruption and parliamentary oppression. In point of fact, however, Lee focused upon another topic. After briefly describing the colony's political structure, he turned to "our staple" and explained how Virginians cultivated tobacco. Lee analyzed each step in the long agricultural routine—sowing, transplanting, weeding, topping, cutting, curing, and packing—for, in his opinion, it was important for people unfamiliar with this culture (perhaps the ministers of George III who were busy devising new ways to tax the colonists?) to understand exactly "how much labour is required on a Virginean estate & how poor the produce."[1]

Lee's preoccupation with the production of tobacco would not have surprised his neighbors on Virginia's Northern Neck (the northern peninsula of Virginia located between the Potomac and Rappahannock Rivers), men like Landon Carter, John Tayloe, and George Washington. After all, it is twentieth-century historians who insist on treating these people as lawyers, as statesmen, and as theorists, as almost anything in fact, except as planters.[2] This essentially political perspective

[1] Lee Family Papers, Mssl. L51, f. 378, Virginia Historical Society, Richmond, Virginia. The essay was not published. See, Pauline Maier's sketch of Lee's political ideas in *The Old Revolutionaries: Political Lives in the Age of Samuel Adams* (New York, 1980), 164-200.

[2] For example, the fullest account of the careers of these Virginians remains Charles S. Sydnor's *Gentlemen Freeholders: Political Practices in Washington's Virginia* (Chapel Hill, N.C., 1952). Like other historians who have written about the great planters—Douglas S. Freeman, Louis Morton, Aubrey C. Land, and Rhys Isaac represent notable exceptions—Sydnor concentrated on poli-

distorts our understanding of the world of the eighteenth-century Virginians. Tobacco touched nearly every aspect of their existence. It was a source of the colony's prosperity, a medium for commercial transactions and payment of local taxes, and a theme of decorative art. Indeed, the majority of the planters' waking hours were spent, as they would have said, in "making a crop."[3] Almost every surviving letterbook from this period contains a detailed description of tobacco production, and even Thomas Jefferson, who never distinguished himself as a successful plantation manager, instructed a European correspondent in the mysteries of cultivating the Virginia staple.[4]

Though Virginians acknowledged the profound impact that tobacco had had upon the colony's social and economic development, they regarded the staple with a critical eye. Many planters readily admitted that the crop's effect upon their lives and the lives of their fathers had not been entirely beneficial. A case in point was the Chesapeake settlement pattern, a use of space that distinguished the people of this region from most other colonial Americans. The earliest Virginians had carved out riverfront estates often located miles from the nearest neighbor. As time passed, colonists spread west and north along the waterways in search of fresh lands on which to establish their sons and daughters. Each generation faced the same problem; each behaved much as its predecessor had done. Crown officials complained that dispersed living invited military disaster and discouraged urban development, but even those Virginians who recognized the desirability of prosperous commercial centers refused to abandon their isolated plantations.[5]

tics and paid virtually no attention to the role of tobacco in shaping Virginia culture. The crop did not even appear in Sydnor's index.

[3] For an example of tobacco employed as a theme of decorative art, see the tobacco finials on a mid-eighteenth-century Chesapeake walnut chest (G59.17.5) in the Winterthur Museum, Winterthur, Delaware.

[4] To G. K. van Hogendorp, with Papers, "On Tobacco Culture," 4 May 1784, in *The Papers of Thomas Jefferson*, ed. Julian P. Boyd (Princeton, 1953), VII, 209-12.

[5] See John C. Rainbolt, "The Absence of Towns in Seventeenth-Century Virginia," *Journal of Southern History*, 35(1969), 343-60; Kevin P. Kelly, " 'In

IV. Tobacco leaves on Virginia paper money

By the middle of the eighteenth century, most planters accepted that dispersed settlement was an inevitable product of a particular type of agriculture. Tobacco may not in fact have caused dispersion—the early planters might have done more to maintain the fertility of their original tracts—but contemporary Virginians nevertheless blamed their staple for scattering men and women across the countryside. In 1775, for example, the anonymous author of *American Husbandry* informed his readers of what every Virginian knew from firsthand experience: "A very considerable tract of land is necessary for a tobacco plantation." The writer estimated that planters required at least fifty acres for each field laborer, for if they possessed less land, "they will find themselves distressed for want of room."[6]

Virginia's dispersed settlement pattern had obvious cultural implications. Social relations among the colony's great planters were less frequent, less spontaneous than were those enjoyed by wealthy town-dwellers in other parts of America. Religious services, no doubt, brought people together, but churches were often inconveniently located. Inclement weather frequently kept planters at home. Militia practice occasionally broke the work routine, and it was not unusual for planters to use these gatherings as an excuse to get roaring drunk. Meetings of the county courts served a social as well as legal function.[7] But however important these events may

Dispers'd Country Plantations': Settlement Patterns in Seventeenth-Century Surry County, Virginia," in *The Chesapeake in the Seventeenth Century: Essays on Anglo-American Society and Politics*, ed. Thad W. Tate and David L. Ammerman (New York, 1980), 183-205.

[6] *American Husbandry*, ed. Harry J. Carman (New York, 1939), 165. This anonymous book was originally published in 1775. Avery O. Craven, *Soil Exhaustion as a Factor in the Agricultural History of Virginia and Maryland, 1606-1860*, University of Illinois Studies in the Social Sciences, vol. 13, no. 1 (Urbana, Ill., 1926); and Carville V. Earle, *The Evolution of a Tidewater Settlement System: All Hallow's Parish, Maryland, 1650-1783* (Chicago, 1975).

[7] An imaginative discussion of the meaning of community in the colonial Chesapeake is Lorena S. Walsh "Community Networks in the Early Chesapeake" (Paper presented at the St. Mary's Conference, St. Mary's City, Maryland, May 1984).

have been, the great majority of the planter's life was spent on his plantation in the company of family, servants, and slaves. Schooling, for those who could afford it, usually occurred at home, the responsibility of private tutors.

Some Virginians found this "solitary and unsociable" existence boring.[8] Like William Fitzhugh, Virginia's most affluent seventeenth-century planter, they relied on libraries to compensate for the absence of "society that is good and ingenious."[9] Sometimes even books must have seemed poor substitutes for regular contact with outsiders. In 1756 Edmund Pendleton, a young and promising lawyer, protested that he had failed to hear an important piece of news because he lived isolated in "a forest."[10]

In this society the cultivation of tobacco in large measure determined the planters' sense of time, their perception of appropriate behavior at particular moments throughout the year. A comparison with the production of other staples helps make the point. Each crop, be it coffee, sugar, or tobacco, possesses a distinct character—almost a personality—and thus places different demands on the people who grow it. Some staples, for example, require a great expenditure of labor over a relatively short period of time, perhaps a month or two of drudgery associated with the harvest; in sugar-making regions especially, this exhausting season can be followed by months of unemployment or underemployment. Other staples generate more balanced work rhythms. Under these conditions the tasks necessary to transform seeds into a marketable commodity are spread over the entire year, and there is no extraordinary crisis period, such as when the sugar cane is cut, which alone determines whether the enterprise will be a success.

[8] "A Letter from Mr. John Clayton Rector of Crofton at Wakefield in Yorkshire, to the Royal Society, May 12, 1688," in *Tracts and Other Papers Relating Principally to the Origin, Settlement, and Progress of the Colonies in North America* . . . , ed. Peter Force (Washington, D.C., 1844), III, no. 12, 21.

[9] Richard Beale Davis, ed., *William Fitzhugh and His Chesapeake World, 1676-1701: The Fitzhugh Letters and Other Documents* (Chapel Hill, N.C., 1963), 15.

[10] Cited in David John Mays, *Edmund Pendleton, 1721-1803: A Biography* (Cambridge, Mass., 1952), I, 102.

Work schedules, of course, influence the timing of other, seemingly unrelated activities. In many countries, the personality of the major crop determines when festivals are held— in other words, when the cultivators and their families have the leisure to organize such events. In the coffee-growing sections of early twentieth-century Puerto Rico, "traditional ceremonies . . . marked a sharp transition from work to nonwork."[11]

In the cultivation of other staples such as tobacco, there is no clear break between labor and leisure. As grown in eighteenth-century Virginia, the crop placed major demands upon the planter and his laborers throughout the year. From the moment they put out the seed to the time that they loaded hogsheads on British vessels, the workers were fully occupied in making a crop. Tobacco was not like wheat, a plant that colonial farmers sowed and simply waited to harvest.[12] The Virginia staple could never be taken for granted. It dictated a series of tasks, any one of which, if improperly performed, could jeopardize many months of hard work. Each step in the annual process required skill, judgment, and luck. No wonder that a French traveler reported that "the culture of tobacco is difficult, troublesome, and uncertain."[13]

By the time this man visited Virginia, the Tidewater planters had established a familiar work routine. Indeed, it did not change significantly over the entire colonial period. It became a piece of customary knowledge, passed from fathers to sons, masters to slaves, American-born blacks to newly imported Africans. As one eighteenth-century observer noted, "This process varies more or less in the different plantations, but the variations are not by any means considerable."[14] This pro-

---

[11] Julian H. Steward et al., *The People of Puerto Rico; a Study in Social Anthropology* (Urbana, Ill., 1956), 200.

[12] See, Harold B. Gill, Jr., "Wheat Culture in Colonial Virginia," *Agricultural History*, 52(1978), 386; Douglas S. Freeman, *George Washington: A Biography* (New York, 1953), III, 195-96; and Rhys Isaac, *The Transformation of Virginia 1740-1790* (Chapel Hill, N.C., 1982), 22-30.

[13] Duc de La Rochefoucauld Liancourt, *Travels through the United States of North America* (London, 1799), II, 84.

[14] Ibid., 85. An excellent discussion of this annual process can be found in David O. Percy, *The Production of Tobacco along the Colonial Potomac*, National

duction schedule, repeated annually throughout a planter's lifetime, on plantations scattered throughout Virginia, was a powerful element in the development and persistence of the tobacco mentality. The cultivation of this staple provided planters with a stock of common experiences; indeed, it sustained a "silent" language, a vocabulary of work imprinted so deeply upon the minds of people who grew it that they were barely conscious of how many assumptions and ideas they actually shared. Richard Henry Lee was probably correct: unless one understands exactly what was at stake at every point—the dangers, the requirements, and the critical, often subtle decisions made by planters throughout the year—one cannot fully comprehend the relation of culture to agriculture or why the later switch from tobacco to wheat so upset the symbolic world of the Tidewater gentry.[15]

I

The production cycle for Virginia tobacco began in late December or early January. The commonly accepted date for planting seed in specially enriched beds was about twelve days after Christmas. The precise timing depended upon a number of variables, but according to one prosperous gentleman, "The best time for sowing the seed is as early after Christmas as the weather will permit."[16] The small seedbeds, not larger than a quarter acre, were usually treated with animal manure, although it was not uncommon for fields to be

Colonial Farm Research Report, no. 1 (Accokeek, Md., 1979). Also, Melvin Herndon, *Tobacco in Colonial Virginia: 'The Sovereign Remedy'*, Jamestown 350th Anniversary Historical Booklet, no. 20 (Williamsburg, 1957). For a modern account of tobacco production throughout the world, see B. C. Akehurst, *Tobacco* (London, 1968).

[15] See Chapter V.

[16] A man identified as Judge Parker is quoted in William Tatham, *An Historical and Practical Essay on the Culture and Commerce of Tobacco*, ed. G. Herndon (Coral Gables, Fla., 1969), 118-19. Tatham's book was published in London in 1800. See also, Curtis Carroll Davis, ed., " 'A National Property': Richard Claiborne's Tobacco Treatise for Poland," *W&MQ*, 3rd ser., 21(1964), 99-110.

fertilized with wood ash. In either case, once he had placed the seed in the ground, the planter covered the entire bed with branches in order to protect the tobacco from possible frost damage. Knowledgeable producers prepared several different "plant-beds," frequently separated by considerable distances. This practice insured that the accidental destruction of one bed by cold, disease, or pests would not deprive the planter of a good crop. But, as with all farming, there were risks. Prudent Virginians understood that the odds against a single plant's survival to maturity were exceedingly high, and during this initial stage of cultivation, "an experienced planter commonly takes care to have ten times as many plants as he can make use of."[17]

The second phase of tobacco cultivation, transplanting seedlings from the beds to the main fields, occupied the full attention of the plantation labor force for several months. The work usually commenced in late April, but, as in all stages of colonial tobacco production, the exact timing depended in large part upon the planter's judgment. He alone decided whether the tiny plants were sufficiently developed to survive movement. Even when the owner of the plantation could not be immediately present—say, at an outlying property run by an overseer—he often sent precise instruction on how to manage such affairs.[18] According to common eighteenth-century wisdom, the tobacco leaves were supposed to be "as large as a dollar." Virginians looked for additional signs of maturity—the thickness of the young leaves or the general appearance of the plants—subtle indicators that one learned to recognize through long personal experience.[19]

However skilled the planter may have been, transplanting was an anxious time for everyone. Chance played an uncom-

---

[17] J.F.D. Smyth, *A Tour in the United States of America* (London, 1784), II, 129. See also, Lee Family Papers, Mssl. L51, f. 378.

[18] "Instructions Given by Richard Corbin, Esq., to His Agent [James Semple] for the Management of His Plantations; Virginia, 1759," in *Plantation and Frontier Documents: 1649-1863; Illustrative of Industrial History in the Colonial and Ante-Bellum South*, ed. Ulrich B. Phillips (Cleveland, 1909), I, 112.

[19] Jefferson, "On Tobacco Culture," *Papers*, VII, 210.

fortably large role in this procedure. Success required frequent rains; soaking moisture loosened the soil and allowed the planter to pull up the seedlings without harming their roots. The work was difficult and unpleasant. Because no one could predict when the rains might fall, one had to take advantage of major downpours, termed "seasons" by colonial Virginians. "When a good shower . . . happens at this period of the year," wrote one well-informed grower, "the planter hurries to the plant bed, disregarding the teeming element, which is doomed to wet his skin."[20] Laborers rushed from the beds to the fields where small tobacco hills had already been laid out. A seedling was dropped on "every . . . hill by the negro-children; the most skillful slaves then . . . planting them."[21] Under perfect conditions, transplanting could be finished by late May, but the job often spilled over into June. William Tatham, an eighteenth-century Virginian who published a detailed description of tobacco cultivation, explained that the fields were seldom fully planted until "the *long season in May*; which (to make use of an Irishism) very frequently happens in June."[22]

As the tobacco ripened in the fields over the summer, the planter and his slaves performed a number of tedious chores. Each plant received regular, individual attention; each task was done by hand. The crop could not be ignored, not even for a week. Producers waged constant battle against weeds, and over the course of the growing season, workers hoed each tobacco hill as many as three times. Since major planters like Landon Carter cultivated more than a hundred thousand separate plants, weeding obviously took a considerable amount of time. After eight to twelve leaves had appeared on each plant—the number depended upon "the fertility of the earth"—the planter ordered his laborers to begin topping.[23]

---

[20] Tatham, *Historical and Practical Essay*, 15.

[21] Smyth, *Tour*, II, 130.

[22] Tatham, *Historical and Practical Essay*, 14. See also, Lee Family Papers, Mssl. L51, f. 378.

[23] Jefferson, "On Tobacco Culture," *Papers*, VII, 210. See also, Smyth, *Tour*, II, 131-37.

This operation, literally the removal of the top of the plant, prevented the tobacco from flowering and thus channeled the plant's energies into the leaves. Tobacco that had been topped put out suckers, secondary shoots that had to be removed lest they rob the developing leaves of important nutrients.

The next step, cutting the tobacco, generated considerable tension on the plantation. The timing of this decision tested the planter's competence, or at least, so he thought. Virginians knew that the operation was supposed to take place sometime in September. The difficulty came in determining the exact date on which to start. As every planter understood, even a slight miscalculation could compromise the entire crop. An early frost, for example, was capable of destroying every unprotected plant, and as the September days grew cooler, the danger of frost obviously increased. On the other hand, to cut unripe tobacco was folly. Immature leaves heavy with moisture seldom cured properly.

And yet, notwithstanding the critical importance of this moment in the production cycle, Virginians offered no precise description of what ripe tobacco actually looked like. Instead, they provided loose guidelines, folk wisdom almost certainly based on experience. When it came to cutting, each planter seems to have relied on his own judgment. He simply sensed when the tobacco was ready for cutting; it had the "right" appearance. According to Tatham, "The tobacco, when ripe, changes its colour, and looks greyish; the leaf feels thick, and if pressed between the finger and thumb will easily crack." He then added, "experience alone can enable a person to judge when tobacco is fully ripe."[24] Richard Henry Lee, a gentleman who possessed the necessary experience, advised growers to look for "spots appearing on the leaf."[25] Other planters adopted different guidelines, a mixture of local custom and informed intuition, none of which guaranteed success.

Colonial Virginians did not refer to the September cutting

[24] Tatham, *Historical and Practical Essay*, 124-25.
[25] Lee Family Papers, Mssl. L51, f. 378.

as a "harvest." The term was inappropriate, for it would have
suggested finality, the completion of the annual agricultural
cycle. But for the tobacco planter, cutting led immediately to
another arduous task, curing, and if he failed at this stage, it
did not much matter how skillfully the transplanting or cutting had been performed. There was no time for either festi-
val or thanksgiving. One English visitor who closely studied
the cultivation of tobacco claimed that proper curing represented the planter's most difficult challenge, "and, for want
of knowledge and care, there are every year many hogs-heads
spoiled, and worth nothing." He insisted, in fact, that "the
curing of tobacco is an art." Another man termed it "an art
most difficult of attainment."[26]

Again, the crucial factor was personal judgment. Slaves
hung the cut tobacco in special curing barns—one can still see
such structures in the South—where it was dried. The trick
was to produce a leaf neither too dry nor too moist. Excess
moisture would almost certainly cause the tobacco to rot during shipment across the Atlantic. But leaves that were allowed
to dry too long became brittle and sometimes disintegrated
before reaching Great Britain.

Experienced planters naturally tried to terminate the curing
process at the moment that the tobacco became dry without
being brittle, pliable without being moist, a time that Virginians called "case." This point, Tatham explained, "can only
be judged of safely by long experience." The problem was
that the condition of the tobacco could change radically from
hour to hour, moving in and out of "case" depending on the
humidity. Wet days supposedly gave the cured tobacco leaves
greater flexibility and thus made them easier for packers to
handle. "This condition," observed Tatham, "can only be distinguished by diligent attention, and frequent handling; for it
often changes this quality with the change of the weather in

[26] Richard Parkinson, *A Tour in America, in 1798, 1799, and 1800* (London,
1805), II, 418, 423; N. F. Cabell, "Some Fragments of an Intended Report
on the Post Revolutionary History of Agriculture in Virginia," *W&MQ*, 1st
ser., 26(1918), 155.

a very short space of time."²⁷ If the colony experienced a particularly rainy fall, however, the planter was sometimes forced to light fires in the curing barn. Though the heat assisted the drying process, it could introduce unwanted problems. As Jefferson reported, "great care is necessary as it [the tobacco] is very inflammable, and if it takes fire, the whole, with the house, consumes as quickly as straw would."²⁸

Following curing, several tedious operations remained before the tobacco was deemed marketable. When the leaves reached "case," slaves quickly "stripped" them from the stalks on which they had hung in the drying barn. Those planters who obtained the highest returns for their tobacco also "stemmed" the leaves. This was a boring job. Plantation laborers, men as well as women, removed "the largest stem or fibers from the web of the leaf," leaving a handsome product that could be easily packed. The speed with which stemming was accomplished depended upon the slaves' "expertness." One had to learn the necessary skills, and "those unaccustomed to it find it difficult to stem a single plant."²⁹ Regardless of the workers' training or disposition, these operations required considerable amounts of time, and during the autumn months it was not unusual for the slaves to labor long into the night over the individual leaves.

Only after these tasks had been completed could the planter begin "prizing." Workers placed layer after layer of leaves in hogsheads manufactured by plantation coopers. Men employing a hand press then "prized" the tobacco until they had compressed it into a nearly solid mass. More leaves were then added, and the process was repeated until the hogshead eventually weighed about a thousand pounds. Sometimes the pressure on the tobacco cracked the staves, bursting the hogshead. Since freight rates were determined by the individual hogshead rather than by total weight, the planter usually elected to take his chances with breakage. No wonder that Tatham

²⁷ Tatham, *Historical and Practical Essay*, 37.
²⁸ Jefferson, "On Tobacco Culture," *Papers*, VII, 211.
²⁹ Tatham, *Historical and Practical Essay*, 40-41.

V. Production of tobacco in eighteenth-century Virginia

concluded that prizing "requires the combination of judgment and experience."[30] These hogsheads were obviously difficult to handle. Virginians generally relied on gravity, rolling the tobacco down to the riverfront. One still encounters eighteenth-century "rolling roads" throughout the Tidewater region. The one that the Lee family used at Stratford, for example, can be traced from the fields down to the place on the Potomac where once a small warehouse stood.

These jobs—stripping, stemming, and prizing—continued throughout the fall. A prosperous Virginia planter, Richard Corbin, advised his plantation manager that with careful planning of the work routine, "the tobacco will be all prised before Christmas, weigh well, and at least one hhd [hogshead] in Ten gained by finishing the Tobo thus early."[31] But Corbin counselled perfection. Often the hogsheads were not ready for shipment to the public warehouses and inspection until well after the New Year.

Not until the following spring, a full fifteen months after the sowing of the tobacco seed, did the planter send loaded hogsheads to the European market. By that time, of course, another crop was in the ground, and he faced a new round of agricultural decisions. The schedule contained few slack periods, no time during which the grower could be completely free of anxieties about the state of his crop. Richard Corbin explained the tobacco cycle to an inexperienced assistant. Sounding suspiciously like a New England Puritan, Corbin observed that "To employ the Fall & Winter well is the foundation of a successful Crop in the Summer: You will therefore Animate the overseers to great diligence that their work may be in proper forwardness and not have that to do in the Spring that ought to be done in the Winter: there is Business sufficient for every Season of the year."[32] And when Richard Parkinson, an Englishman, first arrived in Virginia, planters told him that it required a "year's work to go through the

[30] Ibid., 43.

[31] "Instructions Given by Richard Corbin," in *Plantation and Frontier*, I, 112.

[32] Ibid., 111.

VI. Transporting hogsheads of tobacco to the public warehouses

process" of cultivating tobacco, to which Parkinson later exclaimed, "so it is"! He ticked off a full calendar, each month corresponding to some specific task.[33] This demanding routine barely left time to clear fresh land for future plantings or to cut wood for fences and fuel.

This work cycle affected eighteenth-century planter culture in several significant ways. First, the staple became an arbiter of time, of work and of play. The production schedule contained no clear culmination, no point at which the grower could relax and enjoy the fruits of his labor.[34] As we have seen, even cutting tobacco could not be termed a genuine harvest, for curing followed hard upon the cutting. One task was as important as any other.

Recreational and business activities had to be scheduled around the cultivation of tobacco, fit somehow into the established work routine. The planters resented being called to sessions of the county courts. During the third quarter of the eighteenth-century, these meetings sometimes lasted three to five days and were regarded as an unnecessary waste of time. Even the justices frequently slipped away before the county court had cleared its agenda.[35] And perhaps the rowdy drunkenness that accompanied public gatherings—militia practice, elections, and weddings, for example—can be explained, at least in part, by the participants' awareness that such communal activities were rare and that much work in the fields and barns remained undone.[36] Even personal pleasures revolved around tobacco time. After George Washington dropped the cultivation of tobacco for that of wheat, he discovered that he had more time for fox-hunting, his favorite form of relaxation. As his biographer observes, wheat altered the pace of Washington's life, for in cereal agriculture, "The

[33] Parkinson, *Tour in America*, II, 415-16. See also, Freeman, *Washington*, III, 194-96.

[34] For an analysis of a different agricultural work routine, see Steward et al., *People of Puerto Rico*, 199-200.

[35] A. G. Roeber, *Faithful Magistrates and Republican Lawyers: Creators of Virginia Legal Culture, 1680-1810* (Chapel Hill, N.C., 1981), chapter 3.

[36] D. and A. Rutman, *A Place in Time: Middlesex County, Virginia, 1650-1750* (New York, 1984), 138-42; Isaac, *Transformation of Virginia*, 107-110.

ground was plowed; the grain was planted; after that, nothing need be done or could be done, except keep livestock away, until harvest."[37]

Second, the production of tobacco promoted social cohesion. This claim appears paradoxical, for it seems unlikely that a crop that restricted communal activities, that dispersed the population across the landscape, that heightened the planter's awareness of his own autonomy, could have generated a sense of common identity and purpose. The solution to this puzzle lies in a shared work process. The production of tobacco provided highly individualistic planters with a body of common rules and assumptions that helped bind them together. As one man labored in the fields, whatever the time of year, he knew that other people on other plantations were engaged in similar tasks. A planter did not actually have to see other men at work to know what they were doing. He took such things for granted.

This shared framework of labor experience, a kind of social knowledge, made distant, often unrelated planters appear less alien than they might have been had they been urban artisans or cultivators of other crops. The schedule of tobacco production became a kind of secular litany, and at the drop of a hat, planters recited the steps necessary to transform seeds into marketable leaves. The fabric of rules tied an individual not only to his neighbors but also to an historical continuum of planters who had worked this land. Since time out of mind—or so it must have seemed—Virginians had followed the same calendar, and thus the very process of cultivating tobacco placed a man within a tradition as old as the colony itself. Tatham provided an example of this turn of mind. While conducting research in seventeenth-century documents related to the tobacco trade, he was suddenly overwhelmed by an awareness of the centrality of tobacco in the colony's development. "We learn from these laws," he declared, "how much the subject of this staple was interwoven in the spirit of the times; and how nearly the history of the tobacco plant is allied to the chronology of an extensive and flourishing country,

[37] Freeman, *Washington*, III, 196.

whose measures contribute greatly . . . to give a tone to the affairs of the American union."[38] Predictably, one visitor to Virginia discovered that "the planters never go out of the beaten road, but do just as their fathers did."[39]

By the middle of the eighteenth century, many people both in the colonies and the mother country had come to regard Virginia and tobacco as synonymous. To be sure, the planters grew other crops, such as corn, but these plants never acquired tobacco's prominence. According to one Frenchman who visited Virginia in 1765, "the produce of the Soil is hemp, Indian Corn, flax, silk, Cotton and a great quantity of wild grapes, but tobacco is *the* staple Commodity of Virginia."[40] The evidence in support of this observation seemed overwhelming. One encountered tobacco on the small farms scattered along the colony's back roads, on the vast fields of the great riverfront plantations, on the wharves near the public warehouses. It dominated conversation in Williamsburg and Fredericksburg. No wonder an English traveler labeled tobacco "the grand staple of Virginia."[41] Robert Beverley, a Tidewater planter who generally avoided such extravagant language, called tobacco simply "our staple."[42]

---

[38] Tatham, *Historical and Practical Essay*, 184. The persistence of a distinctive culture also impressed the marquis de Chastellux, one of many well-to-do Frenchmen drawn to America during the revolutionary period. During a visit to Virginia, Chastellux noted, "The Virginians differ essentially from the inhabitants to the north and eastward . . . not only in the nature of their climate, that of their soil, and the objects of cultivation peculiar to it, but in that indelible character which is imprinted on every nation at the moment of its origins, and which by perpetuating itself from generation to generation justifies the following great principle, that *everything which is, partakes of that which has been.*" *Travels in North America, 1780-1782* (Dublin, 1787), II, 174-75.

[39] *American Husbandry*, ed. Carman, 160. For an interesting discussion of the culture of agriculture in the contemporary United States, see, Mark Kramer, *Three Farms: Making Milk, Meat and Money from the American Soil* (Boston, 1980), 3-107.

[40] "Journal of a French Traveller in the Colonies, 1765," pt. 1, *American Historical Review*, 26(1920-21), 743 (emphasis added).

[41] Smyth, *Tour*, I, 32-33.

[42] Robert Beverley to John Bland, 1764, Beverley Letter Book, 1761-1793, Library of Congress, Washington, D.C.

By mid-eighteenth century, therefore, tobacco had acquired considerable symbolic significance in this society.[43] It
came to represent not only a particular agrarian work experience, but also the people themselves, a collectivity of producers. On this emblematic level, tobacco linked the planters,
large and small, those who traded on consignment with the
merchant houses of London and those who sold their crop to
the local Scottish factor. To be sure, the great plant rs owned
more land and slaves, but there do not seem to have been
important economies of scale in eighteenth-century tobacco
cultivation. In other words, the great planter—a Carter or
Corbin—produced more tobacco because he possessed more
laborers, not because bigness in itself offered special advantages. The small planter who owned only a few slaves (or
none at all) merely grew the staple on a smaller scale. The
techniques he employed were the same as those used on the
major plantations. He faced essentially the same problems as
did his more affluent neighbor. He observed the same general
work calendar. And so in some sense, he was just a smaller
version of the great planter. If tobacco came in some quarters
to symbolize a wealthy gentry culture, a society of fast-riding,
fox-hunting gentlemen who frightened the likes of poor James
Ireland into silence, it could also evoke images for the small
man of *becoming* wealthy, of acquiring slaves and an imposing
brick house. Tobacco symbolized economic possibilities and
thereby promoted social cohesion.

II

In colonial Virginia, tobacco also acquired a psychological dimension. The staple provided a medium within which the
planter negotiated a public reputation, a sense of self-worth
as an agricultural producer. In part, the deep personal ties

[43] Rev. Andrew Burnaby, *Travels through the Middle Settlements in North
America, in the Years 1759 and 1760; with Observations upon the State of the
Colonies*, in *A General Collection of the Best and Most Interesting Voyages and Travels in All Parts of the World* . . . , ed. John Pinkerton (London, 1812), XIII,
717.

between the Virginia planter and the staple—the expression of ego through a crop—resulted from the peculiar characteristics of tobacco. As we have seen, its cultivation required continuous personal attention; at every stage the planter made crucial judgments about the crop's development. His attention throughout the year was focused not upon whole fields or even upon specific plants but upon individual leaves. According to Fernando Ortiz, a modern Cuban anthropologist, "This is why tobacco-raising is such a meticulous affair, in contrast to [sugar] cane, which demands little attention. The tobacco-grower has to tend his tobacco . . . leaf by leaf. . . . The ideal of the tobacco man . . . is distinction, for his product to be in a class by itself, the best."[44] The Virginia planters did their best to be present at every step of the process, and however boring life on the isolated plantations may sometimes have seemed, they were seldom in a position to become absentee owners, to delegate fully the responsibilities of agricultural management. Growing tobacco in this society was a personal challenge.

Of course, Tidewater planters recognized that their presence did not in itself guarantee success. Many aspects of tobacco cultivation were beyond their personal control. Regardless of his skills, the planter still had to reckon with luck, with chance factors like pests and weather that undermined the best-laid plans. Such "accidents," as Virginians sometimes called them, were an inescapable part of raising tobacco. In 1768 Henry Fitzhugh, a wealthy planter of northern Virginia, encountered a series of misfortunes in making a crop. In words that other Virginians might just as well have written, he recounted his reverses. "We have had so cold & dry a Summer," Fitzhugh explained, "that nothing could grow, & abt the midle of Augt we had a very violent Rain which drowned a great deal of tobo on low grounds, & caused that on the high land to spot very much." An early frost, "de-

[44] Fernando Ortiz Fernandez, *Cuban Counterpoint: Tobacco and Sugar* (New York, 1947), 24.

stroyed a great deal of tobo in the Backwoods."[45] In such situations the planter could obviously do very little. Landon Carter bore natural adversity with a certain stoicism, as if he thought he deserved better of nature. In 1771 he predicted that he would bring in a fine crop. But then came a "terrible dry spell," and the soil on his plantation baked "into a mere solid Mass." Carter responded to these conditions as best he could, but his efforts proved ineffectual. Fortuna had won. "Had I not been honestly sensible that no care had been wanting nor diligence neglected," Carter confided in his diary, "I should be uneasy more than I am; but as I have nothing of this sort to accuse myself with, I must and do submit."[46]

In fact, however, Carter and his contemporaries were rarely willing to submit. Fatalism was foreign to their outlook. Instead, they believed in the existence of an agricultural *virtù*, a set of personal attributes that ultimately determined the quality of a man's crop. In 1766 the Rev. John Camm, a person whose clumsy efforts to strengthen the Episcopal hierarchy in Virginia had angered the gentry, reported to an English correspondent: "These honest discontented gentry, I am afraid, secretly murmur at the wise Disposer of events, and sometimes seem to give shrewd hints that his affairs would be better managed if they might be entrusted with the direction of them."[47]

This sense of power—and, of course, responsibility—is the major reason why colonial planters came to regard their tobacco as an extension of self. To be sure, "accidents" might ruin a crop or two, but over the long haul there was no explanation other than incompetence why an individual could

---

[45] Henry Fitzhugh to Steuart and Campbell, 28 June and 20 October 1768, Henry Fitzhugh Papers, Manuscript Division, William R. Perkins Library, Duke University, Durham, North Carolina. Permission to quote from this collection was granted by the Perkins Library, Duke University.

[46] Entry of 16 August 1771, in *The Diary of Colonel Landon Carter of Sabine Hall, 1752-1778*, ed. Jack P. Greene, Virginia Historical Society Documents, vol. 4 (Charlottesville, 1965), II, 614.

[47] Rev. John Camm to Mrs. McClurg, 24 July 1766, *W&MQ*, 1st ser., 2(1894), 238.

not produce good tobacco. William Nelson responded almost arrogantly to an English merchant who suggested in 1770 that the soil of Virginia was too exhausted to make a fine export leaf. "You make me smile," Nelson lectured, "when you talk of the Lands being too much worn & impoverish'd to bring good Tobo. . . . I know that a skillful Planter can make it fine from any Land, it being his Part & Interest to improve any that he finds worn or wearing out."[48]

Landon Carter shared Nelson's assumptions about excellent tobacco. When a young man in his neighborhood—an overseer, no less—announced that *only* the "accidents of the rains" could account for Carter's handsome tobacco crop, Carter lost this temper (judging from his diary, a not infrequent occurrence at Sabine Hall). It was personal management, not luck, that had made the difference. He expressed gratitude for "the assistance of heaven" but nevertheless insisted that his superior skills as a planter explained success. "This I assert," Carter fumed, "if our July had not been so drye and hot . . . My *management* would have appeared more conspicuous than that of others; for I dare bet anything that none of the Tobacco tended as they have done can be [as] thick as mine."[49]

The highest praise one could bestow on an eighteenth-century planter was to call him "crop master," a public recognition of agricultural acumen. Many apparently aspired to this rank, but achievement proved elusive. One contemporary observed that growing tobacco was "an art, that every planter thinks he is proficient in, but which few rightly understand." Tatham defined the personal qualities that he, at least, expected of a grower who held this title. A master cultivated his own "estate." An absentee could never acquire the requisite knowledge; the demands of the work schedule were too heavy. According to Tatham, the crop master "understands the whole process of the culture, and gives instructions concerning the various operations, though perhaps he does not

[48] William Nelson to Samuel Athawes, 26 July 1770, Nelson Letter Book, Colonial Williamsburg, Inc., Research Center, microfilm.

[49] Entry of 8 September 1770, in *Diary of Landon Carter*, ed. Greene, I, 482 (emphasis added).

attend personally to their execution." A crop master demonstrated an ability to make quick, accurate judgments about
each stage of production. Possession of these attributes transformed the ordinary planter into a "lord of the soil."[50]

Tatham knew what he was writing about. Eighteenth-century planters worked hard at being—or at least appearing to
be—proficient tobacco managers. Richard Corbin, for example, instructed an assistant on one of his outlying plantations,
"Let me be acquainted with every incident that happens &
Let me have timely notice of everything that is wanted, that
it may be provided."[51] If nothing else, the person who received these orders could assume that his employer was a
would-be crop master, in other words, a demanding boss.

Competition among the great planters for reputation as superior growers became more intense when, in 1730, the
House of Burgesses passed the Tobacco Act. The purpose of
this legislation was most definitely not certification of crop
masters. Rather, the goal was to raise prices by removing
"bad and trash tobacco" from the export market. The lower
house designated some forty public warehouses to be located
on major streams and rivers throughout Virginia. No tobacco
could be exported from the colony, used in settlement of private debts, or offered in payment of taxes unless it had been
officially inspected at one of these warehouses. The inspectors
opened the hogsheads, graded the leaves, and destroyed the
trash. They then issued receipts on all tobacco passed and
stored at the warehouses. These certificates provided Virginians with a kind of paper currency. The receipts often
changed hands several times before someone finally exported
the tobacco to Great Britain.[52]

Passage of the Tobacco Act raised a storm of protest. The
small planters complained of the inconvenience of carrying

[50] Tatham, *Historical and Practical Essay*, 100; *American Museum* (June 1789),
537.
[51] "Instructions Given by Richard Corbin," in *Plantation and Frontier*, I,
111.
[52] Richard L. Morton, *Colonial Virginia* (Chapel Hill, N.C., 1960), II, 511-
13.

James River, Nº 271

Warehouse, the 30th — Day of July 1748

THIS shall oblige us, the Subscribers, our, and each of our Executors and Administrators, to pay, upon Demand, to Cha͞m͞l Allen or his Order, at the above-mentioned Warehouse five hundred vixty one Pounds of good merchantable Arro Tobacco, according to the Directions of the Act of Assembly, *For amending the Staple of Tobacco, and preventing. Frauds in His Majesty's Customs*; it being for the like Quantity received. Witness our Hands,

561

Robt. Burton
Pleab. Cocke

VII. Virginia tobacco note issued at a public warehouse

their tobacco to the warehouses. They also feared that their leaves—perhaps grown on poorer soils with less individual attention—would be more frequently condemned than would the crops of the larger plantations. The great planters, however, supported the legislation of 1730. During the early decades of the eighteenth century, they had seldom expressed much concern about producing a superior leaf. Like the small planters, they seem to have been interested in quantity not quality. They sold their tobacco to merchants who sent vessels directly to their private wharves. At no point did other Virginians review the condition of the crop. But the Tobacco Act dramatically changed the rules. The inspectors were tobacco judges, arbiters of excellence. It is perhaps not surprising that self-conscious statements about excellence postdate this legislation, suggesting of course that certification provided a powerful new incentive for these gentlemen to best their rivals, to establish bragging rights. By mid-century public inspection had become an annual ritual reinforcing the tobacco mentality.

By whatever means, Virginians learned which planters possessed superior judgment, and at critical points in the production process they turned to these crop masters for advice. Cutting the tobacco was such a task. Writers like Tatham provided inexperienced planters with general descriptions of ripe leaves and changes in color and thickness, but somehow books never conveyed adequate information. In frustration, Tatham declared that ripening is "easier to understand than to express." "It is a point," he concluded, "on which I would not trust my own experience without consulting some able crop-master in the neighborhood."[53]

It was certainly wiser to call on a local expert than to trust one's luck. Carter preached this lesson to anyone who bothered to listen. In 1770 John Purcell, "master of the Patrol in this neck," chased a runaway slave into a curing barn belonging to one of Carter's neighbors and discovered, among other things, that the planter's tobacco was "dung" rotten. When Carter heard this story, he immediately ascribed the condition of the crop to poor personal management. The plants had been "cut down not half ripe and of course too thin to stand the sweat of the house. Thus is 9/10 of the tobacco spoilt every year."[54] The planter stood twice condemned. He not only was an incompetent producer but also had failed to consult a crop master.

Even the names given to the various kinds of tobacco testified to the close personal relation between the planter and his crop. People unfamiliar with the cultivation of this staple assumed that colonial Virginians grew only two varieties, Oronoco and sweet-scented. Though this information may have been technically correct, Virginians recognized finer, more personal distinctions. "Question a planter on the subject," one man explained, "and he will tell you that he cultivates such or such a kind: as, for example 'Colonel Carter's sort,' or some other leading crop master."[55] Sometimes visitors reported finding different "species . . . with names peculiar to the situation, settlement, and neighborhoods, wherein they are produced," but on closer inspection one usually discovered that an excellent local tobacco was identified with a specific planter.[56]

[53] Tatham, *Historical and Practical Essay*, 23-24.

[54] Entry of 11 September 1770, in *Diary of Landon Carter*, ed. Greene, I, 487.

[55] Tatham, *Historical and Practical Essay*, 4-5.

[56] Smyth, *Tour*, II, 130. Rutman and Rutman, *A Place in Time*, 40.

Such eponymous practice was certainly prevalent along the lower York River. The planters in this area claimed that they produced the best leaf in the entire Chesapeake region. But according to Andrew Burnaby, an English traveller, the very best York crops came from the fields of Col. Edward Digges. Indeed, Digges enjoyed a reputation for consistent quality that French wine-makers would have envied. Like their products, his tobacco went to market bearing his personal stamp.[57] Digges's tobacco, Burnaby noted, "is in such high estimation that . . . [he] puts upon every hogshead in which it is packed, the initials of his name; and it is from thence called the E.D. tobacco, and sells for a proportionally higher price."[58] As late as 1811, long after Digges had died, Virginians still talked of the extraordinary sweet-scented tobacco "E. Dees" that had made Digges's York plantation famous in the mother country. When the land was sold off early in the nineteenth century, a newspaper advertisement announced, "1,000 acres in York county, the only estate where the famous E.D. tobacco was raised, which never failed to bring in England one shilling on the pound, when other tobacco would not bring three pence."[59]

The centrality of tobacco in the lives of these men spawned a curious system of social ranking, one strikingly different from that normally associated with modern industrial societies. The planter's self-esteem depended—in part, at least—upon the quality of his tobacco. This measure, of course, was highly subjective. It left him vulnerable, especially after passage of the Tobacco Act, to the opinion of other Virginians. However excellent a person regarded his own crop as being, a sharp-eyed rival could always spot flaws. The great Tidewater planters worried about these negative judgments and, as we shall see, took them quite personally. Indeed, the planters seem to have cultivated tobacco as much to gain the respect of merchants and neighbors—in other words, of people with whom they maintained regular contacts—as to please the

[57] See Leo A. Loubère, *The Red and the White: A History of Wine in France and Italy in the Nineteenth Century* (Albany, N.Y., 1978).
[58] Burnaby, *Travels*, 706-707; "Journal of a French Traveller," 743.
[59] *W&MQ*, 1st ser., 15(1906), 38.

VIII. Personal tobacco marks of the leading planters of Fairfax County

anonymous chewers, smokers, and snuffers who ultimately purchased the staple in Europe. In 1737, for example, William Beverley consigned a shipment of tobacco to a leading London merchant accompanied with this request: "I hope it will come to a good market and as it is famous here among the merchants for fine tobacco, I beg that you will sell it by itself without joining with any other that it may obtain a good name and become famous as Mr. Burwell's tobacco."[60]

Even Virginians whose crops were not so renowned as those of Edward Digges took pride in making outstanding tobacco. In fact, the planter's self-respect was so tightly bound up with the quality of his tobacco that it was sometimes difficult to discern whether a man's reputation or his tobacco was being shipped to market. Henry Fitzhugh staked his honor on twelve hogsheads of sweet-scented tobacco. "It was made on the plantation [where I] live," he informed a British merchant, "& therefore as I saw to the whole man[age]ment of it my self, [I] can with authority recom[m]end it to be exceeding good."[61] Philip Ludwell Lee, Richard Henry's brother, modestly called the crop produced at Stratford in 1771 "as fine as ever was made."[62] William Nelson wrote a sharp note in 1766 to a merchant who seemed unappreciative of having received some of "*my* Hanovers stem'd Tobo."[63] The emphasis was on the planter's skill and judgment, on his personal involvement with production. In 1772 Robert Beverley predicted that his plantation would not produce a large crop, but he consoled himself with the thought "that the Quality is remarkably fine."[64]

If the planters of eighteenth-century Virginia had been less personally involved in production, if like the great sugar lords of the Caribbean they had been absentee investors, they might not have been so sensitive to what other men obtained in the marketplace or so worried about comparisons made by neighbors riding past their fields. But this was not the case.

[60] William Beverley to Micajah Perry, 12 July 1737, *W&MQ*, 1st ser., 3(1894), 223. William Beverley was the father of Robert, a planter whose financial affairs are discussed in detail in Chapter IV.

[61] Henry Fitzhugh to James Buchanan, n.d., Henry Fitzhugh Papers.

[62] Philip Ludwell Lee to William Lee, 25 July 1771, Lee Family Papers, Mssl. L51, f. 252.

[63] William Nelson to James Gildart, 26 July 1766, Nelson Letter Book (emphasis added).

[64] Robert Beverley to [?], 27 December 1762, Beverley Letter Book.

IX. An English advertisement for high-quality Virginia tobacco

Within this particular agrarian culture, planters calculated not
only their own standing but also that of their competitors by
the appearance of fully cured tobacco leaves. "I know in this
neighbourhood," Carter declared, "people are very fond of
speaking meanly of their neighbor's Crops and I am certain
mine has been so characterised." Fortunately for Carter's own
self-respect, as he rode about Virginia's Northern Neck gra-
tuitously rating other men's tobacco, he did not "see any so
good [as mine]," and he even ventured "a wager with the best
of them both as to quantity and quality."[65] In this tobacco
culture, Carter's good management publicly demonstrated his
private virtue.

Robert Beverley, Carter's son-in-law, also kept an eye on
his neighbors and in 1774 was able to recommend one of them
to a British correspondent because "he is thought to make
very good Tobacco."[66] Note the passive construction of Beverley's statement. A collective judgment had been made about
this person's crop. No doubt, Beverley had overheard conversations at a public warehouse or at the county court, places

[65] *Diary of Landon Carter*, ed. Greene, I, 474.
[66] Robert Beverley to Samuel Athawes, 1774, Beverley Letter Book.

where planters congregated and where reputations were established. In this agrarian society, Richard Mason did not fare well. According to George Mason, the colony's famed constitutional theorist, "Dick's" failure as a planter called into question his moral character. After all, he "handled his Tobacco in so careless & slovenly a Manner that more than half of it was rotten, & even the best of it . . . will run some Risque at the Warehouse."[67]

Even popular religious persuasion may have been connected to the tobacco mentality. It is possible, for example, that a crop such as tobacco heightened the producer's confidence in his ability to control nature. Leading Virginia planters in the Revolutionry period spoke of themselves as managers, as crop masters, as persons capable, in other words, of making decisions affecting the quality of the finished leaf. One had to know when to top and worm the plants, when to cut the tobacco, how long to let it cure. As little as possible in this work routine was left to chance. Failure, therefore, resulted from personal dereliction, and by the same token, success implied integrity. It is not surprising that members of the Virginia gentry generally subscribed to a calm, reasonable, low-church Anglicanism, a theology that did not challenge their rather inflated notions of human capabilities. How different the experiences of the wheat farmer. He found himself dependent upon natural elements beyond his direct control. The vulnerability of the cultivator, his enforced passivity during much of the growing season, may have convinced him of God's terrible omnipotence.

The most influential evangelical preacher of the eighteenth century, George Whitefield, certainly suspected that there was a relation between forms of agricultural production and a people's receptivity to the "new light." He loved the prosperous cereal farmers of Pennsylvania. "Their oxen are strong to labour," he recorded in his journal, "and there seems to be no complaining in their streets. What is best of all, I believe they

[67] Robert A. Rutland, ed., *The Papers of George Mason, 1725-1792* (Chapel Hill, N.C., 1970), I, 57.

have the Lord for their God. . . . The Constitution is far from being arbitrary; the soil is good, the land exceedingly fruitful, and there is a greater equality between the poor and rich than perhaps can be found in any other place of the known world." How different Tidewater Virginia appeared to Whitefield! The dispersed tobacco planters had neglected building towns of consequence; there were few churches. When Sunday services were held, farmers offered lame excuses why they could not possibly attend. Tidewater society, so full of "wicked men," discouraged even the indomitable Whitefield. "The greatest probability of doing good in Virginia," he concluded, "is among the Scots-Irish, who have lately settled in the mountainous parts of that province. They raise little or no tobacco, but things that are useful for common life."[68]

Not surprisingly, the price they received for their tobacco obsessed colonial planters. The sources of this preoccupation were cultural as well as economic. There is no question that men like Carter and Lee strove to maintain a favorable balance with the British merchant houses. As we shall see, they hated debt. Nevertheless, they were also concerned with the judgment of other planters. Price provided a reasonably unambiguous measure of the worth of a man's tobacco, its quality; and in this sense a high return validated a person's claim as a crop master. Historians who describe these Virginians solely as agricultural capitalists eager to maximize income miss a crucial aspect of the tobacco mentality. These planters competed not only for pounds and pence but also for honor and reputation.

This point should not be misunderstood. It would be foolish to claim that the planters were indifferent to profits or that they were incapable of responding to economic incentives. In some of their commercial correspondence they sound like hard-nosed businessmen, the kind of calculating entrepreneurs whom agricultural economists tell us inhabit rural

---

[68] George Whitefield, *Journals (1737-1741)*, intro. William V. Davis (Gainesville, Fla., 1969), 384, 386-87. The two preceding paragraphs originally appeared in "Back to Sweat and Toil: Suggestions for the Study of Agricultural Work in Early America," *Pennsylvania History*, 49(1982), 241-58 and are reproduced here with express consent of the editor.

America. But while recognizing the desire to maximize returns, one should appreciate other considerations that strongly influenced planter behavior in this society. The mental process of these Virginians was not unlike that of the Balinese peasants whom Clifford Geertz observed placing bets on fighting cocks. "This [symbolic analysis]," Geertz explained, "I must stress immediately, is *not* to say that money does not matter, or that the Balinese is no more concerned about losing five hundred ringgits than fifteen. Such a conclusion would be absurd. It is because money *does*, in this hardly unmaterialistic society, matter and matter very much that the more of it one risks, the more of a lot of other things, such as one's pride, one's poise, one's dispassion, one's masculinity, one also risks, again only momentarily but again very publicly as well."[69] And it was precisely because tobacco mattered in Virginia society so very much that it became in the eye of the major producers a measure of self, a source of meaningful social identity, as well as a means to maintain a high standard of living.

Whatever the source of their curiosity may have been, the planters paid close attention to news of price. Rumors spread rapidly. Whenever Virginians congregated, they traded information about the local market, and though each planter conducted his business in private, everyone seemed to know exactly how much money he had received. These gatherings filled Virginians with considerable anxiety. They wanted to discover how well other producers had done, to establish an index by which they could measure their own performance. To learn that one had settled for a lower price than that offered to competing planters in the area was galling. It amounted to a public loss of face. Robert ("King") Carter, Landon's father and the wealthiest Virginian of his generation, could not bear the thought of losing out to his neighbors. "In discourse with Colonel Byrd, Mr. Armistead, and a great many others," Carter lectured an English merchant, "I un-

[69] Clifford Geertz, *The Interpretation of Cultures: Selected Essays* (New York, 1973), 433-34.

derstand you had sold their tobacco . . . at good rates. I cannot allow myself to come behind any of these gentlemen in the planter's trade."[70] Carter assumed not only that the news of his sales circulated widely but also that lower returns compromised his standing within the community of planters.

Isaac Giberne understood such thinking. Although this Anglican parson was not a typical Tidewater planter, he was very much involved in the local tobacco culture. In 1773 he wrote to William Lee, a former neighbor who was then trying to establish himself as a London tobacco merchant. "In yours of 25th Jany. last," Giberne observed, "you say you can only promise me *Neighbour's Fare* for my Tobaccos last year." That agreement Giberne accepted, but he warned, "Pray remember my good Friend, that as Colo. Frans. Lee is literally and almost my next door neighbour, that my sales do not fall short of his; otherwise your promise fails, as I shall be content in *the Equity* of *his* price, let it be what it will."[71] Again, the basis of Giberne's expectations was not a finely calibrated accounting of return on investment, or even on some vague sense of what tobacco was selling for in Europe, but on what his immediate peers might receive. At stake was Giberne's honor, and, as William Lee well knew, planters kept few secrets about tobacco prices.

Criticism of a man's tobacco, however tactfully phrased, set off frenzied self-examination. Whenever planters received a low price, for example, they assumed that somehow they must be at fault. Their reaction was almost reflexive. The problem, they reasoned, must have been in production, in the management of the labor force—in other words, in them-

---

[70] Louis B. Wright, ed., *Letters of Robert Carter, 1720-1727: The Commercial Interests of a Virginia Gentleman* (San Marino, Ca., 1940), 93-94.

[71] Worthington Chauncey Ford, ed., *Letters of William Lee* (Brooklyn, N.Y., 1891), I, 74. In another part of the same letter (8 July 1773), Giberne declared, "I must say I expected something more than my proceeds for the Tobaccos . . . which went in Walker. Mr. Russell far exceeded those sales. Nor can I understand the difference you mention of the north side of Rappahannock Tobacco. My overseers at Home and at the Glebe, are reckon'd neat Planters, and it is *generally* allow'd our Tobaccos are the more valuable than the Potomack; and yet we get no better prices, or scarcely so good" (I, 73).

selves—and they usually accepted responsibility for the poor showing of their tobacco in the British market. In 1766 the London firm of Steuart and Campbell notified Henry Fitzhugh that some sixty hogsheads of his "own Crop sold much lower" than had the "rent" tobacco made by Fitzhugh's tenants. This was extremely embarrassing for one who had pretensions of being a crop master. The questionable hogsheads displayed his personal seal, "HF," and he had expected they would "all have sold . . . at a very high price." The problem was in the curing. "You say," Fitzhugh declared, "the tobo was very good, & neatly handled but many hhds very much affected with Smoke." This malodorous quality could not have been avoided, the planter argued, since without fires in the unusually moist curing barns, the entire crop would have been rotted. Nevertheless, Fitzhugh promised to do better next time.[72] Robert Beverley received so many complaints about his early crops that he began to doubt whether he would ever become a master grower. Each year he tried to improve the quality of his leaves, until in 1765 he wrote to England in frustration, "I don't think it necessary for a Man to serve his whole life an apprenticeship."[73]

In a sense, the planters were too involved in an endless cycle of production, too caught up in the tobacco mentality to become fully successful capitalists. Their personal judgments reflected the assumptions of a staple mentality. There seems no other plausible explanation for their naiveté about international market procedures.[74] One experienced Virginia

[72] Henry Fitzhugh to Steuart and Campbell, 18 February 1766, Henry Fitzhugh Papers.

[73] Robert Beverley to Edward and Samuel Athawes, 21 September 1765, Beverley Letter Book.

[74] Economic historians discovered—with evident surprise—that eighteenth-century Tidewater planters actually knew very little about the subtleties of the British tobacco market. Aubrey C. Land wrote, for example, "Small producers or great, all were bound to the tobacco market, whose workings *few understood and almost none perfectly.* Many honest planters regarded the marketing mechanism with suspicion and professed to see tobacco production as a kind of bondage to a shadowy, somewhat sinister group of merchants across the water" (Land, "Economic Behavior in a Planting Society: The

merchant complained that the planters held "wild & chimerical notions" about price-setting mechanisms.[75] Indeed, men
who exercised the closest scrutiny over cutting and curing
seem to have been mystified about what happened to their
tobacco once it left America. In 1774, for example, Fitzhugh

Eighteenth-Century Chesapeake," *Journal of Southern History*, 30(1967), 474,
[emphasis added]). In support of this generalization, Land cites Samuel M.
Rosenblatt's fine essay on the London consignment firm of John Norton and
Sons. As Rosenblatt explains, tobacco merchants regularly received a "drawback," or return, on certain customs duties paid on tobacco reexported from
Great Britain. Some of this money should have been credited to the planters
against whom all duties and fees were charged, but most Virginians apparently possessed only the vaguest comprehension of these procedures. In this
case, what they did not know *did* hurt them, for the drawbacks generated
fairly large sums. "The situation as it related to ready cash, discount, and
interest, was very involved," Rosenblatt declares. "While there can be little
question of the merchants' awareness of the profit that came to them when
they had ready money . . . the great body of planters were not so alert. Some
of those who knew of this advantage did not realize its magnitude." Even
such successful planter-merchants in Virginia as Nathaniel Littleton Savage
and William Nelson seemed uncertain how the system operated, and, as
Rosenblatt concludes, "If William Nelson, a leading mercantile and political
figure in the colony, was so poorly informed about the complexities of English customs procedures, it stands to reason that other less business-oriented
Virginians were even more uninformed" (Rosenblatt, "The Significance of
Credit in the Tobacco Consignment Trade: A Study of John Norton & Sons,
1768-1775," *W&MQ*, 3rd ser., 19[1962], 390-94). Since so many of the colony's great planters had studied in the mother country, one cannot convincingly argue that they lacked an opportunity to learn more about the drawbacks. The planters' perceptions of merchants and credit are treated more
fully in Chapters III and IV.
  [75] Francis Jerdone to Alexander Speirs and Hugh Brown, 11 June 1759,
Francis Jerdone Papers, College of William and Mary Library, Williamsburg,
Virginia. William Nelson expressed amazement at the high prices that Scottish traders gave for Virginia tobacco. He could not understand how they
carried on their business and suspected that they knew something about the
mysteries of commerce that even the English merchants did not comprehend.
He explained to Edward and Samuel Athawes, two experienced London merchants, "Depend upon [it], my Friend, they [the Scots] have some secrets in
the Tobo. Trade, that you & I are unacquainted with, or they could not give
such prices here & carry all before as they do" (12 August 1767, Nelson
Letter Book). See also entry of 20 May 1774, in *Diary of Landon Carter*, ed.
Greene, II, 813.

confessed to an English merchant with whom he had dealt for
more than a decade, "I really do not understand your manner
of keeping my Interest Act [Account]."[76] Virginians speculated about factors of supply and demand, but about commercial practices that ate into their profits, they remained ignorant.

III

Two Virginians, Landon Carter and George Washington, left
particularly vivid insights into the psychological dimensions
of the tobacco mentality, especially into the producer's pursuit of honor and reputation through his crops. Like Washington, Carter kept a diary. The master of Sabine Hall, a
large plantation overlooking the Rappahannock River, took
considerable pride in his ability to grow quality tobacco. In
late September, after most of his plants had been cut and
carried to the curing barns, he congratulated himself. "By
being careful and early in topping, worming and suckering,"
Carter wrote, ". . . I have produced I believe as to goodness
as fine tobacco as ever was seen [,] And as to quantity very
large."[77]

Contemporaries learned to play upon Carter's pride. One
clever associate who came to Sabine Hall looking for scarce
planking took care to accompany his request with the observation that Carter's tobacco was "by far the thickest he had
ever seen."[78] Such comment obviously pleased Carter, for he
reproduced every fulsome word in his diary. He could hardly
contain his satisfaction when "some Gentlemen" who sat on
the county court with him expressed admiration for Carter's
fine crop. "One of them," Carter noted, "ignorantly was going
to separate the leaf imaginging it had been double."[79] Inci-

[76] Henry Fitzhugh to Steuart and Campbell, 29 September 1766; Fitzhugh
to Campbell, 5 December 1774, Henry Fitzhugh Papers.

[77] Entry of 23 September 1770, in *Diary of Landon Carter*, ed. Greene, I,
501.

[78] Entry of 8 September 1770, in ibid., 482.

[79] Entry of 6 September 1770, in ibid., 480.

dents like these reaffirmed Carter's reputation as an outstanding manager, a skillful judge of production. But, though he savored even the slightest praise from neighbors, he showed almost no interest in how his hogsheads were actually marketed in England. He craved direct, immediate confirmation of high standing within a local agrarian community.

A bizarre exchange with a British merchant in 1774 revealed the extent to which Carter's self-esteem was bound up with his tobacco. The merchant accused Carter of exporting a low-grade leaf, and, to support this claim, he returned a sample of the planter's latest crop. The offending leaves "rolled up in blue paper" mortified Carter. He examined the leaves and reported that they "smelt very fine." Still, he was uneasy. Carter turned to members of his own family. "Even my daughter," the planter observed, ". . . praised it." But her testimony failed to reassure the master of Sabine Hall. The more he stared at the contents of the blue package, the more anxious he became. "I do suppose by a thousand ways I should have been ashamed of bad tobacco and had thought it must be changed; but I see it is according to my home method of managements and it is very fine." To be sure, the tobacco was "a trifle dusty," but Carter did not think its quality low enough to warrant rebuke. Finally, unable to contain his shame and doubt any longer, Carter bit into the sample. "I took some of it to chew. It is very fine," he repeated, "and [I] shall tie up the rest; for I love a good quid."[80] Other planters probably would not have gone to such lengths to defend their product, but most would have understood why Carter was so upset.

Robert Wormeley Carter certainly understood. Landon's son played upon his father's vanity, and in so doing revealed much about the workings of the tobacco culture. Landon longed for Robert Wormeley's respect. Next to his son, neither merchants nor neighbors mattered, but for complex reasons, the two men constantly quarreled.[81] There is no ques-

[80] Entry of 21 May 1774, in ibid., II, 813-14.
[81] Ibid., I, 48-61.

X. Landon Carter, the master of Sabine Hall

tion that Landon, an aging patriarch, could be an emotional bully. Sometimes tensions between father and son became unbearable and exploded in a torrent of mutual abuse and criticism. Landon upbraided Robert Wormeley—by the 1770s a middle-aged planter with a family of his own—for sloth, gambling, but most of all for filial ingratitude. In his turn, Robert Wormeley accused his father of producing mediocre tobacco. The charge deeply wounded the senior Carter. Within this particular agricultural society such behavior rep-

resented the height of disrespect, for both men fully understood the symbolic role that tobacco played in their culture.

In July 1770 Robert Wormeley visited Sabine Hall and immediately began to point out imperfections in the way his
father cultivated his crop. Why, Landon asked, did the tobacco plants now ripening in the fields not meet his son's
expectations: "I was told by the most insolent as well as most
impudent person amongst men (my son) That was because I
would follow *my own way*." Landon embraced martyrdom.
The "scoundrel [was] determined to abuse his father," and the
plantation tour continued. Landon had broken the soil improperly; his judgment on other aspects of production was
suspect. The senior Carter held his tongue, but in his diary
he vented his emotion. "He has not seen my estate this whole
year," Landon cried, "but in Passing by, and yet he will find
fault because sworn to do it with his father. If I ask him why
richer lands in my neighbourhood don't exceed me in crop-
ping [in quantity] Then I am answered to make better tobacco."[82] On other occasions, Robert Wormeley was less cen-
sorious, but he knew how to defend himself against his
father's barbs.[83] He could not directly insult the master of
Sabine Hall. By calling Landon's tobacco management into
question, his status as a tobacco master, the son accomplished
the same end.

Another, more public incident occurring in the fall of 1771
revealed Landon's extreme sensitivity to criticism of his tobacco. On this occasion he rose in defense not only of his own
staple, but also that of all Rappahannock planters. Carter
sensed trouble soon after a flood swept down the rivers of
Tidewater Virginia, carrying with it most of the annual crop
stored in the public warehouses. Many planters on the James
and Rappahannock lost an entire season's tobacco, and the
House of Burgesses immediately moved to compensate these
people. The assembly did so, however, on the basis of a for-
mula that struck Carter as arbitrary, inequitable, and intol-

---

[82] Entry of 6 July 1770, in ibid., 436-37 (emphasis added).
[83] For example, see ibid., I, 482; II, 615.

erable. The James River planters received twenty shillings per hundredweight of tobacco, the Rappahannock planters only eighteen. Indeed, the House seemed to be saying—albeit implicitly—that the planters in one region were less skilled than those of another.

When he heard the news, Carter fired off a long letter to the *Virginia Gazette*. The reputation of his neighborhood was at stake. To be sure, Carter admitted, the James River planters made larger crops than did those of the Rappahannock. But what did quantity matter? "When we consider," Carter explained, "that the Proficiency of a Planter as to his Skill (which the Goodness of the Commodity alone ought to respect) is best discovered by the *Cleanness, Neatness, Colour, Scent,* and *Substance* of his Tobacco, we shall find that the Largeness of his Crop tended is very seldom so great a Proof of the presumptive Goodness of it as a small Quantity tended." The James planters showed no attention to the appearance of their fields; they waited too long to begin topping. Any self-respecting Rappahannock grower, Carter assured the newspaper's readers, would characterize such practices as "*lazy* and *lawless.*"

For Landon the difference of two shillings was a matter of honor. Indeed, the House of Burgesses seemed to be intent on treating the Rappahannock planters with the same contempt that all Virginians associated with the Parliament of Great Britain. "As to the Injuriousness of such a Disgrace," he wrote, "behold a Legislature undertaking to depreciate the Staple made by (perhaps) one Third of their Community, whom they certainly equally represent in a British Constitution. . . . what Method is there to remove such an *unnatural* Stigma!" During the Stamp Act crisis, Parliament had behaved in this manner. On the grounds of expediency rather than principle, it had attempted to fleece the colonists. And now, the House of Burgesses was proposing to cheat the Rappahannock planters out of 10 percent of their compensation. "*Truth* and *justice*," he reminded the Virginians, "like Liberty and Property, are so Twin-born in their very Natures that whenever one of them is made sick by *legal Authority* the other must pine and languish under the same heavy Stroke." Before this time, Carter recounted with an unmistakable reference to the first great confrontation with British authority, "every Twopenny Act was twopence every Where, whether on James River or Rappahannock."[84] There is no record of what other Virginians thought of Carter's performance. His letter certainly does reveal a high degree of regional loyalty—a spirit of localism that drove southern leaders to distraction throughout the nineteenth century—as well as a disposition to escalate alleged personal wrongs into issues of great political principle. Pride of production and sensitivity to criticism were two sides of the tobacco mentality.

Like Landon Carter, George Washington assumed that a man's reputation was bound up—at least in part—with the quality of the tobacco he grew. After the conclusion of the French and Indian War in Virginia (by late 1758 the war with France no longer threatened the colony's frontier), Washington returned to Mount Vernon determined to become a successful planter. At this point, in 1759, it did not occur to him to cultivate another staple. Virginians grew tobacco, and he saw no reason to doubt that he could make a quality leaf. In 1762 he offered an overseer a monetary incentive to bring in a better crop than normal because of the "well-known intention of the said George Washington to have his tobacco made and managed in the best and neatest manner which in some manner lessens the quantity."[85] To whom Washington's intentions were well known was not spelled out in this agreement, but he probably realized that his Northern Neck neighbors—the Lees, Fitzhughs, and Carters—kept a sharp watch over his progress as a planter. He may have sensed that his credibility as a political or military leader, as a colonial Cincinnatus, was in some important way related to his success on the plantation.[86]

The results of his early efforts discouraged Washington.

---

[84] *Virginia Gazette* (Purdie and Dixon), 3 October 1771.

[85] Cited in Freeman, *Washington*, III, 81.

[86] See, Garry Wills, *Cincinnatus: George Washington and The Enlightenment* (Garden City, N.Y., 1984).

He was a proud man, and no matter how diligently he worked the stubborn soils of Mount Vernon, he could not produce the kind of quality leaves that one saw on the plantations of the James, Rappahannock, and York rivers. In his own eyes, the crucial measure was price. However hard he tried, he still received lower returns than did his friends and neighbors. In bitter frustration, Washington wrote to an English merchant complaining, "I am at a loss to conceive the Reason why Mr. Wormeleys, and indeed some other Gentlemen's Tobaccos should sell at 12d last year and mine . . . only fetch 11½." Washington knew that the results of his sales were no secret. These much publicly discussed prices provided an index to his skills as a producer, and it was with the conventions of Virginia culture in mind that he protested, "Certain I am no Person in Virginia takes more pains to make their Tobo. fine than I do and tis hard then I should not be well rewarded for it."[87]

Hard indeed. Frustration turned to depression. In 1762 Washington wrote of his own failure as a planter. "I confess, he scribbled, "it [tobacco cultivation] to be an Art beyond my skill, to succeed in making good Tobo. as I have used my utmost endeavours for that purpose this two or 3 years past; and am once again urged to express my surprise at finding that I do not partake of the best prices that are going."[88] At this point in his life, Washington was a captive of the tobacco mentality. He could have turned aggressively to other crops in the early 1760s, but to have done so would have made him less a Virginian, less a gentleman. It would have cut him off from the only source of public esteem other than soldiering that he had ever known.

Depression eventually gave way to anger. Throughout his long military and political career, Washington's self-control impressed contemporaries. He sometimes seemed incapable of showing passion of any sort. But in September 1765 his piti-

[87] George Washington to Robert Cary and Company, 3 April 1761, in *The Writings of George Washington*, ed. John C. Fitzpatrick (Washington, D.C., 1931), II, 357.

[88] Ibid., 378 (28 May 1762).

ful tobacco sparked a remarkable outburst. He reminded an
English correspondent, Robert Cary, that the price he had
obtained for his tobacco was "worse than many of my Ac-
quaintances upon this River, Potomack." The comments that
he imagined men were whispering behind his back were too
much for Washington to bear. "Can it be other wise . . . than
a little mortifying to find, that we, who raise none but Sweet-
scented Tobacco, and endeavour I may venture to add, to be
careful in the management of it . . . ," he asked rhetorically,
"should meet with such unprofitable returns? Surely I may
answer No!"[89] These were not words one expected to hear
from the reserved Washington. He eventually decided that if
he could not excel at the planter's trade, not become a crop
master, then he would shift his attention to a different plant.
It is essential to recognize how Washington reached this decision. It was made with the greatest reluctance. He began
with the traditional culture, and for a decade he persisted
without experiencing notable success. Washington was not
drawn into the wheat market simply because he was looking
for a way to maximize returns on his investment in land and
slaves. Rather, he was forced out of the tobacco market. He
wanted Mount Vernon to prosper; he also longed to master
the "Art . . . of making good Tobo."

                                    IV

Thus, at mid-century these Tidewater Virginians were planters. However much political theory they may have read, however familiar they may have been with the writings of John
Locke and the representatives of the Scottish Enlightenment,
however much time they spent impressing one another with
their worldly ways, they remained products of a regional
agrarian culture. Tobacco shaped their society and helped define their place within it. From the perspective of a cultural
anthropologist, the plant possessed immense symbolic significance for the planters and their families. By 1750, this staple

---

[89] Ibid., 427-28 (20 September 1765).

had been tightly woven into the fabric of the colonists' everyday life; it gave meaning to their experience. It reinforced social cohesion within the white community. One would predict, therefore, that any assault on the traditional relation between planter and tobacco would have far-reaching, even revolutionary, implications for the entire society.[90]

[90] On this point, see Marc Egnal and Joseph A. Ernst, "An Economic Interpretation of the American Revolution," *W&MQ*, 3rd ser., 29(1972), 3-32. They correctly observe, "The forward part played by the Northern Neck of Virginia in pushing that colony toward Independence demands an investigation of colonial society far beyond treatises on whig ideology . . ." (9).

CHAPTER III

PLANTERS AND MERCHANTS: A KIND OF FRIENDSHIP

The leading planters of Tidewater Virginia shipped their tobacco to British merchants on consignment. The older gentlemen, planters like Landon Carter who was born in 1710, had witnessed major changes in the marketing of the colony's staple over their lifetime. In 1730 as much as half of Virginia's annual crop was sold on consignment. Each year, however, this figure decreased. The Scots opened stores and purchased ever larger amounts of tobacco directly from the small and medium planters. By 1776 only a quarter of the tobacco exported reached Great Britain on consignment. But this trend can be misleading. The major planters of the Tidewater had little to do with the Scottish factors. Their perceptions of the staple market reflected the consignment experience, and these views—products of a particular social and economic context—generally fit harmoniously and effectively with the central assumptions of the tobacco mentality.

The eighteenth-century gentry perceived commercial relations with British tobacco merchants in highly personal terms. Exchange, they believed, involved a planter's honor, virtue, and independence; it was a form of "friendship." These rhetorical conventions, developed largely out of face-to-face dealings with neighbors, provided the great planters with a framework—a set of idioms—that helped them to comprehend a complex marketing system centered thousands of miles across the Atlantic Ocean. Theirs was not necessarily an accurate picture of how commerce operated. Indeed, by the standards of modern economic theory, these planters may seem perversely "irrational." But the Virginians did the best they could. They construed a reality by generalizing the values of a local culture, and for most of the century these mental categories served them well enough. This cultural conversation between merchants and planters contained obvious contradictions. By receiving credit from British merchant houses, Virginia gentlemen did, of course, compromise their personal autonomy. For most of the century these elements of potential friction lay dormant. As long as everyone involved in the tobacco trade prospered (or thought that they were prospering), the Virginians had no reason to explore the implications of these inconsistencies. In fact, it was only when the merchants announced that they were playing by different rules that the great planters realized how much of their culture was at risk in the marketplace.

I

Virginia gentlemen dreamed of achieving complete personal independence. For the great planters, it was the ideal social condition. Such men took pride in being insulated from the demands of the outside world, of freeing themselves from obligations to people who were not members of their immediate family. In 1726, William Byrd II described the perfect environment to an English correspondent. "I have a large family of my own," the master of Westover explained, "and my doors are open to every body, yet. . . . Like one of the patriarchs, I have my flocks and my herds, my bond-men and bond-women, and every soart of trade amongst my own servants, so that I live in a kind of independence on every one, but Providence."[1] By the standards of a provincial gentry culture, Byrd was doing very well. When, as an old man, St.

[1] Byrd to Charles Boyle, Earl of Orrery, 5 July, 1726, in *The Correspondence of the Three William Byrds of Westover*, ed. Marion Tinling (Charlottesville, 1977), I, 355. Also see, Gerald W. Mullin, *Flight and Rebellion: Slave Resistance in Eighteenth-Century Virginia* (New York, 1972), chapter 1; Rhys Isaac, *The Transformation of Virginia 1740-1790* (Chapel Hill, N.C., 1982), 131-38; Jack Greene, "Society, Ideology, and Politics," in *Society, Freedom, and Conscience*, ed. Richard M. Jellison (New York, 1976), 52-53; Michael Zuckerman, "William Byrd's Family," *Perspectives in American History*, 12 (1979), 253-311.

George Tucker reflected upon the character of colonial Tide-water society, he insisted that "there was no such thing as *Dependence*, in the lower counties."[2]

The great planters' insistence upon their own independence—a condition that they expected other Virginians to observe—contained a striking element of territoriality. Their vast riverfront plantations were, in fact, self-contained communities run by a resident patriarch.[3] The big house, the immense acreage, the scores of slaves gave dramatic outward expression to the centrality of the landowner's personal independence in this culture. Landon Carter, the master of Sabine Hall, bragged in 1759 that he was virtually invulnerable in his "excellent little Fortress . . . built on a Rock . . . of *Independency*."[4] His son-in-law, Robert Beverley, shared Carter's values. "I thank god," Beverley declared in a letter, "I have a very fine Estate, which even with the Crop I have already made will put me in a State of Perfect Independence."[5] Peyton Randolph, one of revolutionary Virginia's most prominent planters, expressed a similar view. Writing to protest the actions of several British merchants, Randolph announced, "I shall never be affected with any Reply that can be made, having an excellent little Fortress to protect me, one built on a Rock not liable to be shaken with Fears, that of *Independency*."[6] By the 1760s the image of the independent Virginian lodged in his plantation fortress had become something of a cliché, a self-deception that contained a good measure of defensiveness.

Daily life on a large estate reinforced the gentleman's sense

[2] "Notes of St. George Tucker on Manuscript copy of William Wirt's *Life of Patrick Henry* (September 25, 1815)," *W&MQ*, 1st ser., 22(1914), 252.

[3] See Daniel Blake Smith, *Inside the Great House* (Ithaca, N.Y., 1980); Edmund S. Morgan, *Virginians at Home* (Williamsburg, 1952).

[4] Jack P. Greene, ed., *The Diary of Colonel Landon Carter*, Virginia Historical Society Documents, vol. 4 (Charlottesville, 1965), I, 19. For a description of Carter's eighteenth-century home, Sabine Hall, see Thomas Tileston Waterman, *The Mansions of Virginia, 1706-1776* (Chapel Hill, N.C., 1946), 127-36.

[5] Robert Beverley to Samuel Athawes, 18 November 1763, Beverley Letter Book, 1761-1793, Library of Congress, Washington, D.C.

[6] *A Letter to a Gentleman in London, from Virginia* (Williamsburg, 1759), 27.

XI. Landon Carter's "Rock . . . of *Independency*," Sabine Hall

of personal autonomy. John Mason, son of the famous Virginia patriot George Mason, left a vivid description of the self-contained world of the great Tidewater planter. His "recollections" were of Gunston Hall, but there is no question that his powerful depiction of economic independence held for other eighteenth-century plantations as well.

> It was very much the practice with gentlemen of landed and slave estates in the interior of Virginia, so to organize them as to have considerable resources within themselves. . . . Thus my father had among his slaves carpenters, coopers, sawyers, blacksmiths, tanners, curriers, shoemakers, spinners, weavers and knitters, and even a distiller. His woods furnished timber and plank for the

carpenters and coopers, and charcoal for the blacksmith; his cattle killed for his own consumption and for sale supplied skins for the tanners, curriers, and shoemakers, and his sheep gave wool and his fields produced cotton and flax for the weavers and spinners, and his orchards fruit for the distiller. His carpenters and sawyers built and kept in repair all the dwelling-houses, barns, stables, ploughs, harrows, gates &c. on the plantations and the out-houses at the home house. His coopers made the hogsheads that tobacco was prized in and the tight casks to hold the cider and other liquors. The tanners and curriers with the proper vats &c., tanned and dressed the skins as well for the upper as for lower leather to the full amount of the consumption of the estate, and the shoemakers made them into shoes for the negroes. A professed shoemaker was hired for three or four months in the year to come and make up the shoes for the white part of the family. The blacksmiths did all the iron work required by the establishment, as making and repairing ploughs, harrows, teeth chains, bolts &c., &c. The spinners, weavers, and knitters made all the coarse cloths and stockings used by the negroes, and some of finer texture worn by the white family, nearly all worn by the children of it. The distiller made every fall a good deal of apple, peach, and persimmon brandy. The art of distilling from grain was not then among us, and but few public distilleries. All these operations were carried on at the home house, and their results distributed as occasion required to the different plantations.

Even when they ventured beyond the boundaries of their own estates—to meetings of the House of Burgesses at Williamsburg, for example—the great planters stoutly maintained their personnal autonomy. This obsession often made them appear prickly to outsiders. Certainly, one trespassed upon a gentleman's independece at one's peril. Andrew Burnaby, an acerbic British traveler, observed in 1760 that "the public or political character of the Virginians corresponds with their private one: they are haughty and jealous of their liberties, impatient of restraint, and can scarcely bear the thought of being controuled by any superior power."[7] This statement was penned before the Stamp Act crisis, and so presumably does not reflect a social persona that Virginians displayed especially for visitors from the mother country.

Personal autonomy allowed no compromise. It was an aspect of planter culture that gentlemen learned early in their childhood. In 1765, Arthur Lee, a young Virginian sent to medical school in Edinburgh, wrote to his famous older brother, Richard Henry, protesting, ". . . liberty & independence [are] to me the most valuable of all blessings, since I know not a more bitter ingredient than dependence that can enter into the cup of life."[8] Arthur may not have inherited Stratford Hall, but his values were unquestionably those of a great Tidewater planter.

Possession of personal independence demonstrated, among other things, that a gentleman was morally sound. One could trust his judgment, especially in political matters. Independent persons, it was believed, stood above the scramble after power and wealth and thus seemed ideally suited to provide leadership for the small planters. This bundle of assumptions was a staple of Country thought, and the centrality of independence in the writings of Bolingbroke, Trenchard, and Gordon may in part explain the popularity of those authors in colonial Virginia. No doubt other gentry turned to the classical writers, especially Cicero, Horace, and Virgil, for the same reasons.

What these authors said about autonomy apparently corresponded to eighteenth-century planter experience. During the Revolution, Richard Henry Lee assumed that only persons "of independent Circumstance" could possibly become true

[7] Andrew Burnaby, *Travels through the Middle Settlements*, in *A General Collection . . .* , ed. John Pinkerton (London, 1812), XIII, 715. Mason's "Recollections" are quoted in Morgan, *Virginians at Home*, 53-54.

[8] Arthur Lee to [R. H. Lee], 20 March 1765, Lee Family Papers, vol. I, Virginia Historical Society, Richmond, Virginia.

patriots.[9] His neighbor on Virginia's Northern Neck, Landon Carter, agreed. "Independence . . .," he scribbled in his diary in 1769, was the foundation "on which Liberty can alone be protected."[10] Independence of mind sometimes cost a great planter profitable offices in the colony's royal government, but such sacrifice seemed a modest price to pay for the preservation of integrity. "I have not one Quality requisite in a Sycophant or a fashionable Toad Eater," Beverley confessed, "for this Reason, I believe my most prudent Method will be to live as I have done, retired & absolutely independent in my Principles, a Situation, tho' not the most lucrative, is certainly the most satisfactory."[11]

Without substantial property, a planter's claim to personal autonomy obviously rang hollow. Perhaps if the colony had developed a genuine titled aristocracy, a social system in which birth to a certain family automatically conferred noble status, the great planters might have been less concerned about visible material success. But, though the sons of Virginia gentlemen usually became gentlemen, there was no guarantee that every male bearing a particular surname would achieve economic or political eminence.[12] This insecurity, which seems to have grown more pronounced on the eve of the Revolution, created curious tensions within gentry culture. Maintenance of the external trappings of independence —big houses, fast horses, sumptuous finery, and the like— forced the great planters to monitor the flow of pounds and pence more closely than they would have liked. Poor management threatened a man's independence; certainly, neighbors might wonder whether the personal judgment of a man who

[9] Cited in Pauline Maier, *The Old Revolutionaries* (New York, 1980), 182. See, William D. Liddle, "'Virtue and Liberty': An Inquiry into the Role of the Agrarian Myth in the Rhetoric of the American Revolutionary Era," *South Atlantic Quarterly*, 77 (1978), 15-38.

[10] *Diary of Landon Carter*, ed. Greene, I, 19.

[11] Beverley to Samuel Athawes, 15 April 1771, Beverley Letter Book.

[12] Charles S. Sydnor, *Gentlemen Freeholders* (Chapel Hill, N.C., 1952); Robert E. and B. Katherine Brown, *Virginia, 1705-1786: Democracy or Aristocracy?* (East Lansing, Mich., 1964).

had fallen on hard times was as sound as it had been when he was prosperous. At the same time, the Tidewater planter was expected to act as if he really did not care about such practical economic affairs. The men who aspired to be crop masters spent a good deal of time worrying about the tenuous relation between public appearance and private reality.

II

The great planters of eighteenth-century Virginia generally agreed that debt compromised a person's independence. Their concern—at least before the mid-1760s—was not that creditors would haul improvident gentlemen before the local magistrates. Rather, for the gentry the problem was more abstract, more internalized, more an expression of deeply held cultural values than of threatened legal proceedings. They feared that the very condition of being in debt exposed an independent planter to external pressure. It weakened the fortress. In 1761 Richard Corbin, the proud father of a new child, wrote to the colony's royal governor, "You will be pleas'd to hear of the Arrival of my Son, . . . I pray to God he may avoid the Errors of his Countrymen, & only know the Evil of being in Debt from the Experience of others."[13]

Even when a creditor said nothing about the state of an individual's accounts, the indebted man knew in his heart that he had become a dependent being, that he had lost a measure of personal liberty. The presence of so many slaves in Virginia, totally dependent beings, made the prospect of losing liberty more poignant than it might have been in the northern colonies. This psychological element made debt intolerable. The great Tidewater planters convinced themselves that being a little in debt was like being a little unfree, a condition no self-respecting gentleman could long tolerate.[14]

[13] Corbin to Robert Dinwiddie, 10 July 1761, Richard Corbin Letter Book, 1758-1768, Colonial Williamsburg, Inc., Research Center, microfilm.

[14] Edmund S. Morgan, *American Slavery—American Freedom: The Ordeal of Virginia* (New York, 1975), 383-84; John Brewer, "Commercialization and Politics," in Neil McKendrick et al., *The Birth of A Consumer Society: The*

Considering their dread of personal dependence, it is not surprising that Virginia gentlemen preached against indebtedness with the same fervor that New Englanders reserved for sloth. In 1758 Corbin warned a son living in England: "Let me recommend to you this One Caution, Never to Run in debt, or exceed the bounds of your allowance, never buy any thing without Money [but] to pay for it immediately."[15] Walter Jones, a young Virginian studying in Scotland, cleverly turned the traditional advice to his own advantage. In 1766 he wrote to his American brother asking for a loan. Walter argued that if one did not pay off one's creditors, "one must be somewhat dependent & a state of dependence in a place where the chief Characteristic is Pride, you will readily perceive not to be the most agreeable."[16] Whether the brother honored this request is not known, but living in a society often characterized as proud, he must certainly have understood young Walter's predicament. When Robert Beverley began his long career as a tobacco planter, he vowed to avoid debt, a condition that he called in a letter to an English merchant "the general Fatality which overwhelmes this wretched Country at this period." He described himself in 1765 as "a young Man just set out in Life." Even at this early stage of his development, Beverley had already "Discovered that the best Method of securing Success is to endeavour to be *perfectly independent*."[17] In other words, success in colonial Virginia resulted as much from the ability to stay out of debt as from hard work.

The words "perfectly independent" provide an important key to understanding gentry attitudes toward the whole issue of credit. Only in an ideal state could a working planter avoid debt. As anyone who consigned tobacco to a British merchant soon learned—indeed, as anyone who sold tobacco to a Scot-

---

Commercialization of Eighteenth-Century England (Bloomington, Ind., 1982), 211-15.

[15] Corbin to son, 21 August 1758, Corbin Letter Book.

[16] Walter Jones to brother, July 1766, Jones Papers, 1752-1787, Colonial Williamsburg, Inc., Research Center, microfilm, no. M-22-3.

[17] Beverley to [Bland?], 8 May 1765, Beverley Letter Book.

tish factor learned—one could never predict what price the market would bring. A planter might require an extension of credit to tide him over until the next crop. His purchases might exceed the returns from the sale of his tobacco. These were the facts of economic life in eighteenth-century Virginia. But even though they normally accepted and gave credit, even though it was an essential part of the commercial world in which they operated, the great planters remained fundamentally suspicious of debt. Financial dependence conflicted with the imperatives of the tobacco mentality. They dealt with this potential source of strain by defining the rules of the marketplace to fit their own customs and experience, which in the Virginia context meant that indebted men still claimed personal autonomy.[18]

Since "perfect independence" proved so elusive, the practical solution for eighteenth-century Virginians was the establishment of what might best be termed an "etiquette of debt," a culturally sanctioned system of rules that told planters to whom they should offer credit and in what amounts. Such judgments pointed up the unusual character of the colony's staple economy. Participation in the world tobacco market simultaneously generated competition as well as cooperation. Since all planters, large and small, produced the same export crop, they were competitors. Some Virginians received higher prices than did others for their tobacco; every grower wanted to beat out his rivals.

At the same time, the staple economy fostered a spirit of cooperation among the colonial tobacco producers. Not only did these people grow the same crop, they also depended to a greater or lesser degree upon foreign merchants for their livelihood. Out of these commercial experiences they developed that spirit of mutuality that sometimes wells up among men who share a work culture. The Populist crusade of the 1890s provides many examples of this phenomenon.[19] "The

---

[18] On this point see M. Egnal and J. A. Ernst, "An Economic Interpretation," *W&MQ*, 3rd ser., 29 (1972), 25.

[19] See Chapter II. On Populism, Lawrence Goodwyn, *The Populist Moment: A Short History of the Agrarian Revolt in America* (New York, 1978); and Steven

small man was frequently a debtor," one Virginia scholar has written perceptively, "but the large man, his creditor, was likely also to be in debt, either to London merchants or to other large men. The large man might make a profit from the small man by marketing tobacco for him, but both were sellers in the end. The very fact that the large man stood to lose along with the small man in a prolonged depression of tobacco prices made him seem all the more appropriate as a spokesman for the whole country."[20] Cooperation and competition were two sides of the same economic culture, and, depending upon the situation in which he found himself, a planter might emphasize one aspect or the other. In other words, even in a society of competitive, autonomous, and materialistic agrarians, there was always the possibility of generating mass movement.

Debt should be interpreted, therefore, within a complex social structure, at once cohesive and yet subject to constant strain. Within this particular context, credit provided important personal links between the great planters and others who lived in their neighborhood. Indeed, beyond the members of one's own immediate family, credit offered a recognized means of structuring social relationships within the white community. Almost all of the colony's freemen were involved in this vast, largely informal network of giving and receiving credit.[21]

The rules governing these exchanges—really cultural conversations—varied according to the borrower's standing within the planter community. The difficulty with this mechanism of ordering society was that no one knew exactly where another person stood in the ranking. No outside agency—

Hahn, *The Roots of Southern Populism: Yeomen Farmers and the Transformation of the Georgia Upcountry, 1850-1890* (New York, 1983).

[20] Morgan, *American Slavery—American Freedom*, 366. Also Peter J. Coleman, *Debtors and Creditors in America: Insolvency, Imprisonment for Debt, and Bankruptcy, 1607-1900* (Madison, 1974), 198.

[21] A. Land, "Economic Behavior," *Journal of Southern History*, 30 (1967), 479. See B. A. Holderness, "Credit in a Rural Community, 1660-1800: Some Neglected Aspects of Probate Inventories," *Midland History*, 3 (1975), 94-115.

there were no banks in the colony—provided credit ratings, and as many Virginians had learned to their regret at one time or another, external appearances could be deceiving. The problem of sorting out debtors was just as acute in the mother country as it was in colonial Virginia. "The greatest weakness of private credit and debt," one English historian explained, "was that the rules and conventions that governed their use were insufficiently clearly defined, and that the mechanisms that did exist for their regulation frequently exacerbated financial uncertainties rather than relieved them."[22] Personal judgments, therefore, formed the basis of the colony's elaborate culture of debt.

However imprecise the rules of etiquette may have been, there is no question that Virginians shared certain basic assumptions about credit. These were local understandings developed within specific neighborhoods. Unless a person led a notoriously scandalous life, his chances of receiving financial assistance from one of the great planters were fairly good. These were usually oral agreements, expressions of trust probably sealed with a handshake. The great planter entered the sum into an account book—sometimes he did not even bother to do that—in expectation that the debtor would eventually repay his obligation. The overwhelming majority of these debts were small, no more than a few pounds.[23] When such sums were involved, a gentleman rarely demanded interest. In fact, a spirit of friendship—albeit between unequal parties—appears to have governed these transactions.[24] On this local level, credit represented a personal favor, a kind of patronage that great planters were expected to provide to worthy neighbors whom they encountered at church, the county courthouse, or militia training.

An obvious, though incomplete explanation why eighteenth-century Virginians developed such an elaborate system of local credit readily springs to mind. Quite simply, they did

[22] Brewer, "Commercialization and Politics," 203.

[23] Coleman, *Debtors and Creditors*, 198.

[24] See Leslie A. Clarkson, *The Pre-Industrial Economy in England, 1500-1750* (London, 1971), 148-50.

not possess enough cash to pay for everything they purchased. Most of the specie they received, even the smallest
silver coin, flowed quickly to the mother country, and while
the colonial government printed paper currency (the Currency Act passed by Parliament in 1764 placed these emis-
sions under severe restrictions), Virginians never enjoyed an
adequate money supply. The operation of the local economy,
therefore, depended upon the informal credit networks. Without them, the planters would have had no way to conduct
normal business, or when the crops were poor, to pay off
their most pressing obligations.[25]

To see these credit arrangements simply as a function of an
inadequate supply of specie, however, obscures the workings
of planter culture. Within a Virginia county community, debt
was an expression of what historian Harold Perkin aptly calls
the "mesh of continuing loyalties." Though the great planters
occasionally pressed local debtors, they were usually willing
to carry these accounts for years. As in other agrarian societies throughout the world, both then and now, a small debt
could symbolize an enduring friendship between patron and
client.[26]

Sometimes, of course, a creditor threatened to sue a delinquent debtor, and the records of the county courts contain
thousands of cases involving small sums. To take a neighbor
before the local magistrates hardly seems an expression of enduring friendship. A closer look at these actions, however,
reveals a curious phenomenon. Usually the plaintiff would
present his claim to the county court and then request "judgment by petition." In response, the defendant informed the

[25] James H. Soltow provides a good discussion of the currency problems
in *The Economic Role of Williamsburg* (Williamsburg, 1965), 107-112. Also, Joseph A. Ernst, "Genesis of the Currency Act of 1764: Virginia Paper Money
and the Protection of British Investments," *W&MQ*, 3rd ser., 22 (1965), 33-
74; Ernst, *Money and Politics in America, 1755-1775; A Study of the Currency
Act of 1764 and the Political Economy of Revolution* (Chapel Hill, N.C., 1973).

[26] Harold J. Perkin, *The Origins of Modern English Society, 1780-1880* (London, 1972), 49; Raymond Firth, ed., *Themes in Economic Anthropology* (London,
1967); Conrad Arensberg, *The Irish Countryman* (1937; rpt. Garden City,
N.Y., 1968).

judges that he needed time "to imparl," to prepare his argument. But debt cases almost never proceeded beyond that point. The parties settled the matter privately. In fact, the courts may have served as a means of officially recording a debt. Whatever may have been involved, the majority of these cases were simply dismissed. Far from upsetting the web of informal relationships in eighteenth-century Virginia, the law helped planters to work out their private differences with mutual forbearance. No one was publicly humiliated. The courts reinforced the conventions of the tobacco culture.[27]

Since historians have not systematically explored these local credit networks—a task that among other things would require the analysis of thousands of wills—how they operated remains a puzzle.[28] Some planters, however, provided clues. In 1771 William Lee, a Virginian who had moved to London, was eager to settle the estate of Philip Ludwell, a member of a prominent Tidewater family, and in his correspondence with Robert Carter Nicholas, Lee inquired why one individual had not paid the seventeen pounds "due ever since the 15th of May 1754." An extension of credit over so many years seemed generous even by Virginia standards. But Lee well understood that each account raised questions of personal judgement. Such was the case of William Hubbard. This man had received two loans from Ludwell, "so that it appears that Mr. Hubbard is on the whole indebted £21 sterling for five years past, however as you say [he] is poor, if you think him really an object of bounty as far as I am concern'd I leave it entirely to you to release him from my share of his debt."[29] Hubbard was obviously a person of good character, and neither Lee nor Nicholas saw any reason to press him.

George Washington provided a particularly good example of the way that the etiquette of debt operated between men of unequal social standing. His neighbor on the Potomac,

[27] A. G. Roeber, *Faithful Magistrates and Republican Lawyers* (Chapel Hill, N.C., 1981), 84-86.

[28] Ibid., 40.

[29] William Lee to Robert Carter Nicholas, 23 May 1771, Lee Family Papers, Mssl. L51, f. 414.

Capt. John Posey, had served with Washington during the French and Indian War, and between 1755 and 1772 his friend was a constant fixture at Mount Vernon. However brave a soldier Posey may have been, it is difficult to imagine a more unworthy object of charity. Largely as the result of self-indulgence, his finances were in a perpetual state of crisis. He drank too much and spent most of his many free moments chasing foxes across the Virginia countryside. In fact, Posey appeared to have possessed none of the personal attributes that accounted for Washington's own eventual success: diligence, foresight, and self-control. Nevertheless, Washington treated Posey as a friend. In the mid-1750s Posey began asking Washington for money. By 1767 he owned him at least £700, an extraordinary sum since Posey already seemed destined for insolvency.[30]

What is so striking about this curious friendship is that Posey showed no shame. He kept returning to Mount Vernon seeking additional loans. However poor a plantation manager Posey may have been, he played the patron-client relationship like an expert. In June 1767 he requested another £500, an advance that would have increased his indebtedness to Washington to well over £1,200. By all rights, Washington should have thrown Posey out by the seat of his pants.

This is not what occurred. After upbraiding Posey for his irresponsibility, Washington apologized because he could not raise the sum of money that his neighbor required. "I find it next to impossible," Washington explained, "to extract any part of the money which is due to me [and] . . . I have struggled to the utmost of my powr for two years past unsuccessfully to raise 4 or £500 to lend to *a very particular friend of mine*, who I know must sell part of his estate without it. . . ."[31] As a gentleman, Washington wanted to take care of his friends. It was his social responsibility, and even when

[30] Douglas S. Freeman, *George Washington: A Biography* (New York, 1951), III, 99-101, 184, 232-34.

[31] Washington to Captain Posey, 24 June 1767, in *Writings of Washington*, ed. John C. Fitzpatrick (Washington, D.C., 1931), II, 457-60 (emphasis added).

XII. *George Washington: Proud Virginian, determined planter*

confronted by the likes of Posey, Washington found it difficult to say "no."

Despite such generosity—or perhaps because of it—Posey's financial affairs went from bad to worse. Hardship, however, failed to diminish his pride or, for that matter, his gall. When Washington asked him for security on several personal loans, Posey accused Washington of "acting as a Money Lender," clearly very ungentlemanly behavior in this culture. To this outrageous charge Washington protested, "in truth the prospect of gain and advantage to myself was not the motive that led me to advance you this money; 'Twas done to serve your family and if possible to save your Estate from dispersion." To suggest that a great planter would attempt to profit from a friend's adversity—or incompetence—was an insult. After Washington cooled down, he offered Posey some long-overdue advice: avoid getting so far in debt that your creditors sue and thereby cause your "honour" to "suffer." Washington's choice of vocabulary provides unexpected illumination into the core values of the tobacco culture. He assumed that Posey's *honor* was at stake, and that if others learned that the horses and the hounds and the house—indeed, everything that the man possessed—were in fact mortgaged, if they discovered that the appearance of prosperity was just that, appearance, then he would *suffer* the humiliation of exposure. It was something Washington himself could not have endured. The master of Mount Vernon counselled his neighbor about the importance of diligence, a homily followed amazingly by a promise to serve as Posey's security for yet another £300.[32]

The relation between these two Virginians came to a tragicomic conclusion in 1771. Posey, as always down on his luck, begged Washington for £12. On this occasion, however, he provided a new excuse; Washington's loans would save Posey from the clutches of an unattractive woman. "I could [have] been able to [have] Satisfied all my old Arrears, Some months AGoe," Posey explained, "by marrying [an] old widow woman in this County. She has Large soms [of] cash by her, and Prittey good Est[ate]—She is as thick, as she is high—And gits drunk at Least three or foure [times] a weak—which is Disagreable to me—has Viliant [violent] Sperrit when Drunk—its been [a] Great Dispute in my mind what to Doe." How Washington responded to this desperate appeal is not

---

[32] Washington to Posey, 24 September 1767, in ibid., 474-75. See also, Washington's correspondence with Robert Stewart, another old friend, in ibid., 397-98.

known. Posey moved to Maryland and apparently ended his days in debtor's prison.[33]

Washington treated his friend with compassion. Though other great planters might have lost patience with Posey, they do not appear to have taken advantage of their poorer neighbors. In this respect the Tidewater gentlemen were quite different from the aristocrats of London and Paris who ran up large debts with the local tradesmen and then ignored appeals for payment. Such arrogance enraged European shopkeepers, and in the late eighteenth century, they demanded social and economic reform. It was people of this class who supported John Wilkes and the London mob.[34] Perhaps if more artisans had lived in the Chesapeake, the great planters would have exploited them. But, in fact, much labor that was done in Great Britain by freemen was delegated in Virginia to slaves. Moreover, the small planters and scattered shopkeepers in the colony would not have tolerated such behavior. These were the men, after all, who voted in local elections. By abusing credit within the local community, the planter elite would have undermined a source of political power.

When both parties to a credit agreement were great planters—in other words, social peers—debt posed an even more delicate problem. For members of this elite group, paying a debt to another gentleman was a matter of personal honor. Even to require financial assistance from another Virginian was an embarrassment, a lessening of one's independence, but once an agreement had been reached, great planters could not endure the thought of tarnishing their reputations with peers by failing to meet an obligation. At least, that is what they claimed. George Washington, who developed a keen sense of his own honor, once informed another Virginian, "To tell a man who had been disappointed from time to time, and at

---

[33] Posey to Washington, 25 May 1771, in *Letters to Washington*, ed. S. M. Hamilton (New York, 1901), IV, 66. Also Freeman, *George Washington*, III, 293-94.

[34] John Brewer, "English Radicalism in the Age of George III," in *Three British Revolutions: 1641, 1688, 1776*, ed. J.G.A. Pocock (Princeton, 1980), 348.

last had waited in confidence of receiving his money from me, that I was unprovided with the means of satisfying his demand, would be galling to me, unjust to him, and what I can no means think of practicing."[35]

Indeed, a central element in what Douglas Southall Freeman, Washington's biographer, labeled "the code of gentlemen's credit," was a willingness to help a deserving planter retrieve his financial standing, to restore his personal honor, even if that act placed one's own finances in jeopardy.[36] Providing a loan, cosigning a note, or posting security for a bill of exchange represented in this agrarian economy an expression of friendship. In a letter written early in 1768, George Mercer candidly reminded his son of the relationship between friendship and money. "Colo. Tayloe's furnishing you," the elder Mercer observed, "in the *genteel manner* you mention, with a letter of credit, was a proof that you have one friend in Virginia, for generally cash is the truest proof of friendship."[37]

Mercer's remark to his son reveals a key aspect of Virginia gentry culture. Col. John Tayloe, the gentleman who had provided the letter of credit, had dealt with the hard-pressed young planter in a "genteel manner," that is, he acted *as if* Mercer still possessed full independence. It was a fiction, of course, but one that was absolutely essential to the maintenance of harmony among the colony's proud and sensitive gentlemen. This was the message that Washington attempted to communicate to Posey: do not get yourself so far in debt that we can no longer pretend that you possess honor. In 1762 Tayloe himself required a substantial sum to settle an account in Great Britain. He turned to his close friend and neighbor, Landon Carter. "I am in great want of money at present to buy some bills [of exchange]," he explained in a short note,

[35] Washington to Posey, in *Writings of Washington*, II, 457-58. On this point see Bertram Wyatt-Brown, *Southern Honor: Ethics and Behavior in the Old South* (New York, 1982), 327-61.

[36] Freeman, *George Washington*, III, 90.

[37] Lois Mulkearn, ed., *George Mercer Papers Relating to the Ohio Company of Virginia* (Pittsburgh, 1954), 205.

"& should be particularly obliged if you would lend it [to] me only for one Month which [I] am persuaded would not be of any disadvantage to you." Tayloe's tone is respectful, though informal. There is no indication that his own honor is at stake, no offer of interest. "If you have it & will spare it," Tayloe concluded matter-of-factly, "I will send my Gardiner early in the Morning for it."[38] Carter provided a "favour" that no true Virginia gentleman could rightly refuse.

To be forced to set these social conventions aside, whatever the reasons, made gentlemen extremely uneasy. In 1758, for example, Richard Corbin found himself in such an uncomfortable situation. Benjamin Harrison, one of Virginia's more prominent planters, owed him money. Even though the two men were social equals, Corbin chose his words with considerable tact. He sounded almost obsequious. One must always be solicitous, Corbin declared, "of Honor of Family and of Fortune." Indeed, if he had not been "importunately urged to bring this business to a Conclusion," he confessed he probably would have let the matter slide. Corbin understood the code. He had no intention of dunning Harrison. Corbin even reminded the other great planter that "I always observed that regard that is due to a Gentleman of your Character."[39] However annoying Harrison's business practices may have been, Corbin studiously avoided the suggestion that either Harrison's behavior or his own had been dishonorable. In relations between great Tidewater planters, it was the creditor, not the borrower, who made excuses.

The most serious government scandal in eighteenth-century Virginia turned on precisely such cultural considerations. John Robinson, a jovial planter whom contemporaries thought quite wealthy, served not only as the Speaker of the House of Burgesses but also as the colony's treasurer. He held these offices from 1738 to 1768, and in political affairs he was the most powerful man in Virginia, royal governors not ex-

---

[38] John Tayloe to Landon Carter, 17 September 1762, Carter Family Papers, 1659-1797, Sabine Hall Collection, University of Virginia, Manuscripts Department, Alderman Library, Charlottesville, Virginia, microfilm, reel 1.
[39] Corbin to Benjamin Harrison, [1758], Corbin Letter Book.

cluded. One of Robinson's tasks was destroying old Virginia currency that had been accepted in payment of local taxes. Colony law mandated that a certain percentage of Virginia paper be retired each year, and since most assemblymen assumed that Robinson was doing his job, they regularly voted to print new money.

But Robinson was not doing his job. After the tax money had been delivered to Williamsburg, he secretly redistributed the currency to great planters such as William Byrd III, Carter Braxton, and Lewis Burwell, men who in the early 1760s were having difficulty making ends meet. Robinson's actions were quite illegal, but his generosity with public funds resulted neither from personal greed nor from political obligation. The leader of the House of Burgesses foolishly misapplied the code of gentlemen's credit. He helped his "friends" preserve honor, to maintain the fiction of personal autonomy when in fact they were on the edge of bankruptcy.

When a full accounting of the treasury in 1766 exposed a shortfall of almost £100,000, the local gentry seemed shocked. Some concluded that unscrupulous Virginians must have taken advantage of Robinson's magnanimity. At the time of the treasurer's death, William Nelson wrote, "It hath griev'd Me to think that so good a Man as he was in private Life, should be prevail'd upon by a set of men he was connected with, & who pretended to be his Friends, to do anything to stain a Character otherwise so amiable." But, as Nelson confessed, Robinson "never could resist an Application to him for money."[40] And "Philautos," writing in the *Virginia Gazette*, described Robinson as a "good old Gentleman"—a good ol'boy in modern southern politics—whose timely assistance "immediately relieved many worthy families from ruin and

<hr/>

[40] Nelson to Edward and Samuel Athawes, 13 November 1766, Nelson Letter Book, Colonial Williamsburg, Inc., Research Center, microfilm. Also, David John Mays, *Edmund Pendleton, A Biography, 1721-1803* (Cambridge, Mass., 1952), I, 181-83; Joseph A. Ernst, "The Robinson Scandal Redivius: Money, Debts, and Politics in Revolutionary Virginia," *VMHB*, 77 (1969), 146-73.

indigence."[41] Here was another great planter who could not turn down a friend.

The Robinson scandal revealed tensions within the tobacco culture of which the great planters themselves were only partially aware. They were willing—indeed, obliged—to assist worthy friends, but they were no fools. Supporting notorious spendthrifts made no sense and, in any case, would have soon exhausted their limited financial resources. The problem was to distinguish between the diligent gentleman fallen temporarily on hard times and the irresponsible rogue, between the appearance of prosperity and the reality of insolvency. In reaching this decision, one had to rely almost completely on external cues, on a person's dress, his horses and carriage, his outward estate. In this materialistic environment, a man's *visible* estate became an index to his virtue, to his moral standing in the community of planters.

The desire to keep up appearances helped fuel an infernal economic spiral. The planter who wanted to preserve his credit in Virginia, his honor, his claim to personal autonomy, found himself under immense pressure to *seem* prosperous. When John Bartram, one of America's first botanists, set off in 1737 to visit two of Virginia's most influential planters, a London friend advised him to purchase a new set of clothes, "for though I should not esteem thee less, to come to me in what dress thou will,—yet these Virginians are a very gentle, well-dressed people—and look, perhaps, more at a man's outside than his inside." As the anonymous author of *American Husbandry* reported with surprise on the eve of the Revolution, "In most articles of life, a great Virginia planter makes a greater show and lives more luxuriously than a country gentleman in England, on an estate of three or four thousand pounds a year."[42] Andrew Burnaby, another English visitor, claimed that the great planters revealed their true character "in acts of extravagance, ostentation, and a disregard of oe-

[41] *Virginia Gazette* (Purdie and Dixon), 25 July 1766.

[42] Peter Collinson to John Bartram, 17 February 1737, *W&MQ*, 2nd ser., 6 (1926), 304; *American Husbandry*, ed. Harry J. Carman (New York, 1939), 174.

conomy; it is not extraordinary, therefore, that the Virginians over-run their incomes."[43]

These commentators did not fully appreciate the driving force behind such extravagance. The great planter's situation demanded not only that he spend a large percentage of his annual income on conspicuous goods and finery, but also that he hide the true state of his finances even from his friends, the people with whom he dealt on the county court or in the House of Burgesses. John Wayles, a tough individual who collected overdue bills in Virginia for British merchants, noted, "no man of any Account makes a Mortgage here but 'tis soon known his Credit is at an end and it affects him like an Act of Bankruptcy."[44] Wayles understood that credit in Virginia had a public face, and to expose the lie behind the mask by pressing a great planter too hard was viewed—in the Tidewater at least—as a betrayal of friendship. One effect of relying upon British merchants for credit was that it freed the great planter from the prying eyes of their neighbors. No one except the gentleman himself knew exactly how his balance stood. Of course, maintaining the show of wealth was expensive, and in his increasingly frenetic efforts to secure honor, many a planter brought himself ever more deeply into debt.

III

Spring in Tidewater Virginia marked a period of intense activity. There was a burst of energy not only in the fields where the slaves were setting out the tobacco plants, but also along the colony's famed waterways. Ships dispatched by the British tobacco merchants arrived, their holds filled with various items that the great Tidewater planters had ordered over a year earlier. Entire families rushed excitedly to the plantation wharves to watch the unpacking of crates.

This dramatic moment linked the provincial planter to the

[43] Burnaby, *Travels*, 715.

[44] John M. Hemphill II, "John Wayles Rates His Neighbors," *VMHB*, 66 (1958), 304.

culture of the mother country. The boxes and barrels contained crystal and wine, colorful china and silver plate, a beautiful dress cut to the latest London fashion for the mistress of the plantation. The vessels might carry a handsome carriage or even a well-bred racehorse.[45] Sometimes they brought bitter disappointment. In 1740 William Byrd II shot off an angry letter to John Hanbury, the merchant to whom he consigned his tobacco, complaining, "I never saw any thing so demolisht as every parcel that belong'd to me was[,] which was partly owning to the careless way of packing, and partly to your masters [Hanbury's ship captain] tumbling them ashoar at Hampton, and tossing them into a warehouse." Byrd's experience was by no means unique. Many a planter had looked forward to a shipment of European goods only to discover that "Every thing that would break of mine was shattered to pieces, and what would not break, was damaged."[46]

The captains of these vessels, usually acting as agents for the British merchants, also brought letters addressed to specific planters explaining why certain goods had not appeared, discussing the quality of the previous season's crop, and lamenting the low prices that the leaf had fetched on the European market. This was a time when a gentleman learned whether he had made a profit or had slipped further into debt. After responding to the merchant's inquiries, a great planter listed items he wished to have purchased on his account. The captain then visited a public warehouse where he picked up the hogsheads that had been consigned to his employer, and within weeks of its arrival, the tobacco fleet departed for home. This brief, unusually busy period represented the great planter's only personal contact with the firms that merchandised his crop. In fact, his well-being depended upon the enterprise of unseen merchants located three thousand miles

[45] See, for example, John Syme's order sent to the firm of Farrell and Jones, 18 June 1761, United States Circuit Court, Virginia District, Ended Cases (1797), Colonial Williamsburg, Inc., Research Center, microfilm.

[46] Byrd II to [Hanbury], 10 July 1740, in *Correspondence of the Three William Byrds*, ed. Tinling, II, 550-52.

away, invisible men who sold the consignment, who provided credit to cover the difference between the profits from the tobacco and the cost of the goods just ordered.

These were intense relationships—at least for the Virginians—and it is probably not surprising that the great planters projected local meanings onto their transactions with the merchants of Great Britain. Within their own, largely self-contained mental world, Virginians found it nearly impossible to perceive the sale of their tobacco as anything but a kind of personal, face-to-face exchange. They generalized assumptions that had evolved out of the peculiarities of a local agrarian experience to an international marketplace. The tidewater planters simply recreated the British merchants in their own image, and in the process, they transformed them into men who understood the meaning of honor and independence, who appreciated that trade was a kind of friendship, and who would do a favor even if that meant sacrificing profit. This was a cognitive process. The planters of mid-eighteenth-century Virginia attempted to tame the unknown by labeling it in terms drawn from their own tobacco culture.

Virginians lectured British correspondents about the code of friendship. If they had enjoyed direct, personal contact with the merchants, they would perhaps have felt no need to spell out the details of the local commercial etiquette. Since the Tidewater gentlemen lived so far from the mother country, however, they took no chances on being misunderstood, and the letters they sent to Great Britain often smacked of didacticism. "I know there is something that may not improperly be called a *Commercial Friendship*," Richard Corbin explained in 1758, "because I feel it glowing in my own breast, which takes its rise from a long Correspondence and is established by a Punctual and Steady Integrity on both Sides."[47] If the merchant agreed to accept a planter's tobacco on consignment, he thereby entered into a reciprocal relationship with the Virginian, a bond of trust.

Other Virginians employed different metaphors to describe

---

[47] Corbin to [?], 13 June 1758, Corbin Letter Book (emphasis added).

XIII. What an English artist imagined a Virginia tobacco wharf looked like at mid-century

the consignment trade, as a gift of the planter to a deserving merchant or as a kind of courtship, but whatever the language they used, the colonists stressed the mutual obligations created by commerce. In 1738, for example, John Custis explained to an English acquaintance why he could not send a few choice hogsheads to John Hanbury. "I believe when you hear my reasons;" Custis wrote, "you will pardon my not complying with your request." The Virginian had previously established a correspondence with another merchant. This man "has allways treated me with the greatest respect and best of usage; and I should be guilty of one of the greatest offenses (viz.) ingratitude; if I should alter my consignmts . . .

it has ever bin my principle to bee steadfast to my old
friends."[48] Custis obviously invested a great deal of himself in
this commercial tie. A merchant who showed the planter "respect" deserved gratitude; profits mattered, of course, but
only within the context of an ongoing friendship.

Robert Beverley also perceived commerce in these highly
personal terms. This young planter expected a British merchant with whom he had established a correspondence to stick
with him through financial adversity, to do so, in addition,
without showing the slightest hesitation. Expression of doubt,
Beverley thought, revealed a lack of trust; it reminded the
planter that he was not as independent as he liked to pretend.
In fact, this Virginian's letter is remarkably like those that
John Posey must have written to George Washington. When
John Bland, the merchant, balked in 1763 at advancing a large
sum to Beverley—he was already £1,200 in arrears—the
planter protested. "When you are in for so many thousands
[of pounds] with People, whom you know not, & who care
not one Farthing for you farther than to gratify their own
Ends; you have an indisputable Right to Act as you Please."
But Beverley was a special friend. Had the Englishman forgotten that "in the Course of Business [,] Obligations were
reciprocall"? Beverley admitted that Bland had "very frequently conferred Civilities upon me," and the Virginian insisted that he was fully prepared "to acquit myself in the Most
gentle Manner for such services[.] But I am of too delicate a
sentiment to accept of any Kindness, when I discover any
Doubt or Backwardness in him who confers it; with me the
Least diffidence amounts to an absolute deniall."[49]

The more he thought about Bland's insulting behavior, the
angrier Beverley became. The Englishman seemed utterly out
of touch with the basic assumptions of the tobacco culture. "I

---

[48] E. G. Swem, ed., "Brothers of the Spade: Correspondence of Peter Collinson, of London, and of John Custis, of Williamsburg, Virginia, 1734-
1746," *Proceedings of the American Antiquarian Society*, 58 (1948), 68, also 79-
80. See, Byrd II to John Hanbury, 22 July 1736 in *Correspondence of Three
William Byrds*, ed. Tinling, II, 494-96.

[49] Beverley to John Bland, 17 December 1763, Beverley Letter Book.

am determin'd never to ship largely to any man," the Virginian warned, "who will not willingly advance £1,000 for me as soon as I ask [for] it [,] not that I shall ever want it unless to make some Purchases, which may occur, & which I do not at present Dream of." Again, it is instructive to compare this letter with the note that John Tayloe sent to Landon Carter. If his neighbor had the amount of money that Tayloe needed, then there was no excuse for not lending it to a friend.[50] Why did Bland fail to see that this was the way credit worked between social equals? Beverley was willing to give the merchant another chance. If Bland mended his ways, if he played the role of the trustworthy commercial friend, Beverley assured him he "shall discover in every Transaction of mine that Justice, Honor & integrity, which were Dayly inculcated into me in the progress of a good Education."[51]

Like Beverley, other Tidewater planters expected their British "friends" to carry them through hard times. A merchant, they insisted, must do nothing *publicly* to call a planter's credit into question. To write privately reminding a gentleman that he owed money was bad enough, but that approach at least allowed the Virginian to save face. When a merchant openly challenged a planter's note, however, the results could be embarrassing. Such actions called a man's credit into question and with it, his honor and independence. Gentlemen did their best to guard against such public exposure. In 1760, for example, George Washington informed a British correspondent that he might have occasion to draw upon the merchant, using an eighteenth-century system of credit that worked much like a modern checking account with an overdraft provision. "Yet," Washington added anxiously, "if at any time a prospect of Advantage should lead me beyond this a little [,] I hope there will be no danger of my Bills returning." Washington thought it quite unlikely that he should ever find himself in such an awkward financial situation—a comment designed to calm the merchant's fears—"for

[50] See above, pp. 102-103.
[51] Beverley to Bland, 17 December 1763, Beverley Letter Book.

my own aversion to running in Debt will always secure me
against a Step of this Nature."[52]

Another leading planter, Henry Fitzhugh, took similar pre-
cautions to protect his public reputation. He had drawn heavily upon James Buchanan to cover the cost of new slaves, and
the Virginian literally begged the Scotsman not to challenge
this action, "as I have never yet had the discredit of a protested bill." Planters like Fitzhugh apparently reasoned that if
the merchant knew that the money had been well spent, he
would show more enthusiasm in preserving a gentleman's
credit. The Virginians were only asking their distant friends
to observe a local code of debt. Fitzhugh, for example, believed that James Russell, an English correspondent, would
loan him £100 "when I assure you that the debt was not contracted for extravagant living &c. (which is now generally the
case) but to purchase negroes . . . [and therefore] I am in
hopes you will not protest my Bill but will advance me whatever the proceeds of my tobacco falls short. . . ."[53] There is a
certain irony about these letters. In their effort to maintain
independence before their colonial peers—and presumably
before other merchants as well—the great planters revealed
just how deeply dependent they actually were.

Tidewater planters insisted that they upheld their side of
these reciprocal commercial friendships. They thought of
trade itself as a kind of personal favor, in the sense that a
successful doctor or lawyer might say to a younger colleague,
"I'll throw a little business your way."[54] The planters assumed that any merchant would be more than happy to
receive their annual consignment of tobacco, and so, by

[52] *Writings of Washington*, ed. Fitzpatrick, II, 349.

[53] Fitzhugh to James Buchanan, [n.d.]; Fitzhugh to James Russell, 2 August 1757, Henry Fitzhugh Papers, Manuscript Division, Duke University,
Durham, North Carolina. Also, John Baylor to Norton and Sons, 16 September 1760, in *John Norton and Sons Merchants of London and Virginia* . . . ,
ed. Francis Norton Mason (Richmond, Va., 1937), 10.

[54] Marcel Mauss provides some provocative suggestions on this type of exchange in his *The Gift* (New York, 1969; originally published in French in
1925).

selecting one correspondent over another, the Virginian demonstrated friendship. In 1762 Beverley told a newly established British merchant, John Jordan, that "you may depend upon my Remembrance of you in one of your vessels." The remembrance, of course, was a few hogsheads of choice tobacco, and considering the cultural significance of this staple in Virginia, it was a gift to which the planter obviously attached some importance. On another occasion, Beverley explained that he could not bring himself to drop a merchant because the planter "imagined myself in gratitude obliged for many Civilities to direct the Bulk of my Consignments through his hands."[55] George Braxton, another Tidewater planter, assured a correspondent that his "genteel Behavior shall always meet with due acknowledgements & the most grateful Returns."[56] As usual Landon Carter took the logic of friendship a step further, at least, rhetorically. He boasted that even if a certain merchant failed to show him proper "reciprocation," Carter would fulfill their original agreement, which, after all, had been established "upon principles of honour."[57]

Exactly what "reciprocation" meant posed a problem for all parties involved. The merchants certainly provided services to the Virginians that strict business practice would not have required. The correspondents placed the planters' children in schools, checked on their progress from time to time, and settled minor legal matters associated with probate or transfer of property. On their side, the Virginians not only sent their best tobacco, but also tried to defend the merchant's interests in other less obvious ways. The planter gained particular satisfaction if he took the initiative, thus showing that he looked out for the merchant's colonial affairs even though not specifically charged to do so. In 1761 Beverley accidentally discovered at a meeting of the General Court in Williamsburg that

[55] Beverley to John Jordan, 3 March 1762; Beverley to John Bland, 11 August 1765, Beverley Letter Book.

[56] Cited in Frederick Horner, *The History of the Blair, Banister, and Braxton Families Before and After the Revolution* (Philadelphia, 1898), 145.

[57] *Diary of Landon Carter*, ed. Greene, I, 375.

XIV. Typical eighteenth-century bill of exchange

a certain Anthony Steward was about to attach some of John Bland's American property. Beverley immediately spoke up in defense of his English correspondent. "I instantly agreed to become your Bail . . . ," Beverley reported, "rather than your Interest should suffer from your Correspondents in this Country."[58]

Robert Carter Nicholas constantly did favors for his English friend, John Norton. On one occasion Nicholas purchased some excellent tobacco for Norton, a transaction that cost the Virginian both money and time. When he reported what he had done, Nicholas observed, "I never expected to make any Money by these Adventures; if I could Save myself [by fulfilling Norton's expectations for a large shipment of tobacco] and serve my Friend by them, it was all I expected."[59] It probably comforted the Tidewater planters to think that if they behaved so honorably, their commercial friends must be doing the same for them in the mother country.

The planters' letterbooks reveal the Tidewater Virginians were so busy personalizing commerce, so intent on making relations with distant British merchants conform to assumptions derived from a local tobacco culture, that they did not take time to learn how the international tobacco trade actually worked. "The Virginians are content if they can but live from day to day; they confine themselves almost entirely to the cultivation of tobacco," an English visitor observed, "and if they have but enough of this to pay their merchants in London, and to provide for their pleasures, they are satisfied, and desire nothing more."[60] Though this outsider may have exaggerated the Virginians' contentment, he recognized that concentration on the production of a single staple had limited their mental horizons.

Men who strove to become crop masters, who spent hours

[58] Beverley to John Bland, 16 November 1761, Beverley Letter Book.

[59] Cited in Samuel M. Rosenblatt, "Merchant-Planter Relations in the Tobacco Consignment Trade: John Norton and Robert Carter Nicholas," *VMHB*, 72(1964), 458.

[60] Burnaby, *Travels*, 717.

in the fields overseeing the details of cultivation, seem almost naive in their dealings with merchants, as if the trust they invested in their "commercial friends" was sufficient to guarantee a profit. In an extraordinarily frank letter to his son written in 1768, John Mercer touched on this problem. Mercer reflected on his long experience as a planter. "I have lost many thousand pounds by it, but as my [law] practice so wholly engrossed me, I never cou'd attend to consider the matter thoroughly till I quited [the law]," the father explained. But having retired from the practice of law, "I am now convinced that every man, who will not carefully attend his own business [planting] . . . will lose by it. Few people keep regular accounts & therefore don't know what their crops stand them in, & they often imagine them clear gains, after the overseer's share [is] deducted, when if everything else that ought as properly to be deducted was so, they wou'd find, they did not amount to the interest of their money."[61]

The planters wanted to believe in their commercial friends, to create, in fact, a harmonious, trusting relationship. Beverley, for example, thought challenging his correspondent's judgment a distasteful experience, "not only because I frequently find arguments not convincing, but because I really wish to preserve the utmost Harmony in our future Correspondence." It was Beverley's hope—one shared by other great planters as well—that merchants and planters "for the future . . . determine invariably to put the most favorable Construction upon each others words."[62]

The planters' apparent ineptitude in handling their business affairs surprises the modern reader. A few economic historians have even felt compelled to defend the Virginians, arguing that despite occasional lapses the planters were "rational" in calculating return on capital. That may be so. The Tidewater gentlemen did purchase new land and slaves when the opportunity arose; they saw the relationship between these investments and expanded production. These men were

[61] Mulkearn, ed., *George Mercer Papers*, 212-13.
[62] Beverley to Samuel Athawes, 15 April 1771, Beverley Letter Book.

clearly not fools.[63] The problem may lie in the word "rational," at least in the way that twentieth-century economists seem to use that term. By their own lights, the great planters behaved in a perfectly rational manner. They took the assumptions of a particular social environment, a world in which a handshake was sufficient to seal a deal, in which no one paid close attention to record-keeping, in which even small loans were thought to involve personal honor, in which people strove at all costs to preserve their independence, and projected this bundle of values and understandings onto an international market. This was what was going on when Landon Carter lectured a merchant about "principles of honour."

IV

British consignment merchants who loomed so large in the Virginia economy were middling sorts by the standards of the eighteenth-century business community. None possessed fabulous wealth, and when compared to the grandees who controlled the West Indian sugar trade, the operations of the tobacco merchants seem quite modest. Tobacco sold on consignment usually flowed to London or Bristol rather than to Glasgow or Liverpool. The so-called "southern" consignment merchants specialized in superior grades of tobacco, the types preferred by English and Irish smokers.[64] The bulk of

[63] Jacob M. Price, *Capital and Credit in British Overseas Trade: The View from the Chesapeake, 1700-1776* (Cambridge, Mass., 1980), 16. The fullest analysis of the workings of the international tobacco market in the mid-eighteenth century is Price, *France and the Chesapeake; A History of the French Tobacco Monopoly, 1674-1791, and of Its Relationship to the British and American Tobacco Trades* (Ann Arbor, 1973).

[64] Jacob M. Price, "Capital and Credit in the British-Chesapeake Trade, 1750-1775," in *Of Mother Country and Plantations: Proceedings of the Twenty-Seventh Conference in Early American History*, ed. Virginia Bever Platt and David Curtis Skaggs (Bowling Green, Ohio, 1971), 7-36. Price's carefully researched studies of the Chesapeake trade provide invaluable insights into the structure of British commerce. In addition to *France and the Chesapeake* and *Capital and Credit*, one should also examine Price, ed., *Joshua Johnson's Letterbook, 1771-1774: Letters from a Merchant in London to His Partners in Maryland*, London Record Society (London, 1979); "The Rise of Glasgow in the Chesapeake Tobacco Trade, 1707-1775," *W&MQ*, 3rd ser., 11(1954), 179-

the lesser tobaccos—that grown by Virginia's small planters—
was transshipped through Scotland to the Continent.

The major London houses of the mid-eighteenth century
can be divided into four distinct groups: those owned by
wealthy Quakers like John Hanbury; the "old English firms"
run by men such as John Bland, Lyonel Lynde, Samuel
Athawes, and John Norton; the "Scots" like John Buchanan
and James Russell; and newly established American houses
which in this period did not amount to much.[65] Unfortunately, though we know a good deal about the tobacco trade
in aggregate—how many pounds were sold in a certain year,
for instance—we possess little information about specific merchants. Of their vast Virginia correspondence, little survives.

However disappointing the merchants' surviving personal
papers may be, there is good reason to suspect that these men
did not view credit and debt in the ways that Virginia planters did. They employed the same commercial vocabulary, but
British businessmen of the mid–eighteenth century attached
different meanings to these common terms. Their perceptions
grew out of their participation in a rapidly expanding, extremely volatile economy. To be sure, they were not creatures
of a fully industrialized society, but the financial world in
which they operated was vastly more complex than anything
a Virginian would have directly experienced. Successful merchants, even middling ones, had to master impersonal credit
arrangements, new forms of investment, and sophisticated
banking procedures.[66] The very volume of their daily trans-

---

99; and "Who Was John Norton? A Note on the Historical Character of
Some Eighteenth-Century London Virginia Firms," ibid., 19 (1961), 400-
407.

   [65] Price, "Capital and Credit," 7-12.

   [66] Ibid., 22-24; B. L. Anderson, "Money and the Structure of Credit in
the Eighteenth Century," *Business History*, 12(1970), 85-101; Anderson, "Pro-
vincial Aspects of the Financial Revolution of the Eighteenth Century," ibid.,
11(1969), 16-22; Peter Earle, *The World of Defoe* (London, 1976); P.G.M.
Dickson, *The Financial Revolution in England: A Study in the Development of
Public Credit, 1688-1756* (London, 1967); J.H. Plumb, *The Growth of Political
Stability in England; 1675-1725* (London, 1967); Leslie W. Pressnell, *Country
Banking in the Industrial Revolution* (Oxford, 1956).

actions would have staggered those Virginians who wrote of "something . . . called a Commercial Friendship."

The tobacco merchants, in fact, found themselves at the center of a far-reaching social change that historians label the "Consumer Revolution." At mid-century the population of the mother country began to expand at an accelerating rate. And it did so without adversely affecting the country's standard of living. Average working folk discovered that they could purchase items that within their fathers' memories had been luxury goods. There was a sudden popular demand for American imports, especially for sugar and tobacco, as well as for English manufactures. This was the society that produced a Josiah Wedgwood, mass advertising, and consumer fads. To keep up with this unprecedented market, English financiers, manufacturers, and merchants developed an elaborate system of credit, a financial structure that for the first time in the country's history wove isolated hamlets and scattered farms into a recognizable national economy. In London bills of exchange that had originated in outlying cities and counties were bought and sold, traded and discounted, processed as expeditiously as possible so that people living in distant parts of England—people who were complete strangers—could take part in the growing swirl of commerce.[67]

But, as merchants of all varieties learned, opportunities to make large profits also brought tremendous risks.[68] At any given moment, much of a merchant's operating capital was tied up in book debts, really a form of credit than allowed customers to pay for goods over six or twelve months at a small interest charge. Without such devices commercial expansion in this period would have been impossible. During the eighteenth century, the British government never minted sufficient specie to meet the needs of the business community,

[67] E. A. Wrigley and R. S. Schofield, *The Population History of England, 1541-1871: A Reconstruction* (Cambridge, Mass., 1981); D. C. Coleman, *The Economy of England, 1450-1750* (Oxford, 1977); Perkin, *Origins of Modern English Society*; McKendrick et al., *Birth of a Consumer Society*; B. L. Anderson, "Provincial Aspects of the Financial Revolution."

[68] Brewer, "Commercialization and Politics," 209-10.

and in the absence of an adequate money supply, private credit instruments, particularly bills of exhange, circulated as a sort of unofficial currency. The system worked well enough so long as the merchant did not have to cover large, unanticipated demands for cash. He and his partners possessed little margin for error. A solid house might suddenly fall into bankruptcy simply because it did not have sufficient funds on hand to make good on a particular bill of exchange. It did not matter that the firm had built up impressive paper assets. The problem was liquidity. British merchants constantly worried lest the failure of a major house in London, Amsterdam, or Paris set off panic, a crisis of confidence over which they exercised no control, destroying smaller merchant houses along the entire financial chain.[69]

For tobacco merchants, therefore, the price of providing Virginians with credit was chronic insecurity. It was a risk that they were obviously willing to take. The profits in the tobacco trade were considerable. Nevertheless, the liquidity problems that these merchants faced were more serious than those of houses engaged solely in domestic trade. A large amount of their working capital was tied up with customers who lived on the other side of the Atlantic, and even in the best of times (when Britain was at peace and ships avoided major storms), correspondence with a Virginia planter took at least six months. Despite these drawbacks, however, tobacco houses aggressively sought new American business, especially when the European demand for the crop kept prices high. They even pushed credit upon compliant Virginians. In 1768 William Cunninghame and Company of Scotland, for example, instructed its factors in Virginia to offer easy credit as a way of beating commercial rivals, for "such advances will assist toward enabling you not only to retain the former customers but also to engross the whole business."[70]

[69] T. S. Ashton, *Economic Fluctuations in England, 1700-1800* (Oxford, 1959), 108-10.
[70] Cited in T. M. Devine, *The Tobacco Lords: A Study of the Tobacco Merchants of Glasgow and Their Trading Activities, c. 1740-90* (Edinburgh, 1975), 60.

When the price of tobacco fell or panic ran through the British financial community, many merchants sorely regretted their generosity. In 1773 one London trader cautioned a business associate living in Virginia, John Hatley Norton, "against what has been the ruin of so many in this country, viz. launching out into new trades or stretching your old ones to an extent beyond what your capital will bear. I speak this because I know a little how things are carried on in the commercial world & I know that a man may drive a considerable & prosperous trade, may carry annually £1,500 to the credit of profit & loss, and yet, if his seeming profits are in outstanding debts in a distant country, he may be obliged to stop & find all his golden dreams come to nought." The Englishman added poignantly that Norton's own father, a respected tobacco merchant, "sometimes hardly knows which way to turn himself for money to make good his payments."[71] That same year an equally successful merchant, Samuel Athawes, informed his Virginia agent "of the terrible Crash which happened last Summer in England & lately a great House in Holland has given way which has pulled down many here likewise." Even a man of Athawes's standing was desperate. "Those who carry on extensive Business without a proportionable Capital," he counselled, "must expect [,] if they think at all [,] confusion will be the consequence [,] for in the Lottery of enterprising I have always thought the Blanks [non-winning slips] were too numerous for a Prudent or Sensible man to venture in it."[72]

V

Within Virginia society a highly personal culture of debt had evolved well before the Stamp Act crisis. The planters' understanding of credit grew out of their own experiences, ac-

[71] John Frere to John Hatley Norton, 23 March 1773, John Norton and Sons Papers, 1750-1902, Colonial Williamsburg, Inc., Research Center.

[72] Samuel Athawes to William Allason, 19 February 1773, in "The Letters of Wiliam Allason," ed. D. R. Anderson, *Richmond College Historical Papers*, 2(1917), 149.

tual exchanges that had taken place in their neighborhoods. These dealings were heavily laden with moral judgments and even the smallest transaction could raise far-reaching questions about one's honor and independence. These perceptions and the rhetorical conventions that accompanied them were products of a distinct social environment.

This system of cultural meanings functioned well enough in prosperous, or even moderately prosperous times. But it could easily short-circuit. Indeed, as some contemporaries recognized, the structure of the tobacco trade could generate severe tensions between growers and sellers. In his book *The History of the British Plantations*, published in 1738, William Keith explained that though merchants and planters "cannot subsist without the other's Aid" and though "we suppose them to deal honestly and fairly by each other," the commerce could produce suspicion and hostility. "When a covetous Desire to over-reach and to grasp at an immoderate Gain, happens to appear on one Side or the other," this former customs official and governor of Pennsylvania observed, "it gives such Discouragement to the Losers, as in some measure affects the whole Trade."[73]

In the normal conduct of eighteenth-century business, the Tidewater planters were often the "Losers," though their sloppy bookkeeping sometimes disguised the fact. As long as the merchants held out the possibility of easy credit, as long as they sustained the fiction of the planters' economic autonomy, the Virginians were reasonably content. During the 1760s and 1770s, however, the character of this commercial conversation changed dramatically. When hard-pressed British merchants began to call insolvent Tidewater gentlemen to account, the planters acted like "friends" betrayed. It was during this period of unprecedented economic strain that the Virginians discovered that the local meanings that they had developed to make sense out of credit relations were just that—*local* meanings.

[73] William Keith, *The History of British Plantations in America* (London, 1723), 180.

CHAPTER IV

LOSS OF INDEPENDENCE

In 1751 George Washington accompanied his dying brother to Barbados. It was the first time that the young man had seen anything of the world beyond the Chesapeake. Much of what he encountered surprised, even shocked Washington. The great sugar planters did not live quite so well as he had expected. "How wonderful," he marvelled, "that such people shou'd be in debt! and not be able to indulge themselves in all the Luxuries as well as necessaries of Life [.] Yet so it happened Estates are often alienated for the debts."[1]

In only a few years Washington heard visitors make similar observations about the great tobacco planters of the Tidewater. Indeed, the master of Mount Vernon found himself in debt to the merchants to whom he consigned his crop. Indebtedness was nothing unusual in Virginia. Throughout the century planters had occasionally experienced bad years when their tobacco did not cover their expenditures. After 1750, however, the level of personal debt rose precipitously, and as it did, the planters became increasingly uneasy. The merchants whom Tidewater gentlemen described as "friends" were transformed into adversaries, into persons who did not fully understand the local etiquette of credit. Commercial tensions persuaded men like Washington that their own personal autonomy was somehow threatened by the people who merchandised their staple. Lurking behind this confrontation—often no more than a dark suspicion—was a fear that the tobacco culture itself was at stake.

Debt became the focus for a new kind of discourse between planters and merchants. Individual gentlemen developed a vo-

---

[1] *Diaries of George Washington 1748-1799*, ed. John Fitzpatrick (Boston, 1925), I, 27-28.

cabulary to deal with the challenge, a set of economic idioms associated with personal autonomy, principles of honor, even natural rights. These exchanges were not in themselves political. In fact, before the late 1760s the great planters saw debt largely as a private problem, and on those few occasions when they united to protest commercial policy, they attacked the merchants, not the king or Parliament. For the moment Virginians separated these matters from the constitutional debate that flared in the House of Burgesses. But with each passing year the possibility that the planters would merge these two discourses, turning economic idioms to political purposes and thus providing a moral catalyst for independence, became increasingly apparent.

I

Sometime around the middle of the eighteenth century, the character of the tobacco market began to change. At first, no one recognized that anything unusual had occurred. To be sure, before 1725 the planters had endured a prolonged depression, but during the middle decades of the century large purchases by the French introduced an element of predictability to the market. The price of tobacco moved up and down in ways that the planter could anticipate—what one historical geographer calls "cycles of boom and bust"—and the colony's major producers made important decisions about capital investment on the basis of these familiar trends.

But after 1750 the system short-circuited. The planters lost market stability. The length of the boom and bust cycle contracted to only eight years, catching many gentlemen off balance. The problem was the depth of the depressions and their frequency, which made full recovery difficult before the start of a new downturn. These accelerated price swings made traditional investment formulas obsolete, and before the great Tidewater planters could adjust to these unprecedented market conditions, they often found themselves deeply immersed in debt.[2] Even before passage of the Stamp Act, these Virginians sensed that their economic world was in jeopardy. In 1758—just to cite a single example—Robert Carter of Nomini Hall informed an English creditor, "I have experience that the produce of my land and negroes will scarce pay the demand requisite to keep them. I have sold part to sink the debts due against me."[3]

Though the causes of this economic instability remain obscure, it seems clear that the great planters were only partially responsible for the situation in which they found themselves. Their continued prosperity depended upon world market forces largely beyond their control. In this period, unusually violent fluctuations created havoc in European financial centers. Great Britain had, of course, experienced panics earlier in the century. The infamous South Sea Bubble of 1720 destroyed many private fortunes.[4] After such crises, however, the national economy quickly rebounded, and the mid-century was a period of general prosperity.

The Seven Years' War (1756-1763) brought uncertainty to the British financial community. Huge government expenses coupled with an interruption of international commerce severely upset the economy. Cessation of hostilities in 1763 brought on depression, not prosperity, as many contemporaries had predicted. A financial crisis that originated in Amsterdam sparked a run on British banks and holding companies, and in a matter of weeks, credit tightened, interest rates soared, and commodity prices tumbled. Especially hard-hit

[2] Carville V. Earle, *The Evolution of a Tidewater Settlement System: All Hallow's Parish, Maryland, 1650-1783* (Chicago, 1975), 215-18. Charles Wetherell has recently called the "boom and bust" model into question, suggesting that historians of eighteenth-century Maryland and Virginia have mistaken random price fluctuation for cycles. See his " 'Boom and Bust' in the Colonial Chesapeake Economy," *Journal of Interdisciplinary History*, 50(1984), 185-210.

[3] Cited in Louis Morton, *Robert Carter of Nomini Hall* (Williamsburg, 1941), 262. For a good general account of this economic crisis in Virginia, see, Robert Polk Thomson, "The Merchant in Virginia 1700-1775" (Ph.D. diss., University of Wisconsin, 1955), chapter 7.

[4] John Carswell, *The South Sea Bubble* (London, 1960); P.G.M. Dickson, *The Financial Revolution in England* (London, 1967).

merchants fell into bankruptcy. The great planters, already reeling from a series of extremely poor crops (the late 1750s were drought years), not only found credit difficult to obtain, but also faced an unexpected demand for payment on debts incurred over the previous decade. In 1764, according to one Maryland newspaper, "The bankruptcies in Europe have made such a scarcity of money, and had such an effect on credit, that all our American commodities fall greatly."[5] These pressures affected some planters more seriously than others. The small producers, those who obtained credit from resident Scottish factors, may have weathered the crisis better than did some of their gentry neighbors. There was a slight recovery in 1764, but as one historian of the British economy reports, "The year 1764 saw general prosperity. . . . But, as with most post-war booms, there was a speedy reaction; the following year saw the beginning of a depression that dragged on for the rest of the decade."[6] Tobacco prices staged a recovery in the late 1760s, a temporary upswing that served to disguise just how vulnerable the Virginians were.

A second major European panic occurred in 1772. This time, however, the crisis followed a short boom during which the great planters purchased large amounts of British goods on credit. This buying spree left everyone, merchants as well as planters, dangerously overextended, and when desperate merchants demanded payment on old debts, many prominent Virginians were forced to sell slaves, even entire plantations, to satisfy their creditors.[7]

One can estimate the aggregate amount of planter indebtedness with a fair degree of accuracy. After the Revolutionary War, negotiators concluded that the Americans owed British

    [5] Cited in T. S. Ashton, *Economic Fluctuations* (Oxford, 1959), 127.
    [6] Ibid., 152; M. Egnal and J. Ernst, "An Economic Interpretation," *W&MQ*, 3rd ser., 29(1972), 26-28; A. H. John, "War and the English Economy, 1700-1763," *Economic History Review*, 2nd ser., 7(1955), 342-43; Calvin B. Coulter, Jr., "The Virginia Merchant" (Ph.D. diss., Princeton University, 1944), 226-40.
    [7] Richard B. Sheridan, "The British Credit System of 1772 and the American Colonies," *Journal of Economic History*, 20(1960), 161-86.

citizens about £3 million, of which the Virginians alone were responsible for £1.4 million. It is important to view the planters' situation in comparative perspective. Though they accounted for only 21 percent of the country's population in 1776, they held approximately 46 percent of the officially documented debt claims. Whether British claimants inflated the amounts due them in hopes of making a killing is not known. There is no question, however, that the per capita Chesapeake debt—Virginia and Maryland—was nearly twice than that of Britain's other mainland colonies. Moreover, the total amount of money that the planters owed grew spectacularly after 1750. Between 1766 and 1776, it doubled. On the eve of national independence the Chesapeake colonists carried a debt estimated at more than 2.5 times the value of annual British imports.[8]

What percentage of this debt was specifically the responsibility of the great Tidewater planters is difficult to discern. The small growers, enticed by offers of easy credit from Scottish factors, certainly carried much of the new indebtedness. Nevertheless, the gentlemen who sold their tobacco on consignment also increased their dependence upon British creditors. An examination of postrevolutionary debt claims reveals that in 1776 at least ten of Virginia's great planters owed £5,000 or more. This was a huge sum. In the £1,000 to £4,999 range appear such familiar names as Jefferson and Washington. According to one historian who has analyzed the British Treasury records, "At least fifty-five of the individuals from whom £500 or more was claimed were members of the House of Burgesses from 1769 to 1774."[9]

[8] Jacob Price, "Capital and Credit in the British-Chesapeake Trade, 1750-1775," in *Of Mother Country and Plantations*, ed. Virginia Bever Platt and David Curtis Skaggs (Bowling Green, Ohio, 1971), 7-9; Price, *Capital and Credit in British Overseas Trade: The View from the Chesapeake, 1700-1776* (Cambridge, Mass., 1980), 6-15; T. M. Devine, *The Tobacco Lords* (Edinburgh, 1975), 59; Sheridan, "British Credit System," 167-75.

[9] Sheridan, "British Credit System," 183; Emory G. Evans, "Planter Indebtedness and the Coming of the Revolution in Virginia," *W&MQ*, 3rd ser., 19(1962), 517-21.

What these figures indicate, of course, is that the problem of gentry indebtedness in Virginia was bad and getting worse. Though some modern economists may see this deficit as a sign of a robust economy—lots of people making lots of deals—the great planters found the expanding level of debt unsettling. Their reaction is not surprising. After all, these gentlemen did not have access to the statistical summaries that we take for granted today. They relied on hunches and rumors. They barely knew the state of their own accounts; about their neighbors' they could only guess.[10]

A major reason for the exploding debt after 1750 was the planters' rising expectations as consumers. The Virginia gentlemen of Washington's generation insisted on importing goods from the mother country that their fathers and grandfathers could not have afforded, perhaps not even obtained. After mid-century the Tidewater gentry defined luxuries as necessities and indulged their desires. Members of the planter elite subscribed to *Country Magazine* and other smart British periodicals depicting the latest styles.[11] In an amazingly short time, goods described in these publications appeared in the great houses of the Chesapeake. William Eddis, author of *Letters from America*, exclaimed in 1771 "that a new fashion is adopted earlier by the polished and affluent American [he was referring specifically to the great planters of the Chesapeake] than by many opulent persons in the great metropolis."[12]

Eddis probably exaggerated the Anglicization of American taste, but he spotted an important consumer trend. The great planters were, in fact, spending large sums of money on imports. In 1753 one resident merchant informed a British correspondent, "our Gentry have such proud spirits, that nothing will go down, but equipages of the nicest & newest

[10] See, Robert Heilbroner, "The Deficit," *New Yorker*, 30 July 1984, 47-48.

[11] Douglas S. Freeman, *George Washington: A Biography* (New York, 1951), III, 116.

[12] William Eddis, *Letters from America*, ed. Aubrey C. Land (Cambridge, Mass., 1969), 57. Also, Joseph A. Ernst, *Money and Politics in America* (Chapel Hill, N.C., 1973), 13, 46, 66-67.

fashions. You'll hardly believe it when I tell you that there are sundry chariots now in the country which cost 200 Guineas, & one that cost 260."[13] And in 1762, Robert Beverley, a planter who bragged of self-control, ordered a set of "china of the most fashionable sort." Almost as an afterthought, Beverley volunteered that if he had to spend the rest of his life on an isolated Virginia plantation, he was determined to make it as "commodious" as possible.[14] Beverley's consumption of finery was neither unusual nor imaginative. He ordered items that he saw in neighboring plantations, Sabine Hall and Mount Airy, for example. Anyone who has visited Tidewater Virginia knows the splendor of these homes, the magnificence of the great planters' personal possessions. Rural asceticism obviously held little appeal for men like Beverley and Washington, and it was not until the eve of the Revolution that they began seriously to contemplate the virtues of the simple life.

Francis Fauquier, Virginia's lieutenant governor (1758-1768), had no doubt as to the cause of the planters' rising debt. It was not, as some Virginians had insisted, the result of a flood of paper money. "I am entirely of opinion," Fauquier informed the Lords of Trade in 1762, "there is a much more fundamental Cause for this Rise, to wit, the Increase of the Imports, to such a Height that the Crops of Tobacco will not pay for them, so that the Colony is so far from having Money to draw from England that they are greatly in Debt already to the Mother Country, which Debt is daily increasing." The governor expressed no optimism about the planters' immediate financial prospects. They seemed to have lost control over their expenditures and were swept along by a desire to live well whatever the costs. "This is a truth," Fauquier noted, "which some of the most thinking Gentlemen of the Colony see and acknowledge, but at the same time, is so disagreeable a truth to the generality that they shut their Eyes

[13] Francis Jerdone to William Hamilton, 20 September 1753, "Jerdone Letter Book," *W&MQ*, 1st ser., 11(1902-1903), 238.

[14] Beverley to [?], 27 December 1762, Beverley Letter Book, 1761-1793, Library of Congress, Washington, D.C.

against it, and what is to be done to remedy it I know not. I
fear they are not prudent enough to quit any one Article of
Luxury."[15]

John Wayles, a Virginian who among other things collected
debts for British merchants, supported the governor's analysis. In 1766 Wayles chronicled changes that had occurred in
planter buying habits over the previous quarter century. During the 1740s, he declared, a gentleman in Virginia would
never have run up a debt of £1,000. But now, Wayles estimated, "Ten times that sum is . . . spoke of with Indifference
& thought no great burthen on some Estates. Indeed in that
series of Time [,] Property is become more valuable & many
Estates have increased more than tenfold." New wealth stim-
ulated expensive tastes. "In 1740," he recounted, "I don't remember to have seen such a thing as a turkey Carpet in the
Country except a small thing in a bed chamber, Now nothing
are so common as Turkey or Wilton Carpetts, the whole Fur-
niture of the Roomes Elegant & every Appearance of Opulence. All this is in great Measure owing to the Cred[i]t which
the Plant[e]rs have had from England & which has enabled
them to Improve their Estates to the pitch they are Arriv[e]d
at, tho many are ignorant of the true Cause."[16]

And to keep up with the "consumer revolution," the great
planters required additional slaves. One way to compensate

[15] Colonial Office, Public Record Office, London, England, 5/1330, Colonial Williamsburg, Inc., Research Center, microfilm. Richard Corbin blamed
the colony's paper money for the rise in planter indebtedness. In 1767 he
claimed that paper currency had driven out specie and "introduced a Train
of Luxury & extravagance. Debts were wantonly Contracted, when they
cou'd be so easily paid in this fictitious representation of Money; and to this
is owing the present distress of individuals, the great debts they owe are
Melancholy . . . this makes them very importunate for a Loan office, but
what relief they can receive to borrow of one to pay Another I do not Understand." Corbin to John Roberts, 15 May 1767, Richard Corbin Letter
Book, 1758-1768, Colonial Williamsburg, Inc., Research Center, microfilm.

[16] John M. Hemphill, "John Wayles Rates His Neighbors," *VMHB*,
66(1958), 305. See also, William Allason to James Dunlop, 24 February 1763,
in "The Letters of William Allason," ed. D. R. Anderson, *Richmond College
Historical Papers*, 2(1917), 125.

for chronically low tobacco prices was to expand production, and in Virginia, that meant increasing the number of laborers in the fields. Tidewater gentlemen bought new slaves as the opportunity presented itself, sometimes spending several hundred pounds in a single purchase. The planters, who seldom had that much money on hand, begged British merchants to cover this unusual expenditure. In return, Virginians promised more and better tobacco, but as many learned from painful experience, the acquisition of fresh Africans created staggering financial risks. Death or sickness could quickly transform an apparently wise capital investment into bankruptcy.[17]

Part of the explanation for the hostility of some great planters toward slavery—and Jefferson was by no means the only one who despised the institution—was that it brought Virginians into permanent debt. In 1761 Beverley wrote eloquently on the subject of slavery: " 'Tis something so very contradictory to Humanity, that I am really ashamed of my Country whenever I consider of it; & if ever I bid adieu to Virginia, it will be from that Cause alone."[18] Personal indebtedness, of course, was only one of several arguments that planters used against slavery. Many gentlemen said nothing at all. The point is that the Virginians' uneasiness over their growing financial dependence could cause them to question the efficacy of a central prop of the tobacco culture, in this case unfree labor.

[17] Devine, *The Tobacco Lords*, 59.

[18] Beverley to Edward Athawes, 11 July 1761; on Beverley's difficulty in paying for the slaves he purchased on credit see his letters to Samuel Athawes, 18 November 1763 and to John Bland, 17 December 1763, Beverley Letter Book. Arthur Lee expressed similar sentiments. Writing to his brother on 20 March 1765 from Edinburgh, Arthur explained, "The extreme aversion I have to slavery & to the abominable objects of it with you, the Blacks; with the lamentable state of dependence in which I perceive America must for many years be held by Britain make me dread a return to America notwithstanding I am drawn to it by the strongest ties of family affection & patriotic love." Lee Family Papers, vol. I, Virginia Historical Society, Richmond, Virginia. See, J. P. Greene, "Society, Ideology, and Politics," in *Society, Freedom, and Conscience*, ed. R. M. Jellison (New York, 1976), 66-68.

II

By the 1760s many great Tidewater planters—no matter how prosperous they seemed—expressed concern about the effect of debt on their lives. To call this a crisis would be an exaggeration. Good years followed poor ones. Some planters were worse off then were others. Still, there was an increasing awareness among the gentry of the fragility of the trade that had sustained the colony since its founding. Central to this sense of foreboding was the merchant-planter relationship. Indeed, as various gentlemen struggled to remain solvent, they reassessed the meaning of commercial reciprocity. The threatened loss of personal autonomy—or perhaps the recognition that their independence had been a commercial fiction all along—made them unusually irritable. They began to feel trapped. "The Colony is greatly indebted to Great Britain," Lieutenant Governor Fauquier informed his London superiors in 1765, ". . . which renders them uneasy, pevish and ready to murmur at every occurrence."[19]

A good many planters certainly fit Fauquier's general description. William Nelson seemed particularly agitated by his financial situation. In 1767 he wrote to his British correspondents, "You are kind not to complain to me, yet I feel the Uneasiness of being behind . . . as much as if you did, & I will try hard to remove it."[20] In comparison with his social peers, Nelson was actually doing rather well. It was the very condition of dependence that worried him.

Robert Beverley reacted angrily to these changing economic conditions. In 1764 he learned that his major British correspondent was cutting back on credit. This was betrayal. Why now, Beverley wailed, when things were going so badly for the Virginians? Several years earlier the great planters might have adjusted to such an alteration in policy. The colony had been prosperous, and in Beverley's estimation, there would have been "a Possibility of this wretched Country (as it cer-

[19] C.O., P.R.O., 5/1345, ff. 80-81.

[20] Nelson to Edward Hunt and Son, 12 August 1767, Nelson Letter Book, Colonial Williamsburg, Inc., Research Center, microfilm.

tainly is in its Present situation) once more moveing upon its
own Leggs—But I dread very Much from the Appearances of
this Day that it will be condemned forever to a state of *Vassalage & Dependence.*"

Even writing these words—"Vassalage & Dependence"—
must have caused Beverley anguish, for not only had he been
raised in a culture that stressed the primacy of personal autonomy, but also he saw no way of escaping his creditors.
"For 'tis beyond a Doubt," he observed, "that the Produce of
no Estate, when our Staple is given away upon such miserable
Terms, can never work out any Debt of Consequence."[21] Beverley discovered what Landon Carter's improvident sons
would confront a few years later: A Virginian planter without
liquid assets must "learn the art of Parrying duns."[22] To find
themselves beholden, to endure being dunned by British
friends from whom the planters had expected "cheerfull com-
pliance," was a continual source of irritation. As William Nelson declared in 1766, "To remain in Debt I could never bear
but with the greatest Pain."[23]

British tobacco merchants must have been doing some
grumbling of their own during this period. After all, business
was business; debts legally contracted had to be paid on demand. The Virginians' insistence on projecting personal values onto these agreements only roiled normal commercial intercourse. The British found their complaints self-serving;
their rhetoric excessive.

The conversation, however, was two-sided. On their part,
the great planters appeared to have convinced themselves that
the merchants were consciously discriminating against them.

[21] Beverley to John Bland, 1764, Beverley Letter Book, emphasis added.
[22] *The Diary of Colonel Landon Carter*, ed. Jack P. Greene, Virginia Historical Documents, vol. 4 (Charlottesville, 1965), Ii, 641.
[23] Nelson to Bosworth and Griffith, 12 November 1766, Nelson Letter
Book. Also, Henry Fitzhugh to Steuart and Campbell, 29 July 1766, Henry
Fitzhugh Papers, Manuscript Division, Duke University, Durham, North
Carolina. For an analysis of the finances of one leading Tidewater family, see
Emory G. Evans, *Thomas Nelson of Yorktown: Revolutionary Virginian* (Wil-
liamsburg, 1975), chapter 2.

Any slight—real or imagined—could set off a tirade. When Beverley received some poorly made goods from London, for example, he exclaimed, "why I am not to enjoy the same Priviledge [as Englishmen] I know not, unless it arises from the Distance from Thence."[24] Like other colonists, Beverley demanded his rights as an Englishman.

Nothing, however, bothered the great Tidewater planters as much as a challenge to a bill of exchange. This commercial instrument was a draft on a merchant's account. If the planter had deposited funds in England, or if his future crops seemed likely to turn a good profit, then the merchant routinely honored his bill of exchange. But when a merchant "protested" a bill, he indicated that the Virginian was already so heavily into debt that he had become a credit risk. Great planters, of course, saw the protest as a public expression of lack of trust, a humiliation that called their integrity into question, and during the 1760s, these unhappy occurrences became increasingly common. One example reveals how Virginians greeted the news of a protested bill. In 1768 Richard Corbin wrote to Mann Page, a prominent Tidewater planter, to tell him that "Mr. Hanbury [the London merchant] had protested your bill for £301/14/9." Corbin assured Page, "I have expostulated with Messieur Hanbury upon this unfair Treatment. I think we are both treated ill. . . ."[25] Corbin wanted to distance his own behavior from that of the outsiders who had violated the local code of credit.

Experiences like these helped persuade the consignment planters that their friends in the mother country had turned against them. Like spurned lovers, the Virginians spoke of their former objects of affection with suspicion, even hostility. "Merchants have no gratitude," Landon Carter complained in 1768, "let the correspondence be ever so long and profitable to them." British correspondents seemed to define reciprocity in a way that no gentleman would, and in Carter's

---

[24] Beverley to John Bland, 11 August 1765, Beverley Letter Book.
[25] Corbin to Mann Page, 31 August 1768, Corbin Letter Book.

estimation, the merchants of Great Britain could not even be counted on to pay "a bill for a man who has made no Tobo."[26]

A few years later Carter described changing merchant-planter relations in much greater detail. When he received an unsatisfactory letter from John Backhouse, a British merchant, the Virginian described Backhouse as a man "whom I used to call my friend." But Carter had seen the light. "I see that which I used to call friendship," Carter scribbled in his diary, "only subsisted when I lived low and kept myself within my Consignment." What the planter seems to be saying is that he received better treatment so long as he stayed out of debt. Carter could remember only one merchant who "broke an honest man to me." "All the rest are much in trade and I fear that is a Profession that kicks Conscience out of doors like a fawning Puppy," recounted the master of Sabine Hall. "Perhaps they may [have] Charity to relieve a perishing object in their View, but as to friendship they know it not in the least instance where their gains are concerned. I am now quite Satisfied This Gent [Backhouse], has a dry way of doing business and, though he never tells you so because it would be against his interest, yet you feel when he is cool to you by all that he sells, buys, or does for you. Therefore, though my expected life cannot Promise to effect it, as soon as I get out of his debt I must sell at home."[27]

For the most part the discourse between planters and merchants was private. During the 1760s Virginians generally addressed their protests to specific British correspondents. Occasionally, however, a commercial issue proved capable of temporarily uniting dispersed planters, and the hostility toward the merchant community welled up in the House of Burgesses. These confrontations seldom involved constitutional principles. Indeed, the souring of commercial relations between merchants and planters had the peculiar effect of in-

[26] Carter to [Thomas], Lord [Fairfax], 20 June 1768 Landon Carter Papers, Roll I, Virginia Historical Society, Richmond, Virginia.

[27] Entry for 20 May 1774, in *Diary of Landon Carter*, ed. Greene, II, 812-13.

itially deflecting the Virginians' anger away from the British government, particularly away from Parliament.[28]

Such was the intense battle waged in 1763 over Virginia's currency. During the French and Indian War, the colonial government printed thousands of pounds of paper money, bills which, as we have seen, the overly generous John Robinson supposedly destroyed. So long as the Virginia currency maintained a stable value in relation to the British pound sterling, the merchants did not complain too vociferously about colonial paper. But when in the early 1760s the local money fell dramatically against the British pound, the merchants demanded immediate relief. They claimed that indebted planters would attempt to pay off old sterling obligations with less valuable paper, and when the Virginia assembly dragged its heels on this matter, arguing that the supply of paper currency was not responsible for the shift in exchange rates, the major tobacco merchants of Great Britain took their case directly to Parliament.

Tidewater planters regarded the merchants' behavior as treachery. By lobbying the Parliament, the British revealed a deep lack of trust in the integrity of Virginia's leading gentlemen. The merchants, in fact, seemed intent on unilaterally redefining traditional economic ties, on substituting statute for personal negotiations. In short, the tobacco merchants were not acting like true commercial friends. The House of Burgesses—the legislative voice of the great planters—dispatched an irate protest to Governor Fauquier. The Virginians reaffirmed their "dependence upon Great Britain [which] we acknowledge and glory in as our greatest happiness and only security." But, as they reminded Fauquier, "it is the dependence of a part upon one great whole." These proud gentlemen refused to bow to the interests of a few well-con-

[28] Thad W. Tate, "The Coming of the Revolution in Virginia," *W&MQ*, 3rd ser., 19(1962), 337; A. Land, "Economic Behavior in a Planting Society," *Journal of Southern History*, 33(1967), 483-84; Gordon Wood, "Conspiracy and the Paranoid Style, Causality and Deceit in the Eighteenth Century," *W&MQ*, 3rd ser., 39(1982), 401-41; William D. Liddle, " 'Virtue and Liberty,' " *South Atlantic Quarterly*, 77(1978), 15-38.

nected merchants. Indeed, such over-mighty subjects threatened to usurp the prerogatives of the monarch. They were attempting to rule Virginia, to bring it under their control, and, the legislators declared, if the king appreciated the planters' recent sacrifices during the French and Indian War, he would now protect them from the merchants' "unreasonable clamour against our paper Bills of Credit."[29]

These complaints seemed especially curious since, according to the Virginians, the merchants had not the slightest reason to be uneasy about receiving their money. This logic led to conspiratorial conclusions, for if the economic interests of the merchants were in fact secure, then these men must have some hidden purpose in mind. As early as June 1763, the Virginia Committee of Correspondence, a committee of leading local political leaders, suggested that the merchants were plotting against the colony. In a detailed letter sent to Virginia's agent in London, the committee advanced a proposition: "Let us suppose that paper money was no legal Tender in the payment of Debts." Who would stand to gain from such a policy? Was it not peculiar that the only people demanding a withdrawal of Virginia currency were "the Merchants, & many [of] your designing men who have large outstanding Debts due to them in the Colony & having sold their Goods at the most extraordinary Advance during the War, are now desirous of reaping the Benefit of a low Exchange."

And why would the merchants want to undermine the great planters' economic independence? The answer, of course, was that the "designing" men coveted the Virginians' land and estates. The legislators who penned this report feared a plot to strip wealthy Virginians of their property. "If the Debtor should stand out the whole Process [of debt collection] & suffer him [the British creditor] to levy his Execution," the committee speculated, "who are to be the purchasers? Only such as can provide Specie. How few they would be in Number we can easily suggest & they would

[29] Report of the Burgesses to Francis Fauquier, 1763, C.O., P.R.O., 5/1330.

undoubtedly have it in their power to combine together & purchase [it] on their own Terms, which must inevitably terminate in the ruin of the Debtor so that possibly a man of £90,000 Fortune in Land & Slaves owing only £1,000, might by these means be reduced to Beggary."[30]

Virginia's leading planters knew the answer to the committee's rhetorical questions. Robert Beverley, for example, accused a leading tobacco merchant, Samuel Athawes, of ignoring the responsibilities of "true Friendship."[31] The immediate cause of Beverley's outburst was Athawes's failure to credit the Virginian's London account with full interest. The young merchant—he had just taken over the business from his father—may have made an honest mistake. But from Beverley's perspective, such actions provided evidence of a general effort to reduce the great Tidewater planters to utter economic dependence. The plot had been in progress for some time. As early as 1763, Beverley notes that the colonists had become "a pitifull set of animals." And who was to blame for their suffering? "This proceeds more from the machinations of those very Merchants who draw their Subsistence, as it were, from our very Vitals," Beverley explained, "being daily ushering in Innovations, which the Country in general must submit to because they are in Debt in England."[32]

As planter indebtedness mounted, the notion of a merchant conspiracy apparently gained credibility in Virginia. Beverley flayed another merchant as a member of the commercial "fraternity," endeavoring "to oppress & destroy the few Priviledges & Comforts of Life which this miserable Colony enjoys."[33] And in 1765 Beverley angrily announced, "I am of Opinion our being ·so much incumbered arises wholly from their [the merchants'] own Conduct, for they dispose of our Commodities upon such wretched terms, that I am Conscious

[30] "Proceedings of the Virginia Committee of Correspondence, 1759-67," *VMHB*, 11(1904), 348.
[31] Beverley to Athawes, 17 October 1770, Beverley Letter Book.
[32] Beverley to John Bland, 5 April 1763, ibid.
[33] Beverley to [?], 1763, ibid.

upon the strictest Frugality & Oeconomy 'Tis impossible for us to keep the Ballance of Trade in our favour."[34]

These were not the musings of a crank. When a French visitor toured Virginia in 1765—just in time to witness Patrick Henry's fiery attack on the Stamp Act—he learned that tobacco produced huge returns for the royal government and the British merchants, but not, alas, for the Tidewater planters. No doubt, the local gentlemen filled the Frenchman's ear with complaints, and he left America fully convinced that the people who merchandised tobacco oppressed the planters. The "whole weight" of the tobacco trade fell upon the Virginian, "who is kept Down by the lowness of the original price and the Ext[r]avagance of the Charges."[35] In 1766 Archibald Cary, a prominent colonial planter, insisted that British merchants would not even allow the impoverished Virginians liberty to experiment with new crops, in other words, to discover an escape from the crushing burden of debt. Cary believed that merchants "take every step in their power to keep the Planters imploy'd in the Commodity [tobacco], and often refuse to purchase their Hempe by which means many People are deterred from Cultivating it, for want of a Certain Market."[36]

Even Thomas Jefferson, a man usually regarded as a model of enlightened reason, subscribed to the merchant conspiracy. In 1786 he was pleased to be rid of merchant tyranny as he was to be free of parliamentary oppression, and in a letter to a French admirer, he explained how before the Revolution British tobacco correspondents had actively worked to erode the planters' liberty. The plot allegedly unfolded in several distinct steps. First, the merchants had urged Virginians to produce as much tobacco as they possibly could. Good prices were promised; credit flowed easily. The planters trusted their commercial friends in Great Britain, not realizing that abundant credit was the honey to bait the trap of dependence.

[34] Beverley to John Bland, 11 August 1765, ibid.

[35] "Journal of a French Traveller in the Colonies, 1765," pt. 1, *American Historical Review*, 27(1920-21), 744.

[36] Archibald Cary to Edward Montague, the agent of Virginia, 17 April 1766, C.O., P.R.O., 5/1345, f. 134.

But, as the events of the 1760s demonstrated, the merchants had not been concerned with the planters' welfare. They wanted only to maximize their own profits, whatever the consequences for the trusting Virginians. "A powerful engine for this purpose," Jefferson recounted, "was the giving of good prices and credit to the planter till they got him more immersed in debt than he could pay without selling his lands or slaves. They then reduced the prices given for his tobacco so that let his shipments be ever so great, and his demand of necessaries ever so oeconomical, they never permitted him to clear off his debt." Commercial exchange, in fact, deprived the planter of the essential attributes of freedom. "These debts had become hereditary from father to son for many generations, so that the planters were a species of property annexed to certain mercantile houses in London."[37] The tone of Jefferson's statement is bitter; it is the voice of a Virginia gentleman who thinks his trust has been betrayed.

It is the structure, rather than the validity of these arguments that commands attention. Even in their private correspondence these men adopted a Country perspective. Betrayal of public trust by stockjobbers and sniveling courtiers, by people more interested in profit than in virtue, was a theme that ran through the writings of Trenchard and Gordon. The Virginians did not cite these authors in their correspondence. Rather, their sense of injustice grew directly out of experiences that they had had with specific merchants. Like Bolingbroke, they were trying to comprehend their place within a developing capitalistic economy.

III

Conspiratorial thinking was obviously not a phenomenon unique to Virginia gentry culture. Other groups throughout human history have railed against alleged plotters, whether in the form of witches or spies, corporate executives or foreign priests, and have devised various means to protect the com-

[37] "Additional Questions of M. de Meusnier, and Answers," 1786, in *The Papers of Thomas Jefferson*, ed. J. Boyd (Princeton, 1954), X, 27.

munity from the agents of evil.[38] But the unprecedented growth of personal indebtedness in Tidewater Virginia raised issues far more profound than the identification of external enemies. The pressure that British Merchants were forced to apply during this period challenged fundamental assumptions of the tobacco culture. Debt, the gentlemen insisted, compromised personal autonomy, and with it honor, integrity, and virtue. Here, in these intensely personal, often private struggles, one again encounters the strains that ultimately help to explain the receptivity of some wealthy planters to Country political ideas. The Virginia gentry were attempting to preserve a familiar mental world, and it is on this level of analysis that one begins to appreciate how a particular set of economic experiences provoked such an emotional response.

In their correspondence with the merchants, the planters almost reflexively associated the demand for payment with loss of integrity, with subservience, and when a merchant complained about the state of a Virginian's account, the planter usually protested that he had behaved in an honorable manner. In 1755, for example, George Braxton suspected that his honor had been called into question, and he testily informed a British tobacco firm, "I've always acted to be best of my Knowledge consistent with the strictest Rules of Honour & Justice which when I deviated from may I deservedly [be] censured and rebuked by even you."[39] John Page, a respected Tidewater planter, reacted more mildly, but he too associated merchant pressure with personal dishonor. "When

[38] See, Bernard Bailyn, *The Ideological Origins of the American Revolution* (Cambridge, Mass., 1967), 144-59; John Demos, *Entertaining Satan: Witchcraft and the Culture of Early New England* (New York, 1983); Kai T. Erikson, *Wayward Puritans: A Study in the Sociology of Deviance* (New York, 1966); David B. Davis, *The Slave Power Conspiracy and the Paranoid Style* (Baton Rouge, 1969); Richard Hofstadter, *The Paranoid Style in American Politics and Other Essays* (New York, 1965); James H. Hutson, "The Origins of 'The Paranoid Style in America Politics': Public Jealousy from the Age of Walpole to the Age of Jackson," in D. D. Hall et al., *Saints and Revolutionaries: Essays on Early American History* (New York, 1984), 332-72.

[39] Braxton to Bosworth and Griffith, [1755?], in Frederick Horner, *The History of the Blair, Banister, and Braxton Families Before and After the Revolution* (Philadelphia, 1898), 142.

you recollect," he explained to a leading London merchant in 1771, "my first Letters full of an Abhorrence of Extravagance & Debt; & my others full of fair Promises & large Expectations: I fear you begin to suspect my Honour."[40]

The prospect of falling into perpetual dependence upon a merchant threw many Tidewater planters into deep despondence. Their letters of this period often betray apprehension, as if their own private dealings with distant tobacco houses somehow hinted at a larger disaster awaiting their entire society. In 1769 John Baylor promised a correspondent, John Backhouse, to "reduce your great Ballance as fast as possible." And then Baylor anxiously notes, "I hope poor Virginia will again in a few years be able to hold up her head."[41] Benjamin Pendleton told a friend that he could not even face a creditor "without dread."[42] And in 1767 Bernard Moore, a planter whom contemporaries assumed was fabulously successful, confessed privately in a letter, "God knows my case is desperate enough."[43]

Debt—or more precisely fear that other Virginians would discover their embarrassment—drove some great planters almost to the edge of distraction. These proud individuals were seemingly prepared to do anything to preserve the outward trappings of independence, even groveling before the merchants. Baylor begged a British correspondent, "by all that is good & sacred, I will pay you as soon as I possibly can, for I will never make another promise till I have the money either in my own possession or in England."[44]

To be forced to expose one's vulnerability was a psychologically painful experience. In 1766 Richard Corbin found himself on the brink of financial ruin. He desperately needed

[40] John Page to John Norton, 31 July 1771, in *John Norton and Sons*, ed. Francis N. Mason (Richmond, 1937), 172.

[41] Baylor to John Backhouse, 21 July 1769, Backhouse Admr. vs. Baylor Exor., U.S. Circuit Court, Virginia District, Ended Cases, 1798.

[42] Benjamin Pendleton to James Hunter, 13 May 1767, Hunter-Spotswood Family Documents, Colonial Williamsburg, Inc., Research Center.

[43] Bernard Moore to Hunter, 22 April 1767, Hunter-Spotswood Family Documents.

[44] Baylor to John Norton, 18 September 1764, in *John Norton and Sons*, ed. Mason, 11.

£1,000 to preserve his credit, and in a letter to a person who owed him money—one of the more moving statements surviving from this period—Corbin pleads, ". . . *let* me be secure, *let* my Credit be supported, and it is all that I require of you; *Let* me not run any Risque or Hazard, or be brought into any Dispute with any Person upon the Score of my Demand against you; *Let* me be satisfied, & I am sure, my Friend, whatever Indulgence it is in my Power to give consistent with my own Credit, and the welfare of my own Family, I shou'd with Cheerfulness allow you."[45] Corbin's touching letter reads almost like a secular prayer.

Demeaning themselves like this surely must have embarrassed these independent Virginians. And after 1760 it happened with increasing frequency. By 1771 Moore, now nearly overwhelmed by the accumulating burden of debt, beseeched a merchant to send a secondhand "Post Chariot" for his wife, since as this proud planter explained "she has now nothing left even to carry her to Church."[46] Even Jefferson had occasionally to beg. In 1771 his shaky financial situation frightened the young planter, and like Corbin, he longed for security. Jefferson wrote to a British merchant declaring, "I mentioned to you that I had become one of several securities for a gentleman of my acquaintance lately engaged in trade." The Virginian had heard that this man was prospering, but one could never be sure. "I would not therefore take any step to wound his credit," Jefferson stated. "But as far as it can possibly be done without affecting that I must *beg* you to have me secured." He had observed the local etiquette of credit, advancing money to a friend even though his own affairs were uncertain, and now he paid the price of living in fear. "Should my friend prove unsuccessful . . . ," Jefferson confessed, "It might sweep away the whole of my little fortune."[47]

---

[45] Corbin to Mr. Hunter, 28 June 1766, Corbin Letter Book (emphasis added).

[46] Moore to John Norton, 28 September 1771, in *John Norton and Sons*, ed. Mason, 193.

[47] Jefferson to Thomas Adams, 20 February 1771, in *The Papers of Thomas Jefferson*, ed. J. Boyd (Princeton, 1950), I, 61.

Chronic indebtedness forced the great Virginia planters to provide excuses for their personal expenditures, for their plantation management, in fact, for a style of life that had become emblematic of gentry culture. Gentlemen who viewed themselves as Old Testament Patriarchs detested having to apologize for private matters. These were concerns over which outsiders rightfully exercised no control. But as John Page, master of Rosewell, learned in 1769, debt brought even a planter's personal life under the scrutiny of British creditors. When he discovered that a tobacco consignment had not covered the cost of goods ordered from London, Page realized that his correspondent, John Norton, required an explanation. The planter insisted that had he "known the Amount of my Debts here, & could have foreseen the Expenses of Electioneering," he would never have purchased so many items. Surely, Page protested, "no Body hates the Thought of being in Debt more than I do," and he expected Norton to take account of Page's personal situation: "the Great Scarcity of money here, the Shortness of my Crops for four Years past, & the necessary Expenses of an encreasing Family joined to the Commencement of Housekeeping in a large House, [which] have forced me to submit to it [debt] for a while."[48] What Norton, who had bills of his own to pay, thought of this arrangement, is not known. In 1764 Henry Fitzhugh urged an English creditor to remember, "I have [a] large family, & the chiefest of my estates [is] entailed on a few of my children so that I [am] under a necessity of purchasing Lands for the others. . . ."[49]

As debt compromised their economic independence, the great planters increasingly substituted promises for performance, as if the mere expectation of profit helped preserve commercial honor. All they needed was a run of luck, a little more time, a more stringent household budget. On the eve of the Revolution, in fact, many gentlemen lived on hope. John

[48] John Page to John Norton, 27 May 1769, in *John Norton and Sons*, ed. Mason, 93-94.

[49] Fitzhugh to John Bland, 1764, Henry Fitzhugh Papers.

Page, for example, assured Norton that "I have a very good Prospect of a Crop, have engaged a Good Overseer, [and] have resolved not to send to England for anything this Year. . . ."[50]

And Henry Fitzhugh, a man who never prospered as a planter, constantly promised what he could not deliver. In 1756 he thanked a correspondent for paying a large bill "when I had not a farthing in your hands," and lest the merchant should be uneasy, Fitzhugh assured him, "you shall not lay long out of your money for I shall not draw [more] till the Tobo. is shipped to you."[51] The Virginian's optimism proved premature. He continued to run substantial deficits, and a decade later he still dreamed of escaping from debt. In 1765 Fitzhugh reported to the firm of Steuart and Campbell that he had just dispatched eighty-one hogsheads of tobacco, "very fine, as I am informed by the Inspectors & others who saw them Inspected, which I expect will sell well as I am informed that good tobo. sells well & is rising." He even bragged, "I am so fortunate as to have a better crop than ever I had & all very forward if no accident happens from this time [,] I shall ship you next year at least 100 hogsheads."[52] On the basis of his own inflated predictions, Fitzhugh ordered more goods and slipped deeper into dependence.

Perhaps one should not make too much of these incidents. Often the planter weathered a particular crisis. He may, in fact, have avoided bankruptcy. Nevertheless, a resentment against the merchants was clearly building. The very structure of the tobacco commerce compelled British correspondents to remind the great planters of their financial dependence. For anyone, these would be unpleasant experiences, but for men like Jefferson they were particularly difficult to bear. And in the years before the Revolution, a growing number of

---

[50] Page to Norton, 27 May 1769, in *John Norton and Sons*, ed. Mason, 94.

[51] Fitzhugh to James Buchanan, 11 November 1756, Henry Fitzhugh Papers.

[52] Fitzhugh to Steuart and Campbell, 18 February 1766, Henry Fitzhugh Papers.

Tidewater gentlemen lived with the memory of having, at least once, been forced to beg.

IV

The experiences of three specific Virginians—George Washington, Robert Beverley, and John Syme—illuminate the cultural character of planter-merchant tensions. Their stories, of course, remind us that we are dealing with people, not abstractions. These gentlemen set out in the 1750s as young adults to become independent producers, to acquire the clothes, housing, and slaves that they knew were necessary to sustain their claim to gentry status. For them, the imperatives of the tobacco mentality became second nature. They aspired to grow a quality leaf. And yet, in each case, these proud, ambitious planters found that the road to personal independence brought them inevitably into dependence upon a British merchant. Their ordeal provides insight into the mental world of other Tidewater gentlemen whose lives are less fully documented.

Debt—or more precisely the shock of discovering that they had lost a measure of personal autonomy—did not in itself transform these planters into revolutionaries. Beverley sat out the conflict. Syme served in the military and in the new state government. And Washington became the most influential man in the republic. What warrants close attention here, however, is not their later political loyalties, but the language that they employed to describe their deteriorating relations with the British merchants. Country idioms increasingly appear in their private discourses with correspondents, and though some gentlemen stopped short of rebellion, their experiences suggest a link between commerce and politics, an understanding of how during the 1770s radical Country thought might have acquired sufficient moral force to bring at least some planters to Revolution.

As noted earlier, George Washington returned from military service in the French and Indian War eager to establish himself as a crop master. His prospects seemed good. He had inherited a well-situated estate, Mount Vernon, and in the late 1750s, he set his slaves to growing tobacco. But try as he would, Washington's agricultural endeavors never prospered. The light soils of Virginia's Northern Neck could not produce quality leaves. A series of particularly poor crops left Washington financially vulnerable. An early sign of trouble occurred in 1760 when a merchant demanded payment on a bill of exchange Washington had written for £90. This was not a large sum of money, but since the young planter did not have it on hand, he was forced to go to court to seek an extension with interest on this obligation. His inability to honor his own bill—now a matter of public record—greatly embarrassed Washington. As Douglas Southall Freeman, his biographer, explained, "Washington was forced to admit that he did not have the cash to discharge the debt. . . . Previously, every man who had called at Mount Vernon with an honest bill had the money in his pocket when he turned his horse's head from the house."[53]

Over the next few years Washington's financial situation steadily deteriorated, and in 1761 he owed Robert Cary and Company nearly £2,000. The growing burden filled the ambitious planter with dread. Though he wanted to fill his estate with impressive English imports, Washington could not tolerate being under another man's control. The knowledge that he was gradually losing his independence alternately triggered testiness and self-abasement.[54]

This was the context for a remarkable letter that Washington wrote to Cary in 1764. The merchant, worried about the Virginian's rising indebtedness, had apparently urged Washington to confront the problem. The request—however diplomatically phrased—elicited a highly emotional response, partly confessional, partly indignant, the kind of spirited rhetoric that one does not usually associate with Washington. The immediate problem was not the debt. Rather, by reminding

[53] Freeman, *Washington*, III, 39. See, Chapter II for a discussion of Washington's early frustrations as a planter.

[54] Ibid., 63, 85-86.

the planter of his obligation, Cary implicitly stated that he did not fully trust Washington. His actions called the planter's personal honor into question, something a true commercial friend would never do.

Washington maintained that the debts he had accumulated were not his fault. "Mischance rather than Misconduct," he insisted, "hath been the cause of it." This military veteran who took the slightest criticism as an affront reminded Cary of the misfortunes he had experienced. Washington listed the excuses: bad weather, low tobacco prices, failure of his neighbors to pay their debts, and the unexpectedly high cost of new land and slaves. Surely, Washington seemed to be saying, an honorable gentleman could not be held accountable for such "unlucky" events.

If Washington had observed the proper etiquette, what then could be said of the British merchant? Cary, in the planter's estimation, seemed oblivious to the reciprocal character of trade. Indeed, he appeared to have operated his business on assumptions that Washington found totally alien. "For I must confess," the Virginian lectured, "I did not expect that a correspondent so steady, and constant as I have proved, and was willing to have continued to your House while the advantages were in any degree reciprocal [,] woud be reminded in the Instant it was discovered how necessary it was for him to be expeditious in his payments. Reason and prudence naturally dictates to every Man of common sense the thing that is right and you might have rested assured, that so fast as I coud make remittances without distressing myself too much my Inclinations woud have prompted me to it."

By dunning his American friend, Cary had strained their relationship. The merchant could easily have avoided this confrontation, however, for he must certainly have known that in Virginia "it is but an irksome thing to a *free mind* to be always hampered in Debt." A free mind! Here was a voice of the Country agrarian. The Virginian was insisting that Cary recognize the planter's personal autonomy—that he sustain a cultural fiction—even though Washington was thousands of pounds in debt. In an impassioned style uncharacteristic of the man, Washington poured out his heart to this distant correspondent who seemed so insensitive to the assumptions of the tobacco culture. "I have already run into much greater prolixity on this head," Washington observed, "than I promised or intended."[55] It was clear that he felt both humiliated and betrayed, and it seems unlikely that this experience did not color his reaction to the pressing political problems of the day.

Robert Beverley's rich correspondence chronicles another great planter's descent into debt. Like Washington, this Virginian expressed optimism about his early financial prospects. And well he should have. Beverley came from a prominent gentry family, had recently been educated in England, and would soon marry one of Landon Carter's daughters. In 1761, the year he returned to Virginia, Beverley wrote to Edward Athawes, a merchant, and judging from the letter's informal tone, a personal friend as well. "I find my Estate is under exceeding good management," he reported; "The Produce this Year is sixty seven hogsheads on my Plantation, & between 80,000 & 90,000 lbs. [of tobacco] Rents, & a considerable Quantity of Provisions." The cost of setting up his household—his years in the mother country had taught him expensive tastes—forced Beverley to borrow money, but he was confident that one good tobacco crop "will set me at full Liberty the next Spring."[56]

In another letter written at this time, the young planter revealed an almost carefree attitude toward debt. He clearly believed that he could avoid the liquidity problems that plagued other Tidewater gentlemen, and in an offhand manner, Beverley observed to John Bland, "I imagine that I am in your Debt, tho' I cant even form a guess, but I should be glad if you would send me in a sheet how the Account stands between us, that I may discharge [it], for 'tis my Intention for

[55] George Washington to Robert Cary and Company, 10 August 1764, in *The Writings of George Washington*, ed. John Fitzpatrick (Washington, D.C., 1931), II, 416-18. Note Washington's testiness in other commercial letters written in this period, II, 42-43, 427-29.

[56] Beverley to Edward Athawes, 11 July 1761, Beverley Letter Book.

the future to run in Debt with no Body whatever. . . ." He assured the English merchant that he could "very easily" stay out of debt since "I find I have a good Estate under good Management."[57] Beverley obviously assumed that he was dealing with a friend, with someone he could trust, and when in the fall of 1761 he ordered a handsome "chariot" for £85, the planter promised to send Bland a large consignment of tobacco next season. "I don't expect," he declared, "that after this year, I shall be under the necessity of borrowing Money either from you or any other Merchant."[58] Full independence was in sight.

But, as on so many plantations throughout Virginia, the crops in the fields did not turn out as well as Beverley had predicted. An unexpected fall in the price of tobacco also took him by surprise, and despite the confident rhetoric of the previous season, Beverley discovered that he still owed considerable sums to the British merchants. The failure to get out of debt was a frustrating experience, and after he had consigned a large shipment of tobacco to Bland in December 1763, Beverley observed that surely so many hogsheads "ought to discharge the Debt."[59] Like Washington, he resented having outsiders remind him of his growing obligations; he was especially sensitive about his inability to achieve financial independence.

By 1764 frustration had spawned fatalism. Beverley wondered increasingly whether he would ever be able to clear his debts. Perhaps a man's good intentions counted for nothing. In fact, the great planters seemed condemned to dependence. In a letter to William Hunter, another merchant, Beverley bluntly stated, "I am afraid we shall not gain much Advantage by the Cultivation of Tobacco." Whereas in 1761 Beverley had treated Athawes and Bland as commercial friends, as social peers who would look out for his interests, he now adopted a defensive tone, and instead of offering Hunter large

[57] Beverley to John Bland, 11 July 1761, ibid.
[58] Beverley to Bland, October 1761, ibid.
[59] Beverley to Bland, 17 December 1763; also, Beverley to Bland, June 1762, ibid.

consignments of valuable Virginia tobacco, he promised simply not to be "a very Burthensome Correspondent."[60]

As Beverley's personal finances grew more tenuous, he was forced to borrow money from his strong-willed father-in-law. This was an extremely unpleasant experience, and in a note to Carter written in January 1766 concerning the loan, Beverley felt compelled not only to apologize for the imposition, but also to defend his honor. "I am sorry," Beverley explained in uncharacteristically stilted prose, "you should give yourself any Uneasiness relative to my Ballance, for 'tho I am indebted several large Sums of Money, I should never be desirous to put any Friend of mine to any Inconvenience." But, as Carter knew all too well, the great planters of their neighborhood had endured several "unfavorable Seasons . . . [which] will not enable the most industrious or opulent Planters in the Country to comply so punctually with their Engagements as they might wish." Beverley argued in effect that his performance did not reflect a flawed character. He still thought himself as worthy as the next gentlemen.

The burden of dependence, however, was taking a heavy psychological toll on this struggling planter. He had reached middle age, and in one letter he even drew attention to an expanding waistline. He had a large family. And as his financial obligations mounted, Beverley dreamed of release. "For my Part," he told Carter, "I hope we shall be able to extricate ourselves from our Difficulties, [for] could we have a tolerable Certainty of getting any Thing for our Tobacco & if I should ever be happy enough to enjoy Independence & Ease, I am determined never to involve myself by my Indolence or Imprudence."[61] The last words were particularly significant. Beverley promised to reform his ways, to make a more strenuous effort to lead a simple, virtuous life, if only he could

[60] Beverley to William Hunter, 5 March 1764, ibid.

[61] Beverley to Landon Carter, 16 January 1766, Landon Carter Papers, Mss. 1, C2462a. To understand why Beverley might have been so distressed by having to borrow money from Carter, see Jack Greene's splendid essay, *Landon Carter: An Inquiry into the Personal Values and Social Imperatives of the Eighteenth-Century Gentry* (Charlottesville, 1965).

restore his credit and independence, if only he could start again.

Like Washington, Beverley understood the appeal of a "free mind." An increasingly intolerable market situation had driven both men to express their hopes and fears—their longing to restore virtue—in language that sounded remarkably like that of some English Country writers. In June 1775, Beverley wrote to Samuel Athawes. The Virginian may ultimately have expressed ambivalence about separation from the mother country, but on this occasion he spoke out for colonial rights. "I have ever been of Opinion," he reminded the merchant, "that as Freemen, our Properties should be exempt from Parliamentary Taxation, & our Persons secured from Punishments, unless inflicted under our own Laws." Only after these liberties had been secured would he agree "in a constitutional way, to the general support of the Empire."[62]

John Syme's story is affecting, though it hardly contains the stuff of tragedy. He was Patrick Henry's half-brother and sometime representative to the House of Burgesses from Hanover County. Had Syme lived in the modern South, he would have been known affectionately as an "ol' boy." He loved fast horses, good dogs, and fancy clothes, and perhaps even more fully than either Beverley or Washington, he manifested the values of the Virginia tobacco culture.[63] As a planter, Syme projected these beliefs onto the merchants who handled his consignments. He assumed that since they were his special friends—really Virginians like himself who happened to live in England—they would conduct their business according to familiar local rules. Indeed, he seemed totally incapable of

[62] Beverley to Samuel Athawes, 4 June 1775, Beverley Letter Book. Also, Robert M. Calhoon, ed., " 'A Sorrowful Spectator of These Tumultuous Times': Robert Beverley Describes the Coming of the Revolution," *VMHB*, 73(1965), 41-55.

[63] See, Syme to Farrell and Jones, 9 June 1753, U.S. Circuit Court, Virginia District, Ended Cases, 1797-98, Jones' Exor. vs. John Syme. Long after the conclusion of the war, various British creditors sued to recover old American debts. As evidence, they presented commercial correspondence, some dating from the 1750s. Of these cases, John Syme's is the most fully documented.

thinking of commercial exchange as other than a highly personal, reciprocal relationship. If Syme did his correspondents a favor, then they owed him one. Moreover, he expected them to respect his personal autonomy, even if that should mean honoring his credit when he was hopelessly in debt. Despite clear evidence that the merchants operated on different standards, Syme clung to an economic perspective that was the product of the Tidewater environment and in the process, compromised the very elements of the local culture he most anxiously sought to preserve.

Syme never experienced financial independence, not even for a single season. Even before dispatching his first crop to the Bristol house of Lidderdale, Harmen, and Farrell, he owed it money, and his earliest surviving commercial correspondence contained excuses for his inabilty to stay out of debt. "I have been Oblig'd to Draw largely on you this year," he reported in June 1753, "which was Occasion'd by my beginning housekeeping." At this stage of his life, the young planter remained confident that he would soon be running his plantations on a profitable basis. There was certainly no reason for alarm. After all, he observed, "I have a Probability of making an hundred hogsheads this year, which shall be sent [to] your house. ... ." Syme seemed particularly anxious to establish a special bond of trust between the merchants and himself. They were to be friends. "What I write you is not with an intention to Deceive you," Syme declared, ". . . as is too often the case, but Desire you will enquire of Col. Randolph into the truth of the Case."[64] Presumably Randolph testified that Syme was indeed an honorable man deserving of generous credit, although Syme's gratuitous comment about planter deception might well have caused the merchants to wonder about his own integrity.

However honorably Syme may have conducted his affairs, he could not clear his debts. In fact, in May 1754 he confessed, "I have again been Oblig'd to draw largely on this Crop, but you may assure yourselves, my Bills will be very

---

[64] 9 June 1753, ibid.

triffling another year, and as I have encreased my Number of Negro's considerably and got the genuine sweet scented Tobacco, my crop will be much greater in Quantity, and much better in Quality. . . ." It was at this point in his correspondence with Lidderdale and his partners that Syme first raised the issue of commercial reciprocity. He urged the merchants—and he did so without sounding obsequious—to treat "my Bills [of exchange] . . . with Due honour. . . ." He did not want to suffer the public humiliation of having his credit protested, and if the merchants were willing to grant him this one favor, he stood ready to advance their commercial interests throughout Virginia. He promised, for example, to meet with "some Gentlemen" living on the York River who had spoken ill of Lidderdale's firm.[65]

Offers of diplomacy did little to improve Syme's personal finances. The cost of the goods he ordered from Great Britain regularly exceeded the returns for his consignment of tobacco. The planter reacted as best he could. He purchased more slaves, cultivated more acreage, produced more tobacco, but nothing helped. His dependence upon Lidderdale grew. In 1755 Syme brazenly attempted to make a virtue out of necessity, informing the Bristol merchants that "it is a Satisfaction to me, that I am in Debt to but one House, and therefore shall be Entirely at Liberty to Devote my Crops & Interest Accordingly."[66]

Unfortunately for this high-living Virginian, Lidderdale and his partners had no interest in supporting improvident colonial planters, and in 1757 they challenged Syme's credit. The move—probably several years overdue—shocked the struggling planter. It was a moment he had desperately sought to avoid. Moreover, these were drought years, and even a crop master would have had difficulty maintaining a favorable balance. "It gives me much concern, to have my Bills protested," Syme complained. How could the merchants hold him accountable for the deficits? "The shortness of the

[65] 27 May 1754, ibid.
[66] 24 April 1755, ibid.

Crop, was what I could not foresee," he cried indignantly, "and as I have always Ship'd you my whole Crop, and done Every thing in my Power for You, I hop'd you would have been so good, as [to] have Honour'd them, notwithstanding my falling so far short. . . ." However angrily the Virginian fulminated against the merchants' betrayal, he recognized that he could not call himself an independent man "till I have pay'd the Old Score."[67]

By 1760 the firm of Lidderdale, Harmen, and Farrell had become Farrell and Jones. But though the personnel changed, the nature of the commercial discourse remained the same. Neither Syme nor the merchants understood the different cultural contexts that gave peculiar meanings to a common vocabulary. Confusion resulted. Syme would berate the merchants for charging too much for insurance and interest or for failing to obtain top prices for his tobacco, and then—often in the very same letter—beg their indulgence. This ambivalent situation produced in Syme a curious mixture of aggressiveness and servility. He once had the gall to suggest that it was the merchants' fault that he had fallen so deeply into debt. "My situation in a Publick Place," the planter explained, "Obliges me to live in a Way, somewhat Expensive whereby I am better able to serve your interests."[68] What were friends for if not to put in a good word for a particular consignment company, and as the great Tidewater planters knew, no one would accept the recommendation of a person who appeared unsuccessful.

With each passing year, Syme became more anxious about the "Old Score." His eagerness to escape the control of Farrell and Jones sometimes clouded his judgment, however, and he presented plans for restoring his full credit that must have struck his British correspondents as bizarre. "You'll Perceive my Crops have increas'd of late," Syme noted in 1760, "which will readily account for my heavy Drafts. This incourages me to think of another scheme to Cultivate my Lands, which is,

[67] 9 February 1757, ibid.
[68] 2 June 1760; also, 15 November 1764, ibid.

if you'll advance me a Sum of Money, at 3 1/2 or 4 per cent
to be laid out in Negroes, their Crops shall be Mark'd with a
distinguishing Mark from the rest, & the Produce annually
remain Untouch'd & go to discharge the Money so advanc'd."
It is not clear from the letterbooks how the merchants reacted
to this idea, but since Syme was already some five or six thousand pounds in debt, they probably did not underwrite a new
major expenditure that depended solely upon Syme's management. In any case, the planter had already undermined his
appeal for a loan by confessing, "I have been & still am, Very
unfortunate in my Slaves dying, having lost as many of my
Men, with these ten years, as Would Amount to 1,000
pounds."[69] There seemed no reason to believe that fresh Africans purchased with the merchants' money would fare any
better than had the others.

By the middle of the decade, Syme had begun to sense that
he too was a slave. He spent much of his adult life in economic bondage to British merchants, and even if that condition resulted in large measure from his own extravagance, it
nevertheless soured his outlook. Time was running out. "I am
now advancing in Life," Syme wrote plaintively to Farrell and
Jones in 1768. "I want to settle my Affairs. If ever I am to do
any thing for my self, now is the time."[70]

But by then, it was too late. To justify a life of economic
failure, Syme adopted a conspiratorial view of commerce.
The merchants, he decided, had singled him out for dishonorable treatment. Though he had offered genuine friendship,
they had plotted his ruin. "If you have no More generosity,
than to Desire me, to sell my Estate," he scribbled, "I am
ready to sell Part of it. Can Any Man in my place, that has
such large Sums Due to him, Act in a fairer Manner?" He
then inquired of Farrell and Jones, no doubt rhetorically,
whether it was really true that "you are endevouring to Ruin
me, at a Time, when Friends ought to be Assisting, to a Person Who had serv'd them & whose Schemes are ripening to

[69] 2 June 1760, ibid.
[70] 25 May 1768, ibid.

much advantage."[71] Without being aware of it, Syme was beginning to sound like a Country pamphleteer shrilly defending his independence against a dark conspiracy.

In one of his last surviving commercial letters written before the Revolution, the planter again asked whether this tobacco firm intended "to Ruin me, or at least Attempt it. Now, [when I am] quite divested of every Sentiment but what [is] Activated by Justice & Equity, was it Generous, was it *right*, to treat your Old Friend in that Manner." They had dragged him to court; they had destroyed his pride. "Was it not Hard, Cruel Hard," he moaned, "to sue an Old & Serviceable Correspondent, for not making immediate Payment of so large a Debt, Accumulated, by so many year's beneficial, greatly beneficial intercourse to your House & such Manifest Loss to me. You Gentlemen had time to Pay Mr. Lidderdale. If any Person upon earth has a *Right* to expect it, I have."[72] Syme was thinking of commerce in terms of rights that any "free mind" in Virginia would have regarded as the foundation of independence. This troubled planter lived on into the 1790s. He served his country in war, his state in political office. But alas, he never escaped the burden of past debt. In 1797 a court ordered Syme to pay Farrell and Jones $53,954.

V

In their privated controversies with British merchants, the great Tidewater planters developed a language of protest—a bundle of perceptions about independence, liberty, and rights—which helps to explain their heightened receptivity to radical Country ideas in the late 1760s and early 1770s. It should be clear, however, that debt did not cause the Revolution. Each planter reacted to external pressures in a way that reflected the peculiarities of his own personality. Syme and Washington became patriots; Beverley remained neutral. Nevertheless, the strains between merchants and planters in

[71] 29 March 1769, ibid.
[72] 28 May 1769, ibid. See, Sheridan, "British Credit System," 183.

this period of escalating indebtedness provided a personal context in which abstractions about liberty and rights, independence and virtue, found meaning. These experiences gave moral force to the general Country idioms of the day.

Moreover, as is now probably clear, the amount of a planter's debt was often of less significance to him than the fact that he was in debt at all. Nor does it seem particularly relevant to argue that debt was of little importance in understanding the coming of the Revolution since in fact many great planters survived their time of financial troubles. That is a judgment that relies upon hindsight. For Syme and the other Tidewater gentlemen the threat to personal autonomy seemed very real.

CHAPTER V

POLITICIZING THE DISCOURSE: TOBACCO, DEBT, AND THE COMING OF REVOLUTION

"Language is one of the principle supports of society," Caledoniensis reminded the readers of the *Virginia Gazette* in March 1769. This observation—one that possesses a peculiarly modern ring—led to unsettling conclusions. "It is a common phrase among the rich," the anonymous writer explained, "and from them adopted by the poor, that a man (naming him) was born a Gentleman." But what, he asked, could that statement possibly mean? One had to earn the right to be called a gentleman. "To talk of a man's being born a Gentleman is as inconsistent as to say he was born a fiddler, and with a fiddle in his arms. . . . no man deserves the appelation *a Gentleman* until he has done something to merit it."[1]

This type of challenge to the hegemony of the great Tidewater planters became increasingly common in the period before the Revolution. Earlier in the century the Virginia gentry would probably have ignored the scribblings of a Caledoniensis. The newspaper might not have even published the essay. But by 1769 conditions were different. The planter elite seemed uncertain, as if its position in Virginia society was not as secure as it might once have been. The problems that confronted these men were by no means imaginary. A gradual shift in large sections of the Tidewater away from tobacco to wheat, a change that had commenced in some places in the 1740s and would continue after the Revolution, had seriously begun to undermine the tobacco mentality. Achieving recognition as a crop master was becoming more difficult, and as

---

[1] *Virginia Gazette* (Purdie & Dixon), 30 March 1769.

some planters sank deeper into debt, they simply gave up the effort to produce Virginia's traditional staple. Neither the transition away from tobacco nor the rising level of indebtedness caused the great planters to support the Revolution. These experiences did, however, help determine how the Tidewater gentlemen ultimately perceived the constitutional issues of the day.

The process was slow and uneven, affecting some planters more profoundly than others. During much of the 1760s thoughtful individuals discussed the cultural crisis that appeared to have overtaken them. They suggested ways to reform Virginia society, but it was not until the end of the decade that the great planters moved decisively from private complaint to group protest. Their Association of 1769 to curtail expensive imports was aimed primarily against British merchants, and though the effort failed to revitalize the tobacco culture, it set the stage for the post-1772 period when these various threads—debt, tobacco, and constitution—dramatically came together. Events politicized an agricultural and commercial discourse. The Country idioms that planters had long employed to defend their personal autonomy from merchants now provided a powerful emotional justification for national independence. Virginia experienced a new beginning, and the men who were able to adjust—the Washingtons and Jeffersons—demonstrated to the likes of Caledoniensis that they truly deserved to be called gentlemen.

I

Sometime during the 1760s, various great Tidewater planters, men who had struggled to preserve honor and independence in their private dealings with particular merchants, became conscious that their personal tribulations were but an expression of a larger, collective experience. The growing awareness that many respected gentlemen were dangerously in debt compounded gentry anxiety. The material symbols of social stability—the graceful mansions dotting the riverfronts, the scores of slaves busily making tobacco, the opulent coaches hurrying along the roads to Williamsburg—became suspect, and the world of the great planters terribly fragile. As George Washington observed in 1769, "many families are reduced, almost, if not quite, to penury and want, from the low ebb of their fortunes."[2] Indeed, not a few of Washington's contemporaries concluded that debt was rapidly undermining the very integrity of the local culture, for as hard-pressed Virginians attempted to preserve their credit, they often ceased to behave like true gentlemen. In their fear of being caught short, the great planters turned on each other, dunning neighbors, threatening legal actions: in fact, acting more like insensitive British merchants than traditional friends.

The growing pressure of indebtedness badly strained the Virginia gentlemen's code of credit. People who had been pushed by creditors in the mother country to reduce their deficits, now turned on other colonists, demanding repayment for past favors. At mid-century a planter of John Mercer's standing could still publicly announce that he hoped no man would put "me to the Blush which a Dun will occasion."[3] By the late 1760s, however, it was much more difficult to treat local debtors with restraint. While Richard Corbin resented having to push other Virginians, for example, he was not willing to compromise his own credit or his family's economic security to save a thriftless neighbor. Consider his dealings with Ralph Wormeley, a planter of distinguished lineage who perpetually lived beyond his means. At an earlier time, Corbin might have indulged Wormeley, reasoning perhaps that a person who owned so much land and so many slaves would someday settle his accounts. After 1766 genteel forbearance was out of the question. When Corbin discovered that British merchants refused to honor Wormeley's bills of exchange, he demanded his £2,600. "These Protests," Corbin explained, "with the Bond debt and the Growing Interest upon the

    [2] Washington to George Mason, 5 April 1769, in *The Writings of George Washington*, ed. John Fitzpatrick (Washington, D.C., 1931, II, 502. See, Myra L. Rich, "Speculations on the Significance of Debt: Virginia, 1781-1789," *VMHB*, 76(1968), 301-17.
    [3] Cited in C. Malcolm Watkins, *The Cultural History of Marlborough, Virginia*, Smithsonian Institution (Washington, D.C., 1968), 50.

Whole, Amounts to a large Sum which together with the
Critical Situation of my affairs makes me very Uneasie." He
recognized that his demands represented a breach of local etiquette, but such considerations had to be set aside, since "a
prudent regard for the Welfare of my own Family and the
Support of my own Credit Obliges me to be very importunate
to secure the Effectual payment of these debts."[4]

Two years later, Corbin took an even harder line with
Wormeley. He stated that "it is necessary it [Wormeley's ac-
count] shou'd be Closed," even if that meant seizing the planter's current tobacco crop. Surely, Corbin suggested, the other
Virginian must understand that these were difficult times,
and if Wormeley wanted to be treated like a gentleman, then,
in financial matters at least, he had better conduct himself like
one. As Corbin declared, "I must endeavor to make the best
Collection I can & so far as the Demand now made on you,
I Confide in your Honor for the punctual performance of it."[5]

Corbin's correspondence with James Hunter, another respected Tidewater planter, further illuminates how a growing
dependence upon external credit disrupted relations between
social peers. In his letters, Corbin referred almost nostalgically to a familiar etiquette of debt. He rapidly shifted his
rhetorical ground, however, and in recognition of the sudden
irrelevance of these old forms, Corbin pressured Hunter to
pay off his large and longstanding debts. These conflicting
elements—a desire to observe tradition while preserving one's
credit—proved almost impossible to reconcile. In his dealings
with Hunter, Corbin adopted an apologetic, even defensive
tone. "I have never yet Pressed you but when I found myself
in danger," Corbin reminded Hunter in 1768. And in an effort to reduce tensions, Corbin promised to return to the old
ways of conducting business as soon as Virginia regained its
prosperity. Corbin explained, "as this danger lessens, I shall
be ready and willing to allow any Indulgence you can in reason ask . . . you may therefore be assured I shall not distress

[4] Corbin to Ralph Wormeley, June 1766, Richard Corbin Letter Book,
1758-1768, Colonial Williamsburg, Inc., Research Center, microfilm.
[5] Corbin to Wormeley, 14 October 1768, ibid.

you till I see a probability of being distressed myself."[6] Corbin did not deny that he had behaved in a manner that the other planter might find objectionable. Rather, he attempted to direct Hunter's anger toward those people in Great Britain who seemed responsible for changing the character of local friendship.

In September Corbin tightened the screws of credit even further. This time he sounded desperate. "The urgency of my Affairs constrains me to be importunate, & to apply to you once more in the Epistolary Way," he informed Hunter. But again, even in this moment of great personal crisis, Corbin noted that he had been compelled by external forces beyond his control to address Hunter "in Terms quite disagreeable to me; it really makes me uneasy; *A failure of Punctuality only once at Home*, is enough to blast . . . Credit, this is a ticklish Situation. . . ." And Corbin closed his letter with an ominous statement: "My Son John who will deliver you this, is desired to take a View of the Negroes enumerated in the Mortgage."[7] The diplomatic wording could scarcely disguise the fact that one great planter was contemplating the sale of another's estate, the wellspring of personal honor and independence in this society.

From other sources one learns that Corbin's dunning of Virginia debtors generated considerable resentment. In a long letter written to his son in January 1768, John Mercer recounted the unhappy tale of a neighbor who had overextended his credit by purchasing too many slaves. Though the man owned a large plantation, he did not possess enough cash to pay his bills. According to Mercer, Corbin offered to rescue the gentleman, to "retrieve his credit," but then, to everyone's disgust, Corbin seized the man's estate.[8] Mercer may have been mistaken about the details of this apparent betrayal of trust. That is not the point. It is of greater interest that

[6] Corbin to James Hunter, 26 February 1768, Richard Corbin, Loose Papers, Colonial Williamsburg, Inc., Research Center, microfilm.

[7] Corbin to James Hunter, 10 September 1768, Corbin Letter Book (emphasis added).

[8] Cited in Lois Mulkearn, ed., *George Mercer Papers* (Pittsburgh, 1954), 206.

Mercer chose to include this piece of news in a rambling, dispirited review of the state of Tidewater society. This Virginian regarded Corbin's predatory behavior as evidence of the decay of gentility. Contemporaries spotted other, even more troubling signs of dissension within the ranks of the Tidewater planters. Again, the source of friction was contraction of British credit. When the merchants squeezed the Virginians, the planters in turn often found themselves forced to choose between bankruptcy or suing a neighbor for an old debt. This was an extremely upsetting experience, and it is no wonder that the hard-nosed Corbin referred to such legal actions as "the last remedy."[9] It is not clear how these cases were resolved. As we have seen, planters traditionally settled disputes over debt out of court, but by the mid-1760s the fear of insolvency may have caused local creditors to take a tougher stand. Whatever may have occurred, contemporaries expressed alarm over the litigiousness. "Poor Virginia," John Baylor wailed in 1764, "what art thou reduced to, held in scorn & derision by the merchants of great Britain & torn to pieces by theirs & our country law suits."[10] William Allason, a resident factor, echoed Baylor's concern. "I believe there never was so many suits pending in this Country as is at this time," he declared in 1764. "Scarcely a prison is allowed to stand, in some Countys the People have agreed to defend one another against the officers. . . ."[11] News of a credit crisis, even rumors, spread panic among the planters, and as John Mercer reported in 1768, in their mad scramble to secure their own estates, "they brought & threatened to bring Suits, so that, to add to the misfortune, the debts will be increased many thousand pounds by Law charges."[12]

[9] Corbin to Edmund Jenings, 16 March 1759, Corbin Letter Book.

[10] Baylor to John Norton, 18 September 1764, in *John Norton and Sons*, ed. Francis N. Mason (Richmond, 1937), 11-12.

[11] Allason to Alexander Walker, 24 June 1764, in "The Letters of William Allason," ed. D. R. Anderson, *Richmond College Historical Papers*, 2(1917), 134.

[12] Cited in Mulkearn, ed., *George Mercer Papers*, 189-90. See, Emory Evans, "The Nelsons: A Biographical Study of a Virginia Family in the Eighteenth Century" (Ph.D. diss., University of Virginia, 1957), 134-36.

Even in such critical circumstances, the great planters had considerable difficulty reconciling a traditional code of debt with the demands of a volatile international economy. In 1765 Robert Beverley sued a planter named Dixon who lived in Spotsylvania County for what he called a "just Debt." Beverley seems to have felt uneasy about the entire proceeding, and when Dixon complained that he had been ill-treated—the case had been moved from Spotsylvania to York—Beverley wrote the man a long letter justifying his actions. "I confess I see not the Cruelty of my Behaviour in Suing you in York Court," Beverley protested. "I was told your own Court never did Business & that York was most expeditious." Moreover, as Beverley pointedly reminded Dixon, he found it extraordinarily distasteful to take a fellow planter before the local justices. Dixon, not Beverely, had forced the issue. "I should not have acted in the Manner I did," Beverley insisted, "had you not repeatedly told me you wou'd not pay me; I then found the Law my only Resource. . . . I had no Design of injuring your Credit, I was only Desirous of recovering those Debts that were due to me that I might in some Measure have it in my Power to discharge those that daily appear against my self." In other words, British creditors, outsiders who did not fully understand the customs of Virginia, had compelled Beverley to file suit against his will. He was not a businessman; he was still a Tidewater gentleman. "I am Sensible, Sir, as you can be," Beverley wrote, "that we *ought* to be as tender with Respect to each others Credit as Possible, nor shall any man act more cautiously in that Respect than myself."[13] The key word in this letter is "ought," for though Virginians like Beverley and Dixon instinctively knew how planters were supposed to behave, they nevertheless acted in ways that called their honor into question.

Other Tidewater gentlemen shared Beverley's uneasiness about the decay of traditional etiquette. They, too, detested having to sue a great planter for money. When in 1765 Lan-

[13] Beverley to Dixon, 26 March 1765, Beverley Letter Book, 1761-1793, Library of Congress, Washington, D.C. (emphasis added).

don Carter was serving as the executor for his brother's estate, he received a letter from William Churchill requesting £300. Churchill added nervously, "[I] hope you will not take it amiss if I should bring suit & assure your self that nothing but necessity should induce me to do such a thing."[14] And even John Syme, who as we have seen was perpetually in debt to British correspondents, could hardly bring himself to take a local debtor to court. In 1766 he reported to Farrell and Jones that he had been "Oblig'd to bring Suits for the Money Due me. I had no other Way to Raise the Needful [sum] but by Selling the Tobacco." Ironically, just a few lines later, Syme begged the Bristol merchants not to sue him, for "to be Sued is grevous to me."[15] This naively generous planter never quite understood why friends could not simply trust one another, thus preserving honor and independence and, above all, avoiding public exposure.

The changing economic environment—one that forced Virginians to sue other Virginians with increasing frequency— bore particularly heavily upon John Mercer. For over a quarter century, this planter-lawyer had ridden from courthouse to courthouse looking out for the interests of the great planters who were his clients. In 1765 advancing age and ill health caused Mercer to retire from his demanding practice, a move that proved financially disastrous, since Mercer lost a steady source of income at precisely the moment that British merchants began pressuring him to pay off his large debts. He reasoned that perhaps his former clients might assist him in this crisis, might show themselves to be true Virginia gentlemen, for as Mercer pointed out, he had never pressed them for the full amount they owed him for his legal services. Their response to his entreaties proved profoundly disappointing. As he explained, "I have attended the bar thirty-six years, through a perpetual hurry and uneasiness, and have been more truly a slave than any one I am, or ever was, mas-

[14] William Churchill to Landon Carter, 25 June 1765, Landon Carter Papers, Roll I, Virginia Historical Society, Richmond, Virginia.

[15] Syme to Farrell and Jones, 20 June 1766, U.S. Circuit Court, Virginia District, Ended Cases, 1797-98.

ter of; yet [I] have not been able, since the first day of last January, to command ten pounds, out of near ten thousand due me."[16]

In utter desperation Mercer ran an advertisement in the *Virginia Gazette* (25 December 1766) in which he publicly took his fellow planters to task for their failure to behave like gentlemen. "The great Number of Debts due to me for the last seven Years of my Practice," he announced, "and the Backwardness of my Clients . . . to make me Satisfaction, would of itself, if I had no other Reason, have obliged me to quit my Practice." He then inquired "whether any Person, who had so many outstanding Debts, was less importunate, or troublesome, to his Debtors. . . ." The question was rhetorical. Mercer had not dunned them, and now, facing bankruptcy, he declared himself reluctant to sue his old friends. "I could not approve the Method of Demand, by the Sheriff, too commonly in Practice, without Necessity," he stated. He begged his clients to help him avoid such unpleasantness. If they failed to honor their obligations, he had no other choice but "to bring Suits, immediately after next April General Court, against all persons indebted to me. . . ."[17] It was difficult for Mercer to suppress cynicism. In Virginia, it seemed, coercion had begun to replace honor; personal autonomy had spawned fiscal irresponsibility.

Some planters even raised the possibility of violence. To suggest that a Carter or Washington was prepared to shoot bill collectors would, of course, be absurd. But lesser, more desperate Virginians apparently contemplated using force to stave off bankruptcy. In 1764 William Allason, a tobacco factor, wrote home asking for "a pair of Pistols," small ones "for the convenience of carrying in a side Pockett." Allason had apparently learned from unhappy experience that, "As it is sometimes Dangerous in Traveling through our wooden Country Particularly at this time when the planters are pressed for old Ballances, we find it necessary to carry with

---

[16] Cited in Watkins, *Cultural History of Marlborough*, 55.
[17] Ibid., 57.

us some defensive Weapons."[18] And two years later, John Wayles, a careful observer of the local culture, informed his British employers, that "Col. N. W. Dandridge & Col. James Littlepage, if their debts are considerable should be look'd After in time, the first has been in Gaol this Summer & the Other go's Armed to protect himself from the Sheriff."[19] Although these were probably isolated cases, the sight of a tobacco planter carrying weapons or a factor arming himself must have disturbed Virginians already worried about the adverse effects of debt upon their society.

More distressing than talk of violence were the advertisements for lotteries that ran with increasing frequency in the *Virginia Gazette.* The great planters, many of them hopelessly in debt and pressed hard by British creditors, organized elaborate drawings in order to obtain even a fraction of their estate's paper value. Since no one in this specie-starved colony possessed enough money to purchase a large plantation outright, an indebted planter sold lottery tickets at generally affordable prices to scores of his neighbors. In 1768 Benjamin Johnson explained in an advertisement why he was promoting "A Scheme of a Lottery." "The reason of my selling on this method is (I assure the public) to pay my debts, and prevent imposition: and [to avoid] that too prevailing custom falling on me, which had on many in this colony, i.e. selling estates by execution at half value. I hope," Johnson, concluded, "it will meet with applause and encouragement."[20]

These contests involved many of the more prominent planters in Tidewater Virginia. Anyone reading the newspapers would have recognized their names. One typical lottery offered 145 tickets at £5 apiece. There were to be fourteen winners, lucky persons who would cart away the great planter's slaves and livestock, take possession of his land and buildings. A lottery for Thomas Moore made available 335 tickets at £20

[18] Allason to Bogle and Scott, 29 July 1764, in "The Letters of William Allason," ed. Anderson, 134-35.

[19] John Hemphill, "John Wayles Rates His Neighbors," *VMHB*, 66(1958), 306.

[20] *Virginia Gazette*, (Rind), 14 April 1768.

each. These affairs were managed by well-known gentlemen, in these examples by the likes of Edmund Pendleton, John Syme, Patrick Henry, R. C. Nicholas, and William Dandridge. The largest lottery of the period involved the magnificent holdings of William Byrd III, a planter who had squandered much of his inheritance at the gaming tables of Williamsburg. Prestley Thornton, Peyton Randolph, John Page, Charles Carter, and Charles Turnbull—all listed in the advertisements as "esquires"—were selected by Byrd to oversee a drawing of 839 winners out of 10,000 tickets, each selling for £5. The grand prize consisted of a forge, mill, and land valued at £8,000.[21]

Despite the enthusiastic newspapers promotions, the lotteries were dismal affairs for the great Tidewater planters. They seldom generated the anticipated revenue. People purchased tickets on credit and then never paid for them. Byrd was forced to appeal for his money in the pages of the *Virginia Gazette*: "I disposed of a fine estate in order to settle my affairs and do justice to every body I had dealings with, but to my very great disappointment, I have not received a third part of the money the tickets sold for."[22] But even if they had been successful, these contrivances for retrieving credit demeaned the gentry. The lotteries exposed their private problems to a curious public. Indeed, for them, they were rituals of humiliation, painful confessions that they were no longer quite the men that they had claimed to be. The drawings tarnished their honor. No wonder that after witnessing the sale of Ralph Wormeley's property in 1766, William Nelson wrote somberly, "These are but Preludes to Vast changes of property among us that must soon take place."[23]

Lotteries served as grim reminders that the world of the Tidewater planters was coming undone, or so it must have seemed. By the late 1760s, credit crises had begun to cast into doubt the very legitimacy of traditional symbols of stability,

[21] See, for example, ibid., 3 October 1767.
[22] Ibid., 26 July 1770.
[23] Nelson to Edward and Samuel Athawes, 13 November 1766, Nelson Letter Book, Colonial Williamsburg, Inc., Research Center, microfilm.

the grand mansions, the sprawling plantations, the handsome coaches. After all, the culture of the great planters depended upon the maintenance of appearance. That is what Caledoniensis meant when he observed that "Language is one of the principle supports of society." If a Virginia gentleman seemed wealthy, then in this materialistic society, he could claim high status. And by displaying the outward trappings of success, he persuaded other Virginians—rich as well as poor—that he was honorable, a person of independent judgment, worthy of credit. External appearances, in fact, provided the currency of social exchange. But then, rather suddenly, for some gentlemen the house of cards came tumbling down. From advertisements of lotteries, from reports of bankruptcy sales, Virginia planters learned that other planters were not what they had seemed or claimed, and as one mordant commentator observed, in this uncertain environment there was "no knowing who to trust."[24]

Even an irascible Anglican minister played upon the theme of social appearance and reality. John Camm, a clergyman who also held a professorship at the College of William and Mary, entered into a pamphlet war with the redoubtable Landon Carter, and in a piece delightfully entitled *A Review of the Rector Detected*, Camm responded to his adversary. Carter had claimed in an earlier publication that one could not tell simply by viewing a planter's outward estate whether he was wealthy or not. "According to the Colonel," the minister wrote, "we cannot know whether the Mr. *Nelson*, Mr. *Page*, and Mr. *Nicholas*, &c. Gentlemen of the first fortune in the Country, be rich or poor, for who knows what Mortgages, Drawbacks, and the like, may have eaten out their Estates?" Camm assumed that Carter's statement was a fatuous excuse for not paying the colony's Anglican ministers a decent wage, and in mock horror, he exclaimed, "This is bad News for the Merchants, and a terrible Blow to the Credit of the Country; for how will the Merchants be able to carry on Trade upon long

[24] 29 January 1765, Corbin Letter Book. See, David Mays, *Edmund Pendleton* (Cambridge, Mass., 1952), I, 144-45.

Credit, if it be impossible for them to know who is rich or who poor by the Possession of large visible Estates. . . ."[25] How indeed! Camm merely demonstrated his ignorance of the private finances of many great planters whom he encountered in Williamsburg. These well-dressed men in their grand carriages may have fooled the clergyman into believing they were rich, but, as a wise old planter like Carter understood, only the sufferance of their creditors allowed many Tidewater gentlemen to maintain "large visible Estates."

The illusion could be smashed in an instant. A great planter's sudden or unexpected fall frequently exposed the lie behind the appearance of prosperity. Such was the case in 1767 when a fire swept through Colonel Tucker's plantation, destroying buildings he had recently put up as security against huge loans. The disaster left him bankrupt; it also may have driven him mad. No one—not even close associates—had known that Tucker's finances were in such desperate shape, and when William Nelson heard what had happened, he could hardly believe the news. "I assure you," he wrote to his British correspondents, "that few things have surprised me so much as the first Information of Colonel Tucker's Affairs being wrong." The gentleman had seemed a perfect model of diligence. "His Assiduity & indefatigable Application to Business which went on with *seeming* success gave me an opinion that he was very rich," and as Nelson confessed, he had secretly chastised himself for not working as hard as Tucker. Nelson concluded that there was a moral here, one for all Virginians: "Fides, We are often deceived by *Appearances*."[26] Of course, the greatest shock of the decade was the discovery that the colony's overly generous treasurer, John Robinson, had supported his apparently well-to-do gentry friends out of public funds and had himself died insolvent.[27]

In 1774 Landon Carter recorded a similar awakening. "I

[25] John Camm, *A Review of the Rector Detected* (Williamsburg, 1764), 9. Also, Landon Carter, *The Rector Detected* (Williamsburg, 1764).

[26] Nelson to Edward Hunt and Son, 29 May 1767, Nelson Letter Book (emphasis added).

[27] See, Chapter III.

was surprised this day," he noted in his diary, "to hear that in the Philadelphia *Gazette* the whole of R[alph] W[ormeley's] estate on Chenandoah [sic], Slaves and all, were to be sold. I say I was surprised because there has been a prodigeous boast of great Profits made there, and not long ago I heard a Gentleman declare his [estate] was then clear of debt. There is nothing like our modes of deceiving ourselves and the world."[28] The great majority of the Tidewater gentry did not share Wormeley's unhappy fate. They muddled through. But that fact did not diminish the impact of tales of catastrophic failure on the survivors. After all, the Tuckers and Wormeleys had struggled to keep up accepted social forms, living far beyond their incomes, and public reports of their ignominious collapse sounded to some contemporaries like an obituary for a foundering culture.

How much the disgrace of a few old Tidewater families affected the way white Virginians perceived the gentry as a whole is difficult to measure. It was a topic that made the great planters edgy, and some of them seemed anxious to distance themselves from individuals whose flagrant extravagance had carried them to the brink of bankruptcy. Not a few Virginians recognized that a group that could not hold onto its property could not long maintain political dominance. In November 1766, for example, the *Virginia Gazette* published a curious piece of social commentary. The author, a talented writer identified only as "R.R.," sensed that less affluent planters were no longer willing automatically to defer to their alleged betters, and with obvious irony, he reported, "I am told that subordination is proper and necessary in all societies, and I am sure nothing entitles a man to superiority so much as family and fortune. Therefore, as some men who are inferiors in fortune have undertaken to judge and blame their superiors in this respect, I think that every great man must be affected with indignation, and endeavour to suppress this

---

[28] *The Diary of Colonel Landon Carter*, ed. Jack P. Greene, Virginia Historical Documents, vol. 4 (Charlottesville, 1965), II, 805.

growing evil."²⁹ But grow it did. Deference could not be taken for granted. The gentry of Richmond County learned this unpleasant lesson in 1771 when they opened the local court of law. The Richmond gentlemen—a group that included Landon Carter—discovered "an Insult of the most Extravagant Nature having been Maliciously offered upon the Bench in which the Justices set to hold Court by daub'g it with Tar and Dung in many places."³⁰

Perhaps one should not make too much of such incidents. The small planters, whatever they may have thought, did not usually insult the colony's leading gentlemen. To persons of Carter's temperament, however, to men already worried that the ruling elite might be losing its hold, slipping into debt and thereby compromising its independence, even minor slights could seem very threatening. Moreover, these chal-

---

²⁹ *Virginia Gazette* (Purdie & Dixon), 6 November 1766; also, 18 July 1766; 12 September 1766; 10 October 1766. The murder during a drunken fight of Robert Routledge, a local merchant, sparked an outburst of angry rhetoric questioning the traditional role of the gentry in Virginia society. The murderer, a nearly bankrupt planter named John Chiswell, was arrested but quickly released on bail by three magistrates who happened to be Chiswell's friends and business associates. "Dikephilos" declared in the *Virginia Gazette* that "Most people at present are really extremely uneasy, on various accounts. They say that one atrocious murderer has already been cleared, by means of great friends; and they are apprehensive that will not be the last opprobrious stain of this kind on our colony." The author appealed to "Gentlemen of proper genius, knowledge, and leisure" to find out what really had happened. Had three leading magistrates abused their powers? "People in general say," the anonymous writer reported, "that every true American justly detested the late intolerable Stamp Act; and that many Gentlemen, who had sufficient confidence in our power, declared they would risk their lives and fortunes to keep off such oppression, and rescue their liberty and property. But now they apprehend that this partiality may be attended with still more dreadful consequences than even that detestable act of power could have been, because this must affect our lives, while that could only affect our estates." *Virginia Gazette*, 18 July 1766. The Chiswell story is fully recounted by Carl Bridenbaugh, "Violence and Virtue in Virginia, 1766; or, The Importance of the Trivial," *Proceedings*, Massachusetts Historical Society, 66(1964), 3-29.

³⁰ Cited in A. G. Roeber, *Faithful Magistrates and Republican Lawyers* (Chapel Hill, N.C., 1981), 112.

lenges suggested the possibility of a radical, new perception of society that few Tidewater planters in the 1760s were willing to entertain. If wealth in itself no longer commanded deference—indeed, if the small planters could no longer be certain that a particular gentleman was really wealthy—then the community would have to be sorted out according to different rules. The gentry would have to demonstrate that it deserved the small planters' respect. As Washington counselled, "it is Works and not Words that People will judge from, and where one Man deceives another from time to time his word being disregarded all confidence is lost."[31]

II

During the 1760s—an exact date is impossible to establish—the great Tidewater planters also began to discuss tobacco in ways that they had not done before. Their comments betrayed doubts about the future of their staple and, by extension, about a set of symbols associated with tobacco. "I am afraid," Robert Beverley declared darkly in 1764, "we shall not gain much Advantage by the Cultivation of Tobacco."[32] He exaggerated, but a growing number of Virginians shared his anxiety. Arthur Lee, a colonist who had gained a broader perspective on the planter's problems from his experiences in England and Scotland, advised his brother Richard Henry: "Tobacco, your present staple, seems to be [a] very precarious commodity."[33]

As Lee's comment suggests, a major source of the Virginians' uneasiness was the low price that they received for their tobacco. To be sure, the market generally rose and fell; good times followed bad. But suddenly in the early 1760s none of the major consignment planters seemed to be doing very well. Gentlemen who prided themselves on having mastered the cultivation of tobacco found themselves heavily in debt. The

[31] *Writings of George Washington*, ed. Fitzpatrick, II, 476.

[32] Beverley to William Hunter, 5 March 1764, Beverley Letter Book.

[33] Arthur Lee to [Richard Henry Lee], 1763, *Lee Family Papers, 1742-1795*, ed. Paul P. Hoffman, 8 reels (Charlottesville, 1966), reel 1.

agricultural skills they had acquired over a lifetime, the ability to judge the precise moment when to cut or prize—these attributes were incapable of restoring the expansive prosperity of early eighteenth-century planters such as Thomas Lee and Robert ("King") Carter. "For my part," George Braxton grumbled in 1756, "I get such small prizes [prices?] for my Tobacco that I would make a Tryal of any commodity rather than wear my Negroes out in making and cultivating a worthless weed."[34]

For men like Beverley and Braxton whose perceptions of the world around them were in large part a function of the tobacco mentality, the sorry state of the colony's agriculture created genuine despair. Not all gentlemen, of course, were quite so despondent, but those who labored under a pile of debt sometimes expressed their frustration in hyperbolic language. From their exaggerated perspective, their culture seemed to have been turned on its head by forces beyond their control. Instead of reinforcing personal autonomy, tobacco generated chronic dependence upon distant merchants. They began to feel trapped. In 1766 an anonymous Virginian declared with cool matter-of-factness, "That this colony is in a declining State, or, I may rather say on the Brink of Destruction, I fear is too evident to the most superficial Observer, to need any arguments to prove."[35] The writer referred not to a specific act of Parliament but to a crisis of confidence that swept through the tobacco culture. The same fatalism echoed in Landon Carter's diary. In 1770 when grasshoppers attacked his tobacco, he observed, "We must submit to all such destruction and do as well as we can, but I believe it will be difficult under such a staple to make a tollerable subsistence. It might be wrong to call them judgments and as these things are by the permission of the great Creator we ought to hope for his mercy."[36]

[34] Cited in Frederick Horner, *The History of the Blair, Banister, and Braxton Families Before and After the Revolution* (Philadelphia, 1898), 141. See also, *Plantation and Frontier Documents*, ed. Ulrich B. Phillips, (Cleveland, 1909), I, 83.

[35] *Virginia Gazette* (Rind), 11 December 1766.

[36] *Diary of Landon Carter*, ed. Greene, I, 435.

Though Virginians who spoke in such despondent terms had difficulty pinpointing the exact source of their society's ills, many suspected that it was somehow related to the cultivation of tobacco. Modern scholars find this a curious conclusion. The total amount of tobacco exported from Virginia was increasing during this period. Nevertheless, even Tidewater gentlemen who may have seen these export figures concluded that something was wrong in the fields. Landon Carter, for example, argued that changes in the colony's climate made it almost impossible for men like himself to produce outstanding tobacco. An unusually cold growing season in 1764 brought to mind a pediction he had heard as a youth, "that Virginia would in time cease to be a tobacco Colony." Six years later Carter still blamed a general cooling trend for the depressed state of the economy. "I cannot help observing," he jotted in his diary, "as I have before done that this climate is so changing [that] unless it return to his [its?] former state Virginia will be no Tobacco Colony soon." Carter worried about the implications of his analysis. What if he were correct? "What then," he asked plaintively, "can we tend?"[37] How could one be a crop master without a crop?

The rational solution—at least in terms of modern economics—was for planters like Carter to drop tobacco. In parts of Maryland people had already made that decision, and apparently some Virginians were prepared to follow their lead.[38] "We also hear," announced the *Georgia Gazette* in 1765, "that the inhabitants of the colony [Virginia] intend to give over the culture of tobacco, as it greatly impoverishes their land, and to introduce a species of agriculture that will be a more general utility, and better adapted to the good of their soil."[39] George Mason could easily have supported this plan. In fact, he advocated a complete break with Virginia's traditional sta-

[37] Ibid., I, 280, 433; II, 635.

[38] Lewis Cecil Gray, *History of Agriculture in the Southern United States to 1860* (New York, 1941), I, 167-68; II, 606-608. Paul G. E. Clemens, *The Atlantic Economy and Colonial Maryland's Eastern Shore: From Tobacco to Grain* (Ithaca, N.Y., 1980).

[39] Cited in Louis Morton, *Robert Carter of Nomini Hall: A Virginia Tobacco Planter of the Eighteenth Century* (Williamsburg, 1941), 143.

ple, and in a letter published in 1769, he challenged "the principal Gentlemen . . . [to] set the Example, that will be quickly followed by the Bulk of the People." Mason knew what had to be done. "If we were to desist purchasing Slaves, and making Tobacco," he calculated, "we shou'd have a Number of Spare Hands to employ in Manufactures, and other Improvements; every private Family wou'd soon be able to make whatever they wanted, for their own Use."[40] All one had to do was accept the necessity of agricultural change.

Few consignment planters of the Tidewater welcomed such advice. They felt as if they were being pulled in different directions. On the one hand, they were deeply troubled by the fragility of the tobacco economy. They hated debt. On the other hand, even when confronted with large deficits or disappointing crops, they found it difficult to desert a known, albeit frustrating, staple for an unfamiliar substitute. Such changes came slowly; they were upsetting. William Tatham understood the continuing hold the tobacco mentality had upon these planters, and while he wished the innovators well, he knew they faced deep-seated cultural resistance. "I have hopes," he explained, "that the obstinacy of habitual practice, and the trodden paths of our ancestors, will prove no obstacle to those experiments, and comparisons, which may be helpful to agricultural knowledge, especially in Virginia . . . if men would but trust themselves a little way beyond the *leading-strings of their forefathers.*"[41]

Early efforts to effect agricultural change in this region were halting, tentative, and unenthusiastic. In the years following the French and Indian War (1758-1759), a few Virginia planters attempted to liberate themselves from tobacco. These trials, however, were conducted with a notable lack of zeal, and when Andrew Burnaby travelled through the colony in 1760, he found most planters cultivating tobacco in exactly the same ways that their fathers and grandfathers had done.

[40] The letter of "Atticus," 11 May 1769, *The Papers of George Mason, 1725-1792* ed. Robert A. Rutland (Chapel Hill, N.C., 1970), I, 108.

[41] William Tatham, *Historical and Practical Essay on the Culture and Commerce of Tobacco,* ed. G. Herndon (Coral Gables, Fla., 1969), 112 (emphasis added).

"Some few," Burnaby admitted, ". . . have been rather more enterprising, and have endeavoured to improve their estates by raising indigo, and other schemes: but whether it has been owing to the climate, to their inexperience in these matters, or their want of perseverance, I am unable to determine but their success has not answered their expectations."[42] If the visitor had bothered to ask John Baylor, a well-known Tide-water planter, Burnaby might have gained greater insight into the failure of indigo. Baylor tried the new crop and disliked it. Indigo was difficult and unprofitable, and as soon as the tobacco market revived even slightly, Baylor announced excitedly that he had returned to "my favourite employment Tobo."[43]

Hemp fared little better. When Col. Adam Gordon toured Virginia in the early 1760s, he was persuaded that the planters would soon give up tobacco. "From the high Duty on that Commodity," the English military officer reported, "its value is fallen, and many people are going upon Hemp, which it is hoped may succeed, if the Bounty is continued."[44] It is not certain to whom Gordon had spoken. Perhaps the men who had time to chat with strangers in Williamsburg overestimated the planters' willingness to produce hemp. Francis Fauquier, Virginia's royal governor, knew better. In 1763 he informed the Commissioners for Trade and Plantation Affairs that "the inhabitants seemed contented with their Staple Tobacco, and cannot as yet be brought to cultivate those articles for which the Society for the Encouragement of Arts and Manufactures in London offer so large Preminums."[45] Virginians working on isolated plantations clung to the cultivation

---

[42] Andrew Burnaby, *Travels through the Middle Settlements in North America*, in *A General Collection*, ed. John Pinkerton (London, 1812), XIII, 717.

[43] *John Norton and Sons*, ed. Mason, 10.

[44] Colonel Adam Gordon, "Journal of an Officer who Travelled in America . . . 1764 and 1765," in *Travels in the American Colonies*, ed. Newton D. Mereness (New York, 1916), 404.

[45] Francis Fauquier, "Answers to the Queries Sent to Me by the Right Honourable the Lords Commissioners for Trade and Plantation Affairs," 30 January 1763, C.O., P.R.O., 5/1330.

of tobacco, hoping, as farmers often do, that chance factors would dramatically raise the price they received for their crops. One good year and no one would have to fiddle with hemp or indigo.[46]

But for many great planters of Tidewater Virginia, the good times never returned, or if they did, only for a season or two. When confronted with record debts—and sometimes only then—the various great planters began sowing wheat where once they had grown tobacco.[47] By 1774 a Fredericksburg merchant, Charles Yates, stated confidently that the planters were determined "to drop planting & turn their Lands to Farming as wheat yields more profit."[48] Though Yates stretched the truth, others noted the transformation that seemed to be taking place.[49] Robert Beverley expressed

[46] Roger Atkinson to Lyonel and Samuel Lynde 25 August 1772, *VMHB*, 15(1907-1908), 354; Robert Beverley to John Bland, 1764, Beverley Letter Book.

[47] About this difficult and continuing transition, the historian Richard B. Sheridan writes, "Tidewater planters, who were burdened with debts that were often passed down from father to son, were compelled to change their agricultural system and to discover new staples that were adapted to worn-out soils. The transition which had been underway since midcentury was painful, even though some planters found a partial solution by growing wheat, settling new plantations in the backcountry, or engaging in manufacturing enterprises." "The British Credit Crisis of 1772 and the American Colonies," *Journal of Economic History*, 22(1960), 184; Paul G. E. Clemens, "The Operation of an Eighteenth-Century Chesapeake Tobacco Plantation," *Agricultural History*, 49(1975), 517-31; Edward C. Papenfuse, Jr., "Planter Behavior and Economic Opportunity in a Staple Economy," ibid., 46(1972), 297-312. See also U. B. Phillips, *Life and Labor in the Old South* (Boston, 1941), 50-51, 98-99; C. Geertz, *Agricultural Involution* (Berkeley, 1963); and L. A. Loubère, *The Red and The White* (Albany, N.Y., 1978).

[48] Cited in Harold B. Gill, "Wheat Culture in Colonial Virginia," *Agricultural History*, 52(1978), 382.

[49] The colony's overall level of tobacco production did not drop in the years immediately preceding the Revolution. Much of the tobacco came, however, from the newly developed lands west of the Tidewater. As Roger Atkinson, a resident merchant, recounted in 1769, "20 years ago . . . the Quantity [of tobacco] was trifling compared with what it is now, for I remember when we took only 500 Hogsheads at these Warehouses, whereas now in a good year the Quantity is 10,000. . . . Now the Quantity here owing to the backland's settlements is amazingly encreased." *VMHB*, 15(1907), 346.

No specific data on the amount of acreage in the Tidewater devoted to

amazement in 1769 at "the great Quantities of our most valuable Lands being so generally employed into the cultivation
of Wheat."[50] One after another, planters of the region com-
mitted themselves more fully to cereal production. In 1767
George Washington stopped planting tobacco altogether and
within a short time had discovered a lucrative local market for
his wheat.[51] His neighbor Robert Carter began switching to
grain in the early 1760s, but for many years—perhaps as a
matter of self-image—he continued to make a few hogsheads
of tobacco. But even that token enterprise ceased in 1774.
Carter informed William Taylor, his agent in Westmoreland

wheat and tobacco are available. We do know, however, that by the 1770s
wheat had clearly become Virginia's second staple. The problem of gathering
more precise statistics is compounded (1) because much wheat produced in
Virginia was consumed there and consequently does not appear on the export
records and (2) because exported wheat went to scattered New World markets (including a growing coastal and overland trade with other American
colonies) and was therefore less well recorded than was the tobacco shipped
almost entirely to British ports. Moreover, the shift from tobacco to wheat
took place at different times and at different rates throughout the Chesapeake
region. Maryland's Eastern Shore clearly led the way. David C. Klingaman
estimates that by the 1760s the grain exports were the "dynamic element" in
the Virginia economy, and the evidence points to an accelerating transition
from tobacco to cereals in the Tidewater area. As Carville Earle and Ronald
Hoffman explain, this change in agricultural production had a significant
impact on urbanization in the Chesapeake colonies. See, Gill, "Wheat Culture in Colonial Virginia," 380-93; Clemens, "Chesapeake Tobacco Plantation," 517-31; Carville Earle and Ronald Hoffman, "Staple Crops and Urban
Development in the Eighteenth-Century South," *Perspectives in American History*, 10(1976), 7-76; David C. Klingaman, *Colonial Virginia's Coastwise and
Grain Trade* (New York, 1975), 98-125; Clemens, *Atlantic Economy and Colonial
Maryland's Eastern Shore*, 111-223; and Allan Kulikoff, "The Economic
Growth of the Eighteenth-Century Colonies," *Journal of Economic History*,
39(1979), 286-88.

[50] Beverley to Samuel Athawes, 6 September 1769, Beverley Letter Book.
While he was travelling through Virginia in April 1773, Josiah Quincy, Jr.,
observed, "The Culture of corn and wheat is supplanting very fast that of
tobacco in this province," "Journal of Josiah Quincy, 1773," *Proceedings*, Massachusetts Historical Society, 49(1915-16), 467. Also, W. A. Low, "The
Farmer in Post-Revolutionary Virginia, 1783-1789," *Agricultural History*, 25
(1951), 122-27.

[51] Douglas S. Freeman, *George Washington: A Biography* (New York, 1951),
III, 179.

and Richmond counties, that tobacco "for several years last passed, yeald no profit to me, but on the contrary, other funds have been applied to support them [tobacco plantations], and to persevere in growing tobacco at those places I apprehend would be a mark of folly and not discretion."[52] Even Edmund Pendleton, a brilliant lawyer of conservative temperament, gave up tobacco at this time. The cultivation of grain presented Pendleton with unanticipated difficulties, and in 1778 he managed to harvest only "Crops of weavel eaten wheat." Fleetingly, he contemplated returning to Virginia's traditional staple, but by that time, as he recognized, it was "perhaps too late."[53]

No doubt, the conversion from one crop to another was neither as sudden nor as dramatic as these examples suggest. Indeed, the great Tidewater planters, especially those of the Northern Neck, had grown wheat for several generations. The problem, as far as they were concerned, was emphasis rather than change. However many acres were actually involved, a shift called into question the planters' self-perception. It was an indication, along with disquieting political and social trends, that the very foundation of the tobacco mentality might be in jeopardy. A familiar symbol system associated with tobacco and kings seemed to be crumbling around them, and in this unsettling atmosphere the colony's leading gentlemen may have been unusually receptive to new ideas about agriculture and government, religion and slavery, all expressions of a traditional culture.

III

In these difficult times, when much of their daily experience seemed discordant with the imperatives of the tobacco men-

[52] Cited in Morton, *Robert Carter*, 262. See esp., 118-48.
[53] Cited in David John Mays, *Edmund Pendleton, A Biography, 1721-1803* (Cambridge, Mass., 1952), I, 117. Some great planters of eastern Virginia migrated west into the Piedmont region and the Shenandoah Valley during this period and there continued to cultivate tobacco. See, Robert D. Mitchell,

tality and their place in a familiar social order appeared inse-
cure, various great planters looked for an escape, a means of
revitalizing a culture that had lost its bearings. Though Tidewater gentlemen fantasized during the 1760s about a new beginning, they did not provide a common or even typical for-
mula for reformation. What unified these responses—
although the planters were not yet aware of it—was a commitment to cultural renewal. John Mercer, an old man nearly
driven to distraction by the accumulating weight of debt, told
his son in 1768 that he would welcome death were he not
responsible for the welfare of his wife and children. His family situation forced him to take a more constructive view of
the future. "I shall look upon myself as commencing *a new
Era*," he declared bravely, "& begin it by settling all my accounts & getting out of debt, as soon as possible." Mercer,
like so many other struggling planters of his generation, was
willing to sacrifice the superficial trappings of gentry status in
order to regain personal honor and independence. "If [it is] to
be done no other way [than] by selling as much of my estate
as will do it," Mercer stood ready, "for I yet have more than
enough to do all the world justice. When that is done and I
can say what I have is my own (however little that may be) I
shall then & not till then, think myself happy."[54] Another
planter expressed the hope in 1764 that "Virginia may again
see the Halcyon days she knew 20 Years ago, when they lived
in peace & pleanty, & feared a Debt in England as the worst
of calamitys."[55]

The West held special attraction for gentlemen who were
down on their luck and yet eager to commence the "new Era."
The open, fresh lands beyond the Tidewater seemed an ideal
location to start again, to clear the slate of old obligations, and

"Agricultural Change and the American Revolution: A Virginia Case Study,"
Agricultural History, 47(1973), 130-32; Joseph Clarke Robert, *The Tobacco
Kingdom: Plantation, Market, and Factory in Virginia and North Carolina, 1800-
1860* (Durham, N.C., 1938), 3-53.

[54] Mulkearn, ed., *George Mercer Papers*, 202-203 (emphasis added).

[55] "Jerman Baker to Duncan Rose," 15 February 1764, *W&MQ*, 1st ser.,
12(1904-1905), 242.

perhaps even to produce a quality leaf again. No doubt they were nostalgic for a time before the French and Indian War when their fathers had patented huge tracts of land. There had been an undeniable boldness about the real estate transactions of men like Thomas Lee, William Byrd II, and Alexander Spotswood. No Virginian entertained this vision of renewal more enthusiastically than did George Washington. Indeed, when advising his shiftless friend Captain Posey, the master of Mount Vernon sounded almost like Horace Greeley. Go West, the great planter counselled, for there is always "an opening prospect in the back Country for Adventurers, where numbers resort to, and where an enterprising Man with very little Money may lay the foundation for a Noble Estate in the New Settlements . . . for himself and posterity." Would not relocating be preferable, he asked Posey, to staggering under "a load of debt" which "must inevitably keep you in continual Anxiety, and dread of your Creditors"?

The answer was self-evident. "Pluck up resolution at once and disengage yourself of these Incumbrances and Vexations," Washington urged, ". . . remove back, where there is a moral certainty of laying the foundation of good Estates to your Children." Posey need not fear he would be alone on the frontier. "You may perceive by the number of Estates which are continually advertised for Sale that you are not the only one under Misfortune and that many good families are retiring into the Interior parts of the Country for the benefit of their Children."[56] The land to the west provided men like Posey an opportunity not only of retrieving their credit, but also—and much more significant—of restoring virtue to a generation of Virginians yet unborn. Here was the old mentality

[56] Washington to Capt. John Posey, 24 June 1767, in *Writings of George Washington*, ed. Fitzpatrick, II, 456-60. In a letter written to Samuel Athawes on 5 January 1773 declaring his intention "to put myself in a state of Independence," Robert Beverley also explained, "I assure you I think seriously of taking Advantage of procuring Lands upon the first Establishment of this new Colony on our Frontier, for I sincerely imagine 20 years hence our sons would think a Tract of suitable Land on the Waters of the Ohio no Contemptible Possession." Beverley Letter Book.

projected onto a new landscape. Solvency would nurture personal autonomy; personal autonomy would assure integrity.

Other sources of cultural regeneration gradually became apparent. Some Virginians, for example, celebrated wheat as a vehicle of personal liberation. The crop was not new, the perception was. For troubled planters cereal production seemed to provide a possibility of severing ties with British tobacco merchants, of escaping from the burden of debt, of reestablishing independence not only for the planters but also for the entire society. Wheat could be sold to other Americans, to Caribbean sugar planters, to Philadelphia merchants. Its cultivation promised to free Virginians from dependence upon English correspondents. In 1772 Roger Atkinson, a local trader, excitedly informed a business associate: "Sir, it is with great Pleasure I acq't you that we have now got another staple of late years, as it were created, viz: Wheat, w'ch will I believe in a little time be equal if not superior to Tob'o—is more certain & of w'ch we shall in a few years make more in Virg'ia than all the Province of Pennsylvania put together, altho' it is their staple commodity."[57] William Allason wrote in less breathless prose, but he well understood the implications of wheat culture for Tidewater society. He was pleased to hear of an unexpectdly large grain harvest in 1774, "and this is the more fortunate as most [planters] had gone more on it [wheat] than heretofore, their dependence on Tobacco being much lessened."[58] Wheat could renew a man's sense of self-confidence. It seems to have done so for Henry Fitzhugh. "I shall not I hope," he declared to a British merchant house to whom he was heavily indebted, "have occasion to draw on you so much for [credit] as I have now got into a way of making large Crops of Wheat at my Back quarters."[59]

For people like Fitzhugh an extraordinary period of cultural redefinition had begun, one which would continue through

[57] Atkinson to Lyonel and Samuel Lynde, 25 August 1772, *VMHB*, 15 (1908), 352.

[58] "The Letters of William Allason," ed. Anderson, 154.

[59] Fitzhugh to Steuart and Campbell, 20 October 1768, Henry Fitzhugh Papers, Manuscript Division, Duke University, Durham, North Carolina.

the postrevolutionary era. Even the language of agriculture changed. Virginians who cultivated wheat no longer called themselves *planters*; grain transformed them into *farmers*. New crops generated new symbols. N. F. Cabell, a man who in the early nineteenth century wrote a short "History of Agriculture in Virginia," described with considerable perspicacity how the movement from tobacco to wheat affected individual Virginians. "Many planters," Cabell declared, "first lessened their crops of tobacco and then abandoned it altogether. Planters thus became farmers, and as such entered on a general course of improvement, but suffered much during the period of transition."[60]

About the character of the planters' suffering, little is known. No doubt some individuals found adjusting to the demands of a new crop difficult. In 1769 Richard Corbin, a leading figure in the royal government of Virginia, complained that "the old beaten path [,] Industry in the Planter's Way, will not suit the present Modern improvement in Husbandry."[61] Corbin was a gentleman who had formerly derived considerable satisfaction from producing a high-grade leaf, but he could not accommodate himself to the changes—political and agricultural—that were now transforming the tobacco culture. Like Wormeley and Beverley, he could not support the Revolution.

IV

As alluring as the West and wheat may have been, most great planters sensed that the revitalization of their culture had to be generated from within themselves. After all, they had succumbed to luxury, and however much one might rail against the merchants for tempting the Virginians with easy credit, one had to admit that the gentry fully cooperated in its own seduction. Renewal required an act of will, a conscious dedi-

[60] N. F. Cabell, "Some Fragments of an Intended Report," *W&MQ*, 1st ser., 26(1918), 155. See also, Gill, "Wheat Culture in Colonial Virginia," 382.
[61] Corbin to Hannah Philippa (Ludwell) Lee, 10 June 1769, Lee Family Papers, Mss. L51, f. 527, Virginia Historical Society, Richmond, Virginia.

cation to the simple life, for only by terminating extravagance could the Tidewater gentlemen truly liberate themselves from dependence upon outsiders. If some of the planters on the eve of the American Revolution sound surprisingly like New England Puritans, it was because they had become convinced that only a radical reformation of personal habits could save them.[62] It was difficult, of course, in this society for any individual to take the lead. Each planter was under tremendous pressure to keep up appearances, if not to impress other Virginians, then to preserve his credit in Great Britain.[63]

So long as men held back, they denied themselves the possibility of transforming individual anger and distress over debt into a powerful vehicle for cultural renewal. Some planters looked to the House of Burgesses to encourage an outpouring of classical virtue. Certainly, as William Nelson declared in reference to a paper currency scheme, the assembly could be expected to review each act from this moral perspective. "I have observed," he wrote, "that when We have a large Quantity of Money in Circulation & it is easily obtained, it serves only to promote & cherish that spirit of Extravagance which hath been our Ruin: No, I think the man that could introduce & establish a new spirit of Frugality, which alone can save us, would deserve more Thanks from us than if he were to make us a present of £200,000."[64]

Nelson himself might have taken the lead in reform. In his own modest way, he provided struggling Tidewater gentlemen with a model of personal behavior. He managed successfully to blend frugality and gentility. As Nelson had demonstrated, in fact, virtue presented the great planters with a means to preserve the traditional tobacco culture. In his funeral sermon for this man, John Camm pointed to Nelson as

[62] See, Edmund S. Morgan, "The Puritan Ethic and the American Revolution," *W&MQ*, 3rd ser., 24(1967), 3-43.

[63] This interpretation was suggested to me by John Brewer's masterful essay "Commercialization and Politics," in N. McKendrick et al., *Birth of a Consumer Society* (Bloomington, Ind., 1982), 212-15.

[64] Nelson to Capel and Osgood Hanbury, 27 February 1768, Nelson Letter Book, Colonial Williamsburg, Inc., Research Center, microfilm.

"an instance, I wish he could not be reckoned a rare instance, of what abundance of good may be done by a prudent and conscientious man without impoverishing himself or his connections, nay while his fortunes are improving." The new era for Virginia's ruling elite simply required self-restraint. "Alas!" Camm exclaimed, "generally speaking, they are not our virtues, but our vices, or, to say [the] least, our follies, which are so costly and expensive as to devour our estates, and exhaust the fountain from which they derive their nourishment . . . this great man had, no doubt, his passions to contend with, as well as other men; but few, I think, have been able, by the help of reason and revelation, to keep them under better regulation."[65] Unfortunately, the majority of Nelson's social peers were weak, and despite his personal example, they continued to live on credit.

Patrick Henry also advocated moral reform. Like Nelson, he concluded that unless the planters practiced frugality and simplicity, they would lose their personal autonomy and in the process expose Virginia to a flood of corruption. Henry seldom supported his arguments with formal references to classical thinkers or English philosophers. Indeed, he may not have researched his positions at all. He spoke like an evangelical preacher, his explosive rhetoric cascading over his listeners until all but the most resistant had been swept away. His performances incorporated general idioms of everyday experience. In his reflections upon Henry's "powerful eloquence" recorded after the Revolution, Edmund Randolph noted, "It was enough to *feel*, to remember some general maxims coeval with the colony."[66] In other words, Henry possessed an extraordinary ability to transform individual discontent, much of it inchoate, into a collective issue.

This is precisely what he did when he first arrived in the House of Burgesses. The electors of Louisa County chose

[65] Funeral Sermon for William Nelson, Waller Family Papers, 1737-1912, Colonial Williamsburg, Inc., Research Center.

[66] Edmund Randolph, *History of Virginia*, ed. Arthur H. Shaffer (Charlottesville, 1970), 181. Also, Rhys Isaac, "Preachers and Patriots," *The American Revolution*, ed. A. F. Young (DeKalb, Ill., 1975), 127-56.

Henry (an unsuccessful tobacco planter turned lawyer) to fill a recently vacated seat in the assembly, and when the new representative reached Williamsburg on 20 May 1765, the legislature was already in session.[67] Henry immediately made his presence felt. Only nine days after being sworn in as a burgess, he introduced the famous Stamp Act resolves, defending them in language so extreme that some Virginians said it smacked of treason. The incident is part of the revolutionary folklore that every schoolchild must learn. But what is usually overlooked in this traditional account is the other business pending before the House that May, legislation that stirred Henry's ire as much as did the Stamp Act. On 17 May several burgesses closely associated with Speaker John Robinson— the man who neglected to burn the Virginia currency—presented a plan that in more modern times would be called a "bail out" program for the colony's most indebted planters.[68] The details of this scheme are not of great concern. The proposer envisioned a public loan office that would assist needy gentlemen, and if Henry had not spoken up, it is possible that they might have had their way.

The new representative refused to let such blatant favoritism pass into law, and on 24 May, he blasted the plan to rescue Virginia's improvident gentlemen. The young Thomas Jefferson, who was present for this speech, recorded what occurred:

> Mr. Henry attacked the scheme . . . on general grounds, in that style of bold, grand, and overwhelming eloquence, for which he became so justly celebrated afterward. I had been intimate with him for the year 1759-60, and felt an interest in what concerned him; and I can never forget a particular exclamation of his in the debate,

[67] The classic account of this session can be found in Edmund S. and Helen M. Morgan, *The Stamp Act Crisis: Prologue to Revolution* (Chapel Hill, N.C., 1953), chapter 7. Also see, George F. Willison, *Patrick Henry and His World* (Garden City, N.Y., 1969).

[68] John Pendleton Kennedy, ed., *Journal of the House of Burgesses of Virginia, 1761-1765* (Richmond, 1907), 350.

which electrified his hearers. It had been urged, that, from certain unhappy circumstances of the colony, men of substantial property had contracted debts, which, if exacted suddenly, must ruin them and their families, but with a little indulgence of time, might be paid with ease. "What sir," exclaimed Mr. Henry, in animadverting on this, "is it proposed, then, to reclaim the spendthrift from his dissipation and extravagance, by filling his pockets with money?" . . . He laid open with so much energy the spirit of favoritism, on which the proposition was founded, and the abuses to which it would lead, that it was crushed in its birth.[69]

A few days later Henry attacked the Stamp Act. Not surprisingly, he brought the same moral fervor to this task as he had to beating down the loan office. Both proposals compromised the colony's virtue. One act represented an external threat to liberty, the other an internal seed of corruption. What is significant is that he kept the two issues separate. He did not talk of debt in constitutional terms. That was a different discourse. But by drawing attention to "dissipation and extravagance," Henry helped Virginians to see that cultural reformation was a collective challenge.

The question of planter frugality dramatically resurfaced a few years later in response to the Townshend Duties. In a terribly misguided effort to obtain revenue from the Americans, Chancellor of the Exchequer Charles Townshend persuaded the House of Commons in 1767 to tax a number of colonial imports such as glass, tea, paper, lead, and paint. When Virginia's royal governor, Lord Botetourt, discovered that prominent local political figures intended to resist Townshend's Revenue Act, he dissolved the House of Burgesses. The representatives responded by marching down the street, reconvening in a private home, and electing Peyton Randolph

[69] William Wirt Henry, *Patrick Henry* (New York, 1891), I, 77. Jefferson appears to have been mistaken on the details of this session. The act passed the House of Burgesses but was defeated in the Council. See, Freeman, *George Washington*, III, 128-30.

moderator. On Wednesday, 17 May 1769, this group drew
up the Virginia Nonimportation Resolution, a document that
was subsequently signed by the colony's "principal gentlemen." Among these were Peyton Randolph, Robert Carter
Nicholas, George Washington, Carter Braxton, Thomas Jefferson, Richard Henry Lee, and Patrick Henry.[70]
The planters agreed not to purchase any items specifically
mentioned in the Revenue Act. But they went well beyond
the strict political requirements of the situation. Anxious
about their mounting personal debts, they pledged to halt
consumption of a long list of luxuries: pewter, clocks, looking
glasses, carriages, joiner's and cabinet work, upholstery of all
sorts, trinkets and jewelry, plate and gold, silversmith's work,
silk and lace, boots and saddles. These were precisely the
kinds of goods that consignment merchants in Great Britain
had obtained for their wealthy Virginia "friends." They were
the badges of gentility. And now the orders would cease.
Townshend unwittingly roused the great Tidewater planters
into transforming private fears over indebtedness into a public
commitment to austerity. Acting alone, none of them would
have had the courage to forgo the purchase of such finery, but
by joining together—by staking their honor—they hoped to
regain their economic independence.

Washington saw more clearly than did many contemporaries that moral regeneration required cooperation. He had
learned from his experience at Mount Vernon of the temptations to purchase expensive British goods. Consumption of
this sort was a narcotic. And it was for these reasons that
Washington wholeheartedly supported the concept of nonimportation, in his words, "because I think there are *private*,
as well as *public* advantages to result from it." In April 1769—
just a month before he signed the Nonimportation Resolution—he wrote a letter to George Mason on this subject, and
in the course of developing his argument, Washington de-

[70] *The Papers of Thomas Jefferson*, ed. Julian Boyd (Princeton, 1950), I, 28-
29; and Merrill Jensen, *The Founding of a Nation: A History of the American
Revolution, 1763-1776* (New York, 1968), 300-305.

scribed the psychology of an indebted Virginia planter. Such a typical gentleman, Washington believed, was perpetually torn between compulsion to order what he could not afford and a desire to reclaim lost independence.

A formal association designed to end the importation of British finery provided Washington's anxious planter with an ideal solution. United action would even benefit "those who live genteely and hospitably, on clear Estates." Such people, Washington declared, "were they, not to consider the valuable object in view, and the good of others, might think it hard to be curtail'd in their living and enjoyments." Washington assumed that though the "extravagant and expensive man" wanted desperately "to retrench his Expenses," he usually could not summon the courage to do so. A general protest against British taxation, however, furnished this hypothetical planter "with a pretext to live within bounds." The gentleman—and one must assume that Washington was speaking autobiographically—had always known that "prudence dictated economy . . . but his resolution was too weak to put it in practice; for how can I, *says he*, who have lived in such and such a manner change my method? I am ashamed to do it; and besides such an alteration in the system of my living, will create suspicions of decay in my fortune, and such a thought the World must not harbour; I will [therefore] . . . continue my course: till at last the course discontinues the Estate, a sale of it being the consequence of his perserverance in error. This I am satisfied is the way that many who have set out in the wrong tract, have reasoned, till ruin stares them in the face."[71] Such were the terrors of a Virginian who lived in a world of external appearances. The only truly independent planter under these circumstances was the one who demonstrated the ability to sacrifice material pleasure for the common good.

Other Tidewater gentlemen fully appreciated the issues

[71] Washington to George Mason, 5 April 1769 in *Writings of George Washington*, ed. Fitzpatrick, II, 502-503. See, J. E. Crowley, *This Sheba, Self* (Baltimore, 1974), 125-57.

that Washington had raised. To be sure, Townshend's attempt to tax them without representation angered the Virginians, but to a large extent, they separated the political from the moral dimensions of nonconsumption. In his response to Washington, for example, George Mason urged the planters to devise a plan that "will promote & encourage Industry & Frugality & discourage all manner of Luxury & Extravagance."[72] He, too, envisioned a cultural renewal, a restoration of honor. Mason echoed the rhetoric of Trenchard and Gordon, but in the Virginia context, the vocabulary of the English Country writers acquired special meaning. The words corresponded to an actual economic experience. John Page agreed. When he heard of the Association of "principal gentlemen," he immediately concluded that whatever else it might achieve, it "must certainly clear us of our Debts."[73] Another planter announced, "It is Industry and frugality with its Attendant Virtue honesty that can relieve us and make us a Happy People."[74] And Robert Beverley was convinced that nonimportation would promote local manufacturing which in turn would help preserve "Our Privileges as Freemen."[75]

Similar arguments and high expectations echoed in the pages of the *Virginia Gazette*. A writer who signed his essay "C.R." enthusiastically supported the Association. Indeed, he declared that the effort to revive public virtue was long overdue. "For it is certain," the writer explained, "that nothing but a discouragement of the present general tendency to those vices, can put us upon an equal footing with our fellow subjects in Great Britain, by restoring to us that weighty situation of being *once more* clear of debt; because it is an incontestable truth, that every debtor does in some measure feel the

[72] "Respecting the Non-Importation of British Goods," 23 April 1769, in *Letters to Washington, 1752-1775*, ed. S. M. Hamilton (Boston, 1898-1902), III, 347.

[73] Page to John Norton, 27 May 1769 in *John Norton and Sons*, ed. Mason, 93-94.

[74] Corbin to Robert Cary and Company, 1 August 1765, Corbin Letter Book.

[75] Beverley to Samuel Athawes, 6 September 1774, Beverley Letter Book.

imperiousness of his creditor." C.R. warned that Virginians of all classes would find giving up expensive imports difficult. The effort required the leadership of the colony's great planters, the very persons who in the essayist's opinion had been most blinded by luxury. This was their opportunity to reestablish moral direction, to earn respect. "If then any Gentlemen should be touched with the restriction that such an association will lay upon their domestic conduct," the writer concluded, "let me [ask him] . . . if he does not think he will find himself doubly compensated by the increase of the prosperity of his country?"[76]

In the same issue of the *Virginia Gazette*, "Brutus" reminded readers that "the prevailing principle of our government is *virtue*." Lest anyone misunderstand his meaning, he defined "virtue." It was a love of country, a foundation to liberty, a quality that allows men to "resist the temptations of ease and luxury, with which liberty is incompatible." Brutus was not talking about paint and paper, items taxed in the Revenue Act, but the fineries listed in the Virginia Nonimportation Resolutions. Nor was he attacking corrupt British hirelings. The problem was internal. Like C.R., he was attempting to tap the guilt and anxiety caused by debt and endow them with sufficient moral force to persuade the great planters radically to alter their personal habits of consumption. "For luxury and idleness," the essayist lectured in familiar Country idiom, "bring on a general deprivation of manners, which sets us loose from all the restraints of both public and private virtue, and diverts our thoughts from examining the behavior and politics of artful and designing men, who meditate our ruin. . . . From immorality and excesses we fall into necessity, and this leads us to a servile dependence upon power, and fits us to the chains prepared for us."[77]

Notwithstanding the rhetorical enthusiasm for Association, the nonimportation movement in Virginia failed. In fact, the results embarrassed almost everyone. In 1770 the *Virginia Ga-*

[76] *Virginia Gazette* (Rind), 1 June 1769.
[77] Ibid.

zette lamented the death of that "glorious association . . . [so] soon forgotten, so basely deserted, and both the letter and the spirit of it kicked out of doors."⁷⁸ During the period in which the agreement had allegedly been in effect the planters actually increased the amount of goods purchased in the mother country. In 1768 British merchants had exported approximately £670,000 worth of goods to the Chesapeake colonies (Virginia and Maryland). By 1770, a year during which the colonists were supposedly busy enforcing the Nonimportation Resolutions, the figure had jumped to nearly a million pounds. And in 1771 the amount of British imports reached an all-time high of nearly £1,225,000.⁷⁹ Some of the "principle gentlemen" who had signed the original document bore responsibility for the debacle. In July 1769, for example, George Washington instructed a British correspondent not to send articles "tax'd by Act of Parliament for the purpose of Raising a Revenue in America."⁸⁰ He said nothing about the other luxury items mentioned in the resolutions. Washington, of course, was not the only gentleman who attempted to minimize the sting of nonconsumption. By the summer of 1770 most Tidewater planters had given up even the pretense of forgoing imported luxuries. An improving tobacco market in the late 1760s had apparently generated hopes of settling "old scores" with the merchants, and for the moment at least, economic self-sacrifice lost whatever appeal it may have had.

To label the Association as nothing more than an example of planter hypocrisy masks its cultural significance. Though the effort failed politically, it did help to crystallize largely inchoate ideas about the moral dangers of dependence. It also provided a vehicle for transforming private fears about debt into a general public concern. And as the articles in the *Vir-*

⁷⁸ Ibid., 8 March 1770.
⁷⁹ Jacob M. Price, "New Time Series for Scotland's and Britain's Trade with the Thirteen Colonies and States, 1740 to 1791," *W&MQ*, 3rd ser., 32(1975), 307-25; James F. Shepherd and Gary M. Walton, *Shipping, Maritime Trade, and the Economic Development of Colonial North America* (Cambridge, 1972); and Jensen, *Founding of a Nation*, 356.
⁸⁰ *Writings of George Washington*, ed. Fitzpatrick, II, 512.

ginia Gazette reveal, Virginians increasingly began to talk of economic problems in the highly charged rhetoric of the radical Country writers.

The migration of a moral vocabulary from private to public discourse was particularly evident in the months following the breakup of the Association. Unwilling to blame themselves for the failure, Virginians turned angrily upon the merchants. There was a certain logic to their recrimination. The planters had never exercised substantial control over the merchants with whom they did business. The British correspondents were certainly under no obligation to observe the Nonimportation Resolutions and thus continued to import many expensive items that the Virginians found irresistible. By focusing their guilt and anxiety on the merchants rather than on the ministers of George III, the great planters insured that the issue of debt remained separate from the debate over constitutional rights and liberties.[81]

Many of these ideological threads came together in a remarkable essay that appeared in the *Virginia Gazette* in October 1771. The author called himself simply "A PLANTER." The piece warned Virginians of a conspiracy of merchants designed to bring them into permanent bondage. He called for vigilance. "It is but a few years," the writer observed, "since we were alarmed with the horrible stamp act. How did we shutter at the image of despotic power, and shrink at the apprehension of abject slavery!" But since that time, the planters seemed to have been lulled into a false sense of security. "We seem to be easy," A PLANTER declared, "and bless our good fortunes, that we are free men, and loyal subjects to the best of Kings; though we all know that we are slaves to the power of the merchants: For who can truly say

---

[81] Thad W. Tate, "Coming of the Revolution," *W&MQ*, 3rd ser., 19(1962), 334-37. William Allason wrote in 1771, "that some Gentlemen of the Assembly are unwilling that the sufferers in the Public Warehouse by the late Fresh [flood], should be reimbursed by the Public, and it is suspected this arrises in the breast of some Patriotick Spirits from a belief that the Tobacco was chiefly the property of the Merchants." Allason to Thomas B. Martin, 5 July 1771, in "The Letters of William Allason," ed. Anderson, 146-47.

he is free, when there is a fixed price set upon his tobacco, and goods he purchases, at rates he does not like?" Only "long custom" could explain why the planters endured such oppression. At last, however, the time had come for Virginians to shake off merchant tyranny, and in words as impassioned as any political pamphlet of the period A PLANTER wrote, "Suffer me then, my dear countrymen, to entreat you, by all that is dear to you, your freedom, love of country, affection for your families, and regard to posterity, no longer to be in bondage, and dependent on those, who neither value you, or your country, any farther than to serve their present wants and purposes."

If the author had done nothing more than bring the full force of the radical Country rhetoric to bear upon the merchant plot, he would have produced an important document. But he pushed the argument further, and in so doing, A PLANTER challenged the basic assumptions that lay behind the gentlemen's code of credit, the very notion of a commercial friendship. Indeed, this anonymous writer did for the consignment merchants what Thomas Paine did for kings; he made them appear petty, selfish, and expendable.

As the essayist realized, many Virginians in 1771 found it difficult to dump their correspondents, or to put it in a slightly different way, to look out for their own interests. Some planters, the writer speculated, "will probably say, 'I have lately made a purchase, my merchant hath given his note to pay the money, and I should use him very ungenteelly to let him suffer.' Others may plead that they are in arrears with him, that they are poor, and if they do not let him have their tobacco, he will sue them, and that would break them."

A PLANTER quickly dispatched these hypothetical objections. He reminded those who felt the need to act with honor that the merchants had never believed in commercial reciprocity. The lesson was clear: "They [the merchants] are very willing to give their notes, because they know it lays a generous mind under an obligation not to let them suffer, and consequently, to let them have tobacco at their own price, or, what is the same thing, as the market is. . . . It is not through any regard the merchant hath for the planter that he gives his note, or advanceth cash on his behalf, but in the end to serve himself, and enslave the other." The very notion that the merchant was the planter's friend amounted to false consciousness. The nature of the marketplace was such that the merchant will inevitably lead "you out of your depth, that he may, when he pleases, sink you, or at any rate make you dependent on him, and take your tobacco at his own price." The writer assured his readers that no one need fear a lawsuit. After all, every Virginian had "a right to spin it [the case] out as far as the thread of the law will bear." That might be two or three years, and by that time normal inflation would make it much easier for the indebted planter to pay off his old bills. A PLANTER concluded, "that which most claims our attention is, that . . . we shall be free from the bondage and tyranny of the merchants. . . ."[82]

Economic conditions in Virginia deteriorated rapidly after 1772. Following a brief resurgence, the tobacco market entered a new depression, and the great planters were more hard pressed than ever to meet their obligations. They had, of course, exacerbated the problem by importing so many goods during the early years of the decade. When the credit crisis of 1772 hit the mother country, the merchants to whom they had consigned their tobacco were caught short. A few overextended houses went bankrupt, and those that survived dunned their American "friends" with a rigor born of panic. The days of recklessly conspicuous consumption were over. "I believe the Virginians have of late altered their manner very much," marvelled a young New Jersey tutor in 1773, "for they begin to find that their estates by even small extravagance, decline, and grow involved with debt, this seems to be the spring which induces the People of fortune who are the pattern of all behaviour here, to be frugal, and moderate."[83]

    [82] *Virginia Gazette* (Rind), 31 October 1771.
    [83] Philip Fithian to Rev. Enoch Green, 1 December 1773, in Philip Vickers Fithian, *Journals and Letters*, ed. Hunter Dickinson Farish (Williamsburg, 1957), 35. On the state of the economy see, Shepherd and Walton, *Shipping*,

These sharp reverses did something that Townshend's Revenue Act had not achieved: they politicized the issue of debt. Up to this time, the great Tidewater planters had focused their hostility largely upon the merchants. Before the early 1770s, in fact, they had not conflated the debate over constitutional rights and liberties with discussion of private indebtedness. As the Virginia gentlemen began to experience severe economic hardship, however, the two discourses merged, and they spoke of tobacco, merchants, and Parliament as if they had all somehow conspired to compromise the planters' autonomy. This was the logic of an argument that Richard Henry Lee advanced in his introduction to John Dickinson's *Letters of a Farmer in Pennsylvania*. Lee claimed that the government of Great Britain "from her exclusive trade to these colonies, and from the manner in which she tied up our manufacturing hands, not only received the entire produce of the lands and labour of these colonies, but has besides involved the people here in heavy debt, which agriculture, without arts, and a trade so confined, will probably never pay. Mr. *Grenville* it seems had the honour of devising this new system of *American* policy."[84] In this context, radical Country idioms—a shrill language of power and bondage, virtue and independence—acquired the emotional intensity necessary to effect cultural renewal. Indeed, the great planters entertained reforms that challenged the very core of the tobacco mentality.

Some Virginians concluded that they could never be truly free so long as they cultivated the region's traditional staple. Tobacco not only retarded the colony's economic development, it was itself a vice, a luxury, a crop inappropriate for

---

Maritime Trade, and Economic Development; Tate, "Coming of the Revolution," 337; Price, *Capital and Credit in British Overseas Trade* (Cambridge, Mass., 1980), 137; and S. Rosenblatt, "Merchant-Planter Relations in the Tobacco Consignment Trade," *VMHB*, 72(1964), 462.

[84] John Dickinson, *Letters of a Farmer in Pennsylvania*, intro. Richard Henry Lee to the Williamsburg edition of *Writings of John Dickinson* (Philadelphia, 1895), I, 292. See also, Richard Henry Lee, "The State of the Constitution of Virginia," Lee Family Papers, Mssl. L51, f. 378.

men who increasingly called themselves republicans. "Our Staple Commodity," declared "Academius" in the *Virginia Gazette* of 5 August 1773, "seems completely adapted for restraining the Progress of Population, and of natural Wealth; as it is a mere Luxury, affords no Aliment, extremely impoverishes the Soil, and requires considerable Extent for it[s] Cultivation." The writer envisioned a society based on a different form of agriculture, one that people could actually consume. Though Academius did not specify a particular replacement, he insisted that "English Husbandry"—whatever that may have meant—was unsuited for the independent yeomen of Virginia.[85] Another essayist, while not calling for a complete abandonment of tobacco, pointed out that wheat farmers would never endure the restrictions and regulations that planters did. "Now can it be imagined," asked "Sobrino," "that any honest Farmer could, with any Patience, bear to have his whole Hogshead of Wheat emptied, hawled about, wasted, and a considerable Toll taken thereout only for one Bushel or two that happened to be badly cleaned at one Head, in the Middle, or any other Part of it?"[86]

In light of these comments, it is interesting to note that one economic historian who has studied the question of planter debt concluded, "We know that the tobacco-growing regions tended to be more revolutionary than the wheat-growing regions in the same states."[87] Edmund Randolph, a leading planter and author of *History of Virginia*, illuminates the possible relationship between the character of agriculture and radical politics. Randolph explained:

> Admidst the agitations of the times, the Assembly were not unmindful of agriculture and were desirous of increasing the facilities of the farmer in a speedy preparation of his crops of wheat for market. That baneful weed tobacco, which had stained our country with all the pollutions and cruelties of slavery, had exhausted the fertil-

[85] *Virginia Gazette* (Purdie & Dixon), 5 August 1773.
[86] Ibid., 17 January 1771.
[87] Price, *Capital and Credit*, 137.

ity of our soil, had swallowed up in its large plantations
vast territories, which if distributed into portions were
best adapted to farm population, was yet the only commodity which could command money for the planter at
a short notice and the only one from which the dexterity
of the British merchant could extract such various emol-
uments and was therefore with him a choice subject of
trade. But it had become obvious that the staff of life was
entitled to legislative stimulus, and a reward of £100 was
voted to John Hobday for the invention of a machine
which pressed out the wheat with ribbed cylinders put
into circular motion by horses.

This is an extraordinary statement. Randolph, a major figure
in the revolutionary movement, believed that a legislative support for a farm machine was a significant event in creating a
republican society. Randolph was not naive. He recognized
that Hobday's invention might not succeed. What Randolph
regarded as important was the symbolism of the subsidy.
Freeing Virginians from the tyranny of tobacco seemed as
essential to him as escaping the oppression of parliament. He
even suggested a mental link between agriculture innovation
and social reform. Randolph observed tentatively that there
had been a causal connection between "the cessation of that
spirit which coveted tobacco as the greatest blessing of our
state" and "the most promising effort which had been ever
made in the legislature for a complete toleration of Protestant
dissenters.[88] It requires quite a leap of imagination to connect
the spread of religious toleration with the erosion of the tobacco mentality, and yet, that is exactly what Randolph did.
   The Virginians were also now prepared to make another
break. After news of the Intolerable Acts reached the colony
in 1774, the leading gentlemen gathered at Raleigh Tavern in
Williamsburg. They resurrected the Association, and a few
months later, a convention of planters endorsed not only the

[88] Randolph, *History of Virginia*, ed. Shaffer, 202-203. Also, *Journals of the
House of Burgesses of Virginia 1773-1776*, ed. John Pendleton Kennedy (Richmond, 1905), 116-17.

THE ALTERNATIVE OF WILLIAMS BURG.

XV. Blending the economic and political discourses: Virginians force local merchants to sign the Association over a hogshead of tobacco

concept of nonimportation, but also of nonexportation. At long last, the great Tidewater planters were persuaded to declare their independence from the merchants of Great Britain, and in the context of tobacco America, that meant revolution.

V

Thus, it seems fair to conclude, though in its nature impossible to prove, that the tobacco mentality provided a psychological ground from which a spirit of rebellion could grow. The horror of debt, made more unbearable by the merchants' dunning, forced planters—now increasingly farmers—to reevaluate a traditional vocabulary of trade. Within the context of a severe credit crisis, familiar words took on new meanings. Old "friends" seemed to have betrayed the trusting Virginians, dishonored them, conspired to undermine their independence. And as the planters sank deeper into debt, some falling into bankruptcy and suffering the humiliation of seeing their possessions sold at public auction, they became convinced that the only sure way to preserve their honor was through a reaffirmation of virtue, a commitment to diligence and frugality, the simple agrarian life.

By focusing attention upon the cultural, as opposed to the economic significance of debt and tobacco, one begins to understand why these particular planters might have voiced radical Country ideas with such passion during this period. After 1773 the Virginians' political ideology resonated with meanings drawn from the experiences of everyday life. It gained power through association with an angry commercial discourse. When the great planters spoke of conspiracy or slavery, they were not mouthing abstractions borrowed from the writings of English Country authors. A source of their apparent hyperbole—though perhaps not the only one—can be found in those private disappointments, humiliations, and misunderstandings recounted so poignantly in the letterbooks.

EPILOGUE

A NEW BEGINNING

The cultural changes begun in the colonial period continued into the period of national independence. To have spoken of the "tobacco mentality" after the Revolution would have made little sense. It was not that Tidewater Virginians abandoned the old staple. Rather, they redefined their relation to tobacco; it no longer provided a source of identity in this agricultural society. In this sense, Robert Beverley had been correct about its being the end of an era. When an English traveler visited Mount Vernon following the war, he described its owner in a manner that reflected the profound shift that had taken place in the agriculture of Tidewater Virginia. "General Washington," he explained, "who *formerly* had been a planter, but *lately* a farmer, had not land left that would bring a crop of tobacco."[1]

On another level, Tidewater Virginia was no longer synonymous with tobacco. It may have been a "tobacco" colony, but it certainly was not a "tobacco" state. The very process of shifting the focus of attention from one crop to another took on symbolic meaning. The colonial crop had been tobacco, a staple now associated with royal government, ruinous debt, slave labor, soil erosion, lack of personal autonomy—in other words, with a host of negative qualities.[2] But wheat helped to free the commonwealth from these burdens. Grain rejuvenated the land, and presumably, the human spirit as well. "Wheat and other corn . . . ," wrote the author of *American Husbandry* in 1775, "are raised principally on old tobacco plantations that are worn out without assistance of

[1] Richard Parkinson, *A Tour of America* (London, 1805), II, 423-24 (emphasis added).
[2] Carville Earle, "A Staple Interpretation of Slavery and Free Labor," *Geographic Review*, 68(1978), 56-59.

much manure. This is a point which deserves attention: exhaust the lands . . . as much as you will with tobacco, you will leave it in order for grain."[3]

Other Virginians stressed the appropriateness of wheat for the new republican society. In his "Report to President Washington on Agricultural Conditions in Northern Virginia" (1791), Dr. David Stuart commented that "people are generally exchanging tobacco for wheat; I flatter myself the face of our Country will soon assume an appearance that will not only do honor to our climate but ourselves." From Stuart's perspective, "the old Tobacco grounds" were merely reminders of the "slovenly" agricultural practices that Virginians had once accepted without second thought, and in the postrevolutionary period the "old" fields evoked no fondness for a lost culture.[4] In 1799 the duc de La Rochefoucauld Liancourt reported that "here, on the James-River, and in fact throughout Virginia, tobacco is yearly replaced by wheat, which becomes gradually almost the general object of culture; and the present fall in the price of wheat does not seem to render the planters less attached to this *change in their system of cultivation*."[5]

Like Dr. Stuart, Jefferson welcomed the transition from tobacco to wheat. He understood the relation between culture and agriculture more fully than did many of his contemporaries, and even before the conclusion of the American Revolution, he decided that the citizens of an independent republic should be discouraged from growing tobacco. His views on this topic were not drawn from the works of European philosophers; they were the product of experiences he had had while growing up on a Virginia plantation. Jefferson recalled that in the year 1758 the planters had exported the largest number of hogsheads in the colony's history. Soon after this, however, they began to cut back on tobacco culti-

[3] *American Husbandry*, ed. Harry J. Carman (New York, 1939), 187.
[4] Gertrude R. B. Richards, ed., "Dr. David Stuart's Report to President Washington on Agricultural Conditions in Northern Virginia," *VMHB* 61(1953), 286, 287.
[5] *Travels through the United States* (London, 1799), II, 84 (emphasis added).

vation, a trend Jefferson applauded. He hated the staple for
the harm he thought it had done to the land and its people.
"It is a culture productive of infinite wretchedness," he declared. "Those employed in it are in a continual state of ex-
ertion beyond the power of nature to support. Little food of
any kind is raised by them; so that the men and animals on
these farms are badly fed, and the earth is rapidly impoverished." By contrast, wheat liberated men from these crushing
burdens. It freed them from the mind-dulling tasks that Jefferson feared would destroy intellectual curiosity and undermine political vigilance. "Besides clothing the earth with her-
bage, and preserving its fertility," he insisted, "it [wheat]
feeds the laborers plentifully, requires from them only a moderate toil, except in the season of harvest, raises great numbers
of animals for food and service, and diffuses plenty and happiness among the whole."[6] Another planter explained: "As the
culture of *wheat*, and the manufacturing of it into *flour* travelled southward, the people became more happy, and independent of British storekeepers who had kept them in debts
and dependence."[7] The message was clear. A cultural revolution was taking place in the fields of Virginia, one that by
providing effective new symbols of agricultural independence
would help insure the survival of the new nation.

The old debts to British merchants were an issue that simply would not go away, plaguing Virginia politics for almost
a quarter century. Though they stated their intention to do
justice to their former correspondents, the planters procrasti-
nated, and during the 1780s the men who ran the state government placed as many obstacles as possible in the path of
merchants eager to sue delinquent planters. The problem embarrassed leaders in other sections of the country, for it was
clear that Great Britain would not fulfill the letter of the peace

[6] *Notes on the State of Virginia* (New York, 1964), 159.

[7] John Beale Bordley, *Essays and Notes on Husbandry and Rural Affairs* (Phil-
adelphia, 1801), 301, cited in Cary Carson, "Homestead Architecture in the
Chesapeake Colonies" (Paper presented at the 41st Conference in Early
American History, Millersville State College, Millersville, Pennsylvania,
April 1981).

treaty until the debts were settled. After 1790, the new United States government allowed creditors to file claims in federal court, but even then the Virginians found ways to delay. The whole sordid business was not fully concluded until the United States created a fund that met at least part of the demands of Virginia's former "friends."[8]

The old indebtedness was not simply a matter of legal maneuvering. The memory of dependence haunted the planters and farmers of the new republic. They continued to show suspicion, if not outright hostility, toward merchants. Jefferson voiced these feelings in a letter to the wife of a young planter. Writing soon after the conclusion of the war, he warned her especially against taking credit, for once she and her husband were in the clutches of the merchants, they might never reclaim their freedom. "No [burden] can be more oppressive to the mind or fortune," Jefferson explained, "and long experience has proved to us that there never was an instance of a man's getting out of debt who was once in the hands of a tobacco merchant." Indeed, he was certain that once the merchant had gained the upper hand, he would lower the prices he gave for the tobacco "so as always to keep the balance against his customer."[9]

But the issue of debt went deeper than hostility toward merchants. By calling attention to the moral implications of planter indebtedness, the colony's revolutionary leaders may have inadvertently undermined the hierarchical order of traditional society. In the long run this had major implications for the reception of republican ideas in Virginia. Certainly, as time passed, it became increasingly difficult to pay deference to the great planters who had squandered fortunes, allowed their mansions to fall into disrepair, or sold off their slaves. In a society in which material possessions counted for so much, a dissolute gentleman forfeited his claim to high social status. Under such conditions, even an illustrious sur-

[8] Charles F. Hobson, "The Recovery of British Debts in the Federal Courts of Virginia, 1790 to 1797," *VMHB*, 92(1984), 176-200.

[9] *Papers of Thomas Jefferson*, ed. Julian Boyd (Princeton, 1954) X, 304-305.

name no longer commanded automatic respect. When Virginians ratified the Constitution of the United States, for example, St. George Tucker realized immediately that the new federal system would allow the British merchants to sue to recover prerevolutionary debts. As he informed his stepsons, one of whom was John Randolph of Roanoke, the change in government would have an extraordinary impact upon the character of local society. The young planters would be forced to drop the traditional values, to become republicans. "The recovery of British debt," Tucker observed, "can no longer be postponed, and there now seems to be a moral certainty that your patrimony will all go to satisfy the unjust debt from your papa to the Hanburys. The consequence, my dear boys, must be obvious to you. Your sole dependence must be on your own personal abilities and exertions."[10]

Those great Tidewater planters—those unable to adjust to political and economic change—had indeed become symbols of decay. None seems to have fallen quite so far, so publicly, as William Byrd III. By the mid-1760s, he was insolvent. Byrd owed his creditors at least £20,000. As we have seen, he attempted to raise money through a lottery, but that scheme failed. He finally assigned his silver plate and plantation slaves to the Bristol firm of Farrell and Jones. Even family members found Byrd's self-indulgence loathsome. He spent his days drinking and gambling in Williamsburg taverns, a relic of a former age, but now universally despised. In 1765 a Frenchman described this pathetic creature. "I soon got acquainted with several of them [the great planters], "he noted in his journal, "but particularly with Colonel Burd . . .

[10] Cited in W. A. Low, "Merchant and Planter Relations in Post-Revolutionary Virginia, 1783-1789," *VMHB*, 61(1953), 317. On the transformation of the content of republicanism see, Joyce Appleby, "The Social Origins of American Revolutionary Ideology," *Journal of American History*, 64(1978), 935-58; Robert P. Sutton, "Nostalgia, Pessimism, and Malaise: The Doomed Aristocrat in Late-Jeffersonian Virginia," *VMHB*, 76(1968), 41-55. The tensions within the postrevolutionary gentry culture are imaginatively explored in Jan Lewis, *The Pursuit of Happiness: Family and Values in Jefferson's Virginia* (Cambridge, 1983), 106-68.

which I soon was like to have reason to repent, for they are all professed gamesters, Especially Colonel Burd, who is never happy but when he has the box and Dices in hand. This Gentleman from a man of the greatest property of any in America has reduced himself to that Degree by gameing, that few or nobody will Credit him for Ever so small a sum of money. He was obliged to sel[l] 400 fine Negroes a few Days before my arrival."[11]

On New Year's Day 1777 William Byrd III went up to his room and shot himself. No one fully ever knows why a person commits suicide. But in this case, the victim's despondency seems to have come from a knowledge that he had no place in the new society. Not long before his death, Byrd wrote to his friend Ralph Wormeley, complaining of "the horrid Disposition of the Times & the frantick Patriotism of those who take the Lead." Wormeley jotted on the letter a telling comment: "He [Byrd] was not trusted. He lost everything."[12]

But this was not the case for Thomas Jefferson. For him, the Revolution promised exciting possibilities not only for Tidewater Virginians, but for all mankind. He envisioned—as Byrd could not—a new republican order, an empire of independent yeomen, producers of wheat. In his *Notes on the State of Virginia*, Jefferson sang the praises of these cultivators who will escape the burdens and errors of the past. "Those who labor in the earth are the chosen people of God . . . ," Jefferson announced, "whose breasts He has made His peculiar deposit for substantial and genuine virtue. . . . Corruption of morals in the mass of cultivators is a phenomenon of which no age nor nation has furnished an example. . . . Dependence

[11] "Journal of a French Traveller in the Colonies, 1765," pt. 1, *American Historical Review*, 26(1920-21), 741-42; David John Mays, *Edmund Pendleton, A Biography, 1721-1803* (Cambridge, Mass., 1952) I, 181-83; Sheridan, "British Credit Crisis," *Journal of Economic History*, 20(1960), 183; Marion Tinling, ed., *The Correspondence of the Three William Byrds of Westover, Virginia 1684-1776* (Charlottesville, 1977), II, 611-13.

[12] Cited in A. G. Roeber, *Faithful Magistrates, and Republican Lawyers* (Chapel Hill, N.C., 1981), 170.

begets subservience and venality, suffocates the germ of virtue, and prepares fit tools for the designs of ambition."[13] Jefferson transformed radical Country ideas into a new agrarian republicanism, an ideology constructed out of the particular experiences of the Virginia planters and distinct from the forms of republicanism that had taken root in other parts of the country. This development helps explain the party strife of the 1790s. Jefferson hated debt, was suspicious of the merchant class, and when his colleague in the new federal government, Alexander Hamilton, brought forth schemes for funding a national debt, the Virginian led the agrarians in revolt.[14]

[13] *Notes on the State of Virginia*, 157.

[14] J. Murrin, "The Great Inversion," in *Three British Revolutions: 1641, 1688, 1776*, ed. J.G.A. Pocock (Princeton, 1980), 417-18; and Lance Banning, *The Jeffersonian Persuasion* (Ithaca, N.Y., 1978).

INDEX

CPSIA information can be obtained
at www.ICGtesting.com
Printed in the USA
LVOW07s1201221117
557309LV00002B/10/P